CURRENT ISSUES IN PUBLIC
SECTOR ECONOMICS

CURRENT ISSUES IN ECONOMICS

General Editor: David Greenaway, University of Nottingham

Current Issues in Public Sector Economics

Edited by

Peter M. Jackson

MACMILLAN

First published 1993
THE MACMILLAN PRESS LTD
Houndmills, Basingstoke, Hampshire RG21 2XS
and London
Companies and representatives
throughout the world

ISBN 0–333–53483–2 hardcover
ISBN 0–333–53484–0 paperback

A catalogue record for this book is available
from the British Library.

Printed in Hong Kong

To my mother and father
Betty and Andrew

Contents

viii   *Contents*

List of Tables

List of Figures

Series Editor's Preface

The *Current Issues* series has slightly unusual origins. *Current Issues in International Trade*, which was published in 1987, and which turned out to be the pilot for the series was in fact 'conceived' in the Horton Hospital, Banbury, and 'delivered' (in the sense of completed) in the Hilton International in Nicosia! The reader may be struck by the thought that a more worthwhile and enjoyable production process would start and finish the other way around. I agree! Be that as it may, that is how the series started.

As I said in the Preface to *Current Issues in International Trade* the reason for its creation was the difficulty of finding suitable references on 'frontier' subjects for undergraduate students. Many of the issues which excite professional economists and which dominate the journal literature take quite a time to percolate down into texts; hence the need for a volume of *Current Issues*. The reception which *Current Issues in International Trade* received persuaded me that it would be worth doing something similar for the other subject areas we teach. Thus each volume in this series is intended to take readers to the 'frontier' of the particular subject area. Each volume contains nine or ten essays, one of which provides a general overview while the remainder are devoted to current issues.

As series editor the main challenge I faced was finding suitable editors for each of the volumes – the best people are generally the busiest! I believe, however, that I have been fortunate in having such an impressive and experienced team of editors with the necessary skills and reputation to persuade first-class authors to participate. I would like to thank all of them for their cooperation and assistance in the development of the series. Like me, all of them will, I am sure, hope that this series provides a useful service to undergraduate and graduate students as well as faculty.

Current Issues in Public Sector Economics is the seventh in the series. This has been an area of some considerable interest over the last decade, with changes in the financing and delivery of public services and changes in the structure of taxation in the UK and elsewhere. These and other issues have helped keep the public sector at the top of the policy agenda. Many of these topical issues are covered in this volume, some covered in *Current Issues in Welfare Economics*. The present volume focuses much more on taxation issues, whilst the emphasis in *Current Issues in Welfare Economics* will be more towards expenditure issues.

The editor of this volume has selected topics where theoretical innovation has been important, as in the case of public choice and preference revelation, as well as topics with a strong policy focus, like income distribution and redistribution and public finance in developing countries. The combination of theory, policy and empirics makes for a well-balanced set of readings, with papers that have been carefully written and carefully edited.

The appropriate role of the public sector in mixed economies is a topic of ongoing interest and will ensure that public sector economics continues to figure as a major final-year undergraduate course. I hope that these essays will be useful and interesting to students of that subject.

University of Nottingham   DAVID GREENAWAY

Ian Walker is Professor of Economics at Keele University and is a Research Fellow at the Institute for Fiscal Studies, London. His research interests include several issues in public and social policy such as the incentives and distributed effects of taxation and social security. His publications include papers in the *Review of Economic Studies* and the *Economic Journal*.

Notes on the Contributors

Richard R. Barnett is Professor of Public Finance and Management at the University of Ulster. He has previously taught at the Universities of Salford and York and at Queen's University, Ontario, and has held the Vivienne Stewart Visiting Fellowship at the University of Cambridge. His research interests lie in the general areas of intergovernmental fiscal relations and the economics and management of public policy.

Richard M. Bird is Professor of Economics at the University of Toronto. His main interest is in public finance and development. His numerous publications in that field include two recent books, *Taxation in Developing Countries*, edited with Oliver Oldman, and *Tax Policy and Economic Development*.

Vani K. Borooah is Professor of Applied Economics at the University of Ulster. He was previously a Senior Research Officer in the Department of Applied Economics at Cambridge University and a Fellow of Queens' College, Cambridge. He has published widely on the topic of political economy and public choice and is a member of the management committee of the European Public Choice Society. His publications include *Political Aspects of the Economy*.

Peter M. Jackson is Professor of Economics at Leicester University. He is also a member of the governing board of the Public Finance Foundation. His research interests include topics in public expenditure analysis and public sector management. His publications include (with C. V. Brown) *Public Sector Economics* and *Political Economy of Bureaucracy*. He is a consultant

xiv

to various organisations on public sec-

Public Money and Management.

David M. King was educated at the Universities of Oxford and York and is now a Senior Lecturer in Economics at the University of Stirling. His chief interest is local government finance. He has been economic adviser on local tax reform to the UK government, and he has also been consulted by other European countries. He has recently worked with the OECD on state and local finance in Eastern Europe. His publications in this field include two-books – *Taxes on Immovable Property* and *Fiscal Tiers: The Economics of Multi-Level Government.*

Peter J. Lambert is a Senior Lecturer in Economics at the University of York and a Research Associate at the Institute of Fiscal Studies in London. His research focuses on the measurement and redistribution of income through the tax and benefit system. He is author of many journal articles and of two books, *Advanced Mathematics for Economists* and the *Distribution and Redistribution of Income: A Mathematical Analysis.*

Rosella Levaggi is an economist with Salford University Business Services. A graduate of the University of Genoa, she followed this up with a D. Phil. in Economics from the University of York. She is a chartered accountant and auditor and was a Research Fellow at the University of York. Her research interests are in applied econometrics, particularly in the field of public finance and intergovernmental relations, and she has recently worked on the development of a general equilibrium model for Italy. She is the author of numerous articles and books, including *Fiscal Federalism and Grants-in-Aid.*

David J. Pyle is a Senior Lecturer in Economics at Leicester University. He was previously a Teaching Fellow at the University of York and an economic adviser to the Home Office. His research interests include the analysis of taxation; the application of economic analysis to the study of criminal law, and management science, especially mathematical programming. He has published widely in these areas and his books include *The Economics of Crime and Law Enforcement* and *Tax Evasion and the Black Economy.*

1 Introduction: The Current State of Public Sector Economics

PETER M. JACKSON

Anyone who sets out to present a collection of essays which cover the current state of a subject runs the risk or charge that a number of important topics have been omitted. Attempting to survey the rapidly expanding boundaries of the domain of public sector economics is, therefore, a risky venture. As the recently published *Handbook of Public Economics* (Auerbach and Feldstein, 1985) demonstrates, the domain of public sector economics covers a vast territory.

When choosing the topics to be treated in this book, care has been taken to be as balanced as possible and to introduce the reader to both theoretical and empirical issues which are often given inadequate treatment, because of space constraints, in the standard textbooks. Undergraduates will find the essays in this volume an accessible route to what is often an impenetrable jungle of technical economics, which tends to characterise (rightly so) the professional economists' literature. Postgraduates should also find the essays a stimulation to encourage them to carry out further research on the many topics which are surveyed here. The essays convey a sense of excitement in public sector economics as many public sector economists grapple with some of the 'big issues' in theoretical and applied economics. A search for solutions to the problems of public sector economics requires the public sector economist to be a good theorist and in command of the most recent applied techniques. In addition the public sector economist who is interested in making a positive contribution to the policy debate must have an appreciation of the fiscal institutions of the country which is being studied.

Analysis of the impact of taxation on the economy has, for many years now, been the substance of much of the core of public sector economics. Indeed, it is only in recent years that the phrase 'public sector economics' has replaced the more narrow topic area of 'public finance', which focused attention on the tax side of the fiscal equation to the exclusion of public expenditure and public choice. In Chapter 2 Jackson surveys a number of topics which deal with the effects of taxation on economic activity. In particular he examines the question of the effects of taxation on savings, capital formation and the financing decisions of firms. These issues are dealt with from both a theoretical and empirical perspective using partial and general equilibrium analysis. The question of public finance in open economics is also considered. It is clear from this review that economists' abilities to solve problems in their subject area go hand-in-hand with theoretical developments taking place elsewhere within the subject. Nowhere is this more evident than in the case of general equilibrium tax analysis which has received a quantum leap in recent years as a result of developments taking place in computable general equilibrium models (see also the essays in Hare, 1988). Any survey of the taxation literature cannot be comprehensive. Students' attention is also directed to the excellent survey by Kay (1990) which covers issues that are not treated in this volume.

Economists have for many years puzzled over the impact of income taxation and income support systems on work behaviour. The question, Is there a disincentive effect from income taxes?, is an important policy question when designing tax systems and one which economists have done much to illuminate. Ian Walker in Chapter 3 presents evidence on the effects of income taxation and income support policies on work incentives in the UK. After outlining the relevant theory and the UK tax and benefit system Walker considers recent fiscal reforms and surveys the UK evidence. He concludes that it seems likely that the recent reforms in the UK have actually worsened the position on work incentives while ostensibly attempting to improve it.

The design of any tax system must take into account not only the size of incentive effects (positive or negative) but also the extent to which taxpayers are likely to comply with the fiscal regime. In Chapter 4 David Pyle considers three questions: What are the compliance costs of the tax system? Why do people try to evade their tax obligations? and What policies should the tax authorities pursue in attempting to enforce compliance? These questions differ from the more traditional treatment of examining the 'black economy' (for an excellent treatment of that topic, see Cowell, 1990). Pyle demonstrates that economic analysis provides insights to the question of how severe penalties should be. Subtle trade-offs between the structure and severity of penalties and their impact upon horizontal equity need to be carefully modelled.

A feature of the recent developments which have taken place in public sector economics, as opposed to public finance, is that economists now pay much more attention to the demand for public goods (public policies) and the supply of public policies. As Jackson (Chapter 2) indicates, these recent developments bring economists into close contact with the political science literature. Richard Barnett, in Chapter 5, examines preference revelation and public goods. Since the publication of Samuelson's seminal papers on the efficient supply of public goods economists have puzzled over how fiscal institutions might be designed that would overcome the difficulties of the preference revelation problems inherent in a Pareto optimal solution. Recent theoretical work on information economics and incentive compatible information structures have given public sector economists clues as to how they might proceed. Barnett reviews this exciting literature and discusses its implication for the empirical estimation of the demand for public goods.

Public choice, which was once a subset of public sector economics, is now often regarded as being a subject in its own right. While Richard Barnett focuses attention on the neoclassical economists' treatment of the demand and supply of public goods, Vani Borooah (Chapter 6) examines the public choice perspective, that is, the demand and supply of public policies. As he ably demonstrates, the public choice perspective brings out the richness of political-economic behaviour and complements the more severe neoclassical approach. Borooah considers why voters decide; the growth of public spending; and the political business cycle.

Much of the discussion in public sector economics assumes a unitary public sector. In reality this is seldom the case. There are multiple levels of government which give rise to complex relationships between the different levels. This is frequently referred to as 'fiscal federalism', though as David King (Chapter 7) points out, the fiscal problems of multi-level government systems are not confined to federal states. Which functions should be assigned to which level of government? How should each level of government be financed? Which taxes should be available to which level of government? What should the grant-in-aid relationship between each level of government look like and how should such grants be designed? These questions are the substance of multi-level government finance and David King's chapter provides a careful review of our current state of understanding them. Some of the questions raised in King's chapter are also touched upon in Barnett's (Chapter 5), especially the issues of grants-in-aid and the way in which these influence the modelling of the demand for local public goods. These two chapters, along with Levaggi's (Chapter 10), can be usefully read in conjunction with one another.

Often the solutions to public sector problems make strong assumptions about the institutional infrastructure of an economy. Well-developed capital markets, low transactions costs and sophisticated political systems for the making of public choices are assumed. These assumptions are, however, often not reasonable for developed countries let alone developing countries (see Newbery and Stern, 1987; Tanzi, 1991). In Chapter 8 Richard Bird considers the problems of public finance in developing countries. As Bird points out, 'the goals or objectives of public finance in developing countries are those of economic policy as a whole'. This chapter integrates some of the themes which are established in the other chapters in the volume: the link between fiscal variables and economic growth; public finance and stabilisation; the issues of income redistribution and the administration of taxes. He shows that in reality the task of the public finance analyst in a developing market economy is more complicated than in either an industrialised market economy or a traditional centrally planned economy: a conclusion hewn out of the experience of someone who has been a longstanding public finance analyst to industrialised and developing economists.

Musgrave (1958) drew a distinction between the three branches of the public sector budget: the allocative branch, which is concerned with the efficient allocation of resources, both inside and outside the public sector; the stabilisation branch, which focuses attention on the use of taxation, public spending and the national debt for short-run demand management of the economy; and finally the distribution branch which uses the instruments of fiscal policy to reallocate incomes (welfares) between individuals in society. No one would argue that this taxonary of branches of the public sector is a description of reality but it does enable the public sector economist to separate out the various policy decisions which governments have to make. Most of the chapters have so far dealt with the allocative branch, though at times the analysis has spilled over into other branches. Bird's chapter ranges across all three branches. The issues of redistribution are dealt with by Peter Lambert in Chapter 9, where he provides a highly accessible route into what is undoubtedly a complex area of the subject. He particularly examines how the economist should proceed when making social welfare comparisons between income distributions. This approach to economic modelling produces results which are of great importance for certain types of income tax reform.

Rosella Levaggi, in the final chapter in the volume, examines the role of asymmetric information in public finance. This is a relatively new topic which Levaggi developed in her PhD thesis. In this chapter she applies the ideas of asymmetric information to an examination of grants-in-aid in a federal system.

2 Taxation, Public Choice and Public Spending

PETER M. JACKSON

'Intelligent and civilised conduct of government and the delineation of its responsibilities are at the heart of democracy. Indeed, the conduct of government is the testing ground of social ethics and civilized living. Intelligent conduct of government requires an understanding of the economic relations involved; and the economist by aiding this understanding may hope to contribute to a better society.' (Musgrave, 1959, p. vi)

2.1 INTRODUCTION

This chapter reviews some of the issues and topics in modern public sector economics which are not covered in the other chapters of this book. Particular attention is given to taxation and capital; the effects of taxation on corporate financing decisions and personal savings; optimal taxation; international aspects of taxation and general equilibrium tax policy models. Modern public choice theory is also reviewed along with the analysis of public spending.

2.2 FUNDAMENTALS OF THE WELFARE STATE

The welfare state is often thought of in terms of its redistribution function. It is, however, possible to justify the existence of the welfare state on efficiency arguments without recourse to references about the redistribution of welfare. This argument is based upon the notion of market failures caused by the existence of

6

public goods and externalities. Few truly pure public goods exist in reality, therefore, does this mean that in practice there is no efficiency argument? Also, are externalities and market imperfections sufficiently significant to justify public sector intervention? Some writers, for example Friedman (1962), have compared the welfare costs of market failures with the welfare costs of public sector intervention (public sector failure). For example, Nozick (1974), following on Hayek's (1944) general arguments about the negative impact of the public sector upon liberty and freedom, points out that means are just as important as ends: i.e. while the ends of public provision might be laudable, achieving them via public provision might be unacceptable because to do so interferes with individuals' rights. The new welfare economics, however, provides an alternative efficiency rationale for public provision which transcends the public goods/externalities basis of market failure. This is founded on the new economics of information with its emphasis upon information asymmetries and principal–agent problems, which are special cases of the more general topic of moral hazard (Stiglitz, 1987). This literature depends heavily upon the work of Arrow (1963) and Akerlof (1970). Individuals as consumers or producers face imperfect information when making decisions. Information is costly to acquire and process. Consumers, for example, are not fully informed about quality or price, while producers are not completely informed about consumers' riskworthiness etc. Principal/agent problems arise when information is not distributed symmetrically. Because of information asymmetries markets can behave badly (i.e. markets fail), which strengthens the arguments for potential public sector intervention on the grounds of economic efficiency. For example, social insurance schemes are an institutional response to the market failures of private insurance markets caused by extreme forms of moral hazard. Principal/agent analysis can also be used to justify the direct public sector provision of services rather than the use of markets aided by regulations or subsidies.

While distributional and efficiency arguments, based upon market failures, do provide a rationale for the existence of the welfare state, modern public finance and public choice theory teaches that these efficiency gains need to be compared against the efficiency losses which arise from the financing and budgeting decisions of governments. Non-lump-sum taxes are distortionary and place a deadweight loss on private sector activities. In the sections which follow, the current state of knowledge about these efficiency costs are reviewed.

2.3   TAXATION AND CAPITAL

In a world of perfect competition and no taxation, differences in risk-adjusted real rates of return on different investments would result in a reallocation of capital and an equalisation of returns. In a world with taxes, it is, however, the real after-tax risk-adjusted rates of return which are equalised across assets in the long run. Neutrality of the tax system requires that the structure of assets (the capital stock) is invariant to changes in tax rates. Non-neutrality implies that the ranking of investments before and after the introduction of taxes (or tax changes) is different, with the usual implication that the after-tax capital stock is less productive.

There is disagreement, however, among economists about the impact of taxation on the cost of capital and hence the efficient allocation of capital between projects. This is also an important issue for understanding the growth performance of an economy and its attractiveness for international capital. If the cost of capital is defined as the minimum pre-tax rate of return that an investment project must earn in order to be profitable, then what is the effect of personal and corporate taxation upon that rate of return?

The answer to that question depends crucially on the assumptions which are made about the firm's financial decisions. According to one view, the total tax burden will fall upon all marginal investment projects, thereby implying a high cost of capital. This is contrasted with the alternative view which suggests that it is only the tax burden on retained earnings which is of any importance. Those who subscribe to the latter view emphasise the importance of financing assumptions. They argue that share issues, debt and retained profits should be regarded as alternative sources of finance. This gives rise to three different definitions of 'cost of capital' to be used in the tax optimising calculations.

The definitions of the cost of capital are expanded if the uses of profit are also considered. These are dividend, inter-payments, profit retentions and share-repurchases. When calculating the tax burden on marginal investment and the minimum pre-tax return required to make it profitable, it is important to know where an additional £1 used for investment is coming from and where it is going. Combining the three sources of profit with the four uses of profit gives twelve different definitions of the cost of capital.

The differences between the two views set out above centres around their use of the notion of the cost of capital. The more traditional view (Harberger, 1962, 1966; McLure, 1979) simply assumed two alternative financing instruments – debt and equity. Shareholders would be prepared to invest an extra £1 into a firm by purchasing new issues of equity (shares) if the returns in the form of dividends exceeded the return on bonds (the alternative use of their funds). If P is the annual dividend from an investment of £1 and i is the annual rate of interest on bonds, then shareholders will be willing to invest up to $P = i$.

The above calculation assumes no taxes. Now assume distributed earnings are subject to a corporate tax rate t_d and in addition to a personal tax rate of t_{dp} (i.e. double taxation of dividends). Further assume that interest income is only taxed at the personal rate t_i. Investment in the marginal investment now takes place up to:

$$(1 - t_d)(1 - t_{dp}) = i\,(1 - t_i)$$

For most countries (Norway being an exception)

$$t_{dp} = t_i$$

Thus,

$$P = \frac{i}{(1 - t_d)}$$

The right-hand side of this equation is the cost of capital. With the introduction of taxation the cost of capital will rise the higher is the tax rate. This causes distortions in the allocation of capital in an economy (and hence has implications for economic growth). In particular, if the tax rate is too high a large proportion of the capital stock will be allocated to the non-corporate sectors or capital will flow out of the country to these areas which do not impose a tax on dividends (Hamada, 1966).

The corporate tax is, however, neutral in the case of debt financing, since it is a burden on intramarginal, and not marginal, investment projects.

The traditional view focused on equity finance (i.e. new share issues) as the dominant source of finance. In reality, however, most corporate finance comes from internal rather than external sources: i.e. retained profits. King (1974a, 1974b, 1977) was the first to depart from the traditional view by analysing the cost of capital for the case of profits retention. This developed the literature of the new view (Bradford, 1980, 1981; Auerbach, 1979, 1983; Fullerton and King, 1984; Edwards and Keen, 1984; Sinn, 1985).

Let t_r be the corporate tax rate on retained profits and t_c be the personal capital gains tax rate. For countries such as the USA, Australia, New Zealand and Switzerland, t_r equals t_d. In the majority of OECD countries, however, t_r exceeds t_d, i.e. imputation systems are used to refund part of the corporate tax to shareholders.

If a firm decides to increase the amount of profit it retains (instead of paying out dividends) in order to finance new investment, then this policy is worthwhile to the shareholder provided that the rate of return on investment is high enough to generate future dividends in excess of the interest income which they would have earned had they received the dividends and invested them in bonds. Retaining profits creates more capital gains and increases shareholders' capital gains tax liability. Thus,

$$P = \frac{1 - t_i}{(1 - t_c)(1 - t_r)}$$

While distortions obviously still exist because of taxation they are not as large as in the case of the traditional view.

A complete treatment of the impact of taxation on the cost of capital would be an extremely complex task since it would need to take into account combinations of alternative sources and uses of funds. This exercise has been carried out by Sinn (1990).

What empirical evidence exists to inform the fiscal economist about the extent to which tax systems favour one type of capital income compared to others? Fullerton and King (1984) studied this question for the US, UK, Sweden and Germany. Others have extended this methodology to other countries: Daly et al. (1984);

Kikutani and Tachibanaki (1986); and McKee, Visser and Saunders (1986). The King–Fullerton methodology determines the tax-inclusive cost of capital (i.e. accounting for the effects of tax provisions such as investment incentives) for a hypothetical project, and compares it with the after-tax return to those providing the funds. The cost of capital, or required rate of return, is expressed as;

$$P = \left[\frac{(1 - A)}{(1 - t)} \cdot (i + d - e) \right] - d$$

where e is the expected rate of inflation; t is the statutory marginal corporate tax rate; i is the nominal discount rate; d is the rate of economic depreciation; A is the present value of grants and allowances which reduce the cost of acquisition of an asset.

What these studies find is that marginal effective tax rates vary considerably according to asset type; the industry in which the asset is used; and the type of financing and source of funds. It is usually the case that machinery is favoured over buildings and inventories; and that debt is more attractive than other sources of finance.

2.4 TAXATION AND CORPORATE FINANCING DECISIONS

Does taxation influence a firm's corporate financing decision, i.e. its choice between debt and equity? Many studies have found no predictable material effects of a firm's tax status on its debt policy (see Myers, 1984; Poterba, 1986; Titman and Wessels, 1988; Fischer, Heinkel and Zechner, 1989; Ang and Peterson, 1986; Long and Malitz, 1985; Bradley, Jarrell and Kim, 1984; and Marsh, 1982). It has, however, been found by Scholes, Wilson and Wolfsen (1989) that tax loss carry-forwards do have a significant effect upon the financial portfolios held by commercial banks.

Theory suggests that firms with low expected marginal tax rates on interest deductions will be less likely to finance new investments with debt. Tax shields (i.e. tax loss carry-forward or investment tax credits) affect average tax rates but have little or no effect upon marginal tax rates.

The problem confronted by many empirical studies which examined debt/equity ratios is that these are stocks concepts which have been built up over time. What is of material interest is to study the effects of taxation on incremental financing decisions, i.e. the actual financing decisions of firms.

Loss carry-forward can have a significant impact on the tax rate facing a firm. Auerbach and Poterba (1986) show that sufficiently generous loss carry-forwards will reduce the tax rate to zero (i.e. marginal tax rate on interest deductions = zero). Firms with high tax loss carry-forwards will be less likely to use debt because they will not be able to use interest deductions. Investment tax credits do not, however, affect the profitability of a debt issue because, on average, firms are profitable and are paying taxes. The only time that tax shields will affect financing decisions is when they change the marginal tax rate on interest deductions.

2.5   TAXATION AND SAVINGS

Taxation of income from capital has the potential of lowering the savings rate of an economy. Controversy exists over the effects of changes in after-tax rates of return to savings. Theory does not give a clear indication of how to choose between these effects so the problem must be resolved empirically.

The theoretical model is straightforward. Individuals maximise an inter-temporal utility function which includes periods while they are in employment and periods of retirement. Maximisation is subject to a lifetime income constraint, which includes labour income, exogenous income and returns to saving. A tax on the returns to savings will change the slope of the budget line, thereby affecting the trade-off between current and future consumption (and hence savings). There is an income effect which raises savings and a substitution effect which reduces savings because the relative price of future consumption has been increased as a result of the tax. Where there are income and substitution effects the net income is ambiguous depending on the strengths of the two effects. If the substitution effect dominates, then policy-makers could direct attention to influence the after-tax return on savings in order to increase savings.

In empirical studies attention is focused on the elasticity of saving with respect to the after-tax rate of return. Earlier views were that the effect of taxes on savings was negligible, i.e. that the uncompensated elasticity of saving was zero. This seemed to be supported by 'Denison's Law', i.e. that saving in the US was a constant fraction of income. Studies by Wright (1969) and Blinder (1975) suggested that the compensated elasticity was low. Howrey and Hymans (1978), Evans (1983) and Friend and Hasbrouck (1983) did not find a significantly large interest elasticity of savings. Henderschott and Peck (1985) found that the after-tax real rate of interest had no effect on the savings ratio. This was confirmed by Montgomery (1986), Blinder (1987), Baum (1988) and Starrett (1988b).

Studies by Boskin (1978), Boskin and Lau (1978) and Summers (1983) find much higher uncompensated elasticities ranging from 0.20 to 0.60. The estimates vary depending upon (a) the definition of saving, (b) the measure of the interest rate, (c) the sample period, and (d) the measure of expected inflation. Summers' (1983) estimates were even larger, ranging from 1.5 to 3.0. Tullio and Contesso (1986) in their study found significant negative uncompensated elasticities of private consumption with respect to the after-tax return on saving – this was for the nominal return and the real return. Beach, Boadway and Bruce (1986) using a life-cycle model introduced the effect of the age distribution of the population. They found a positive effect on saving of the after-tax real return for the young (i.e. the substitution effect was the stronger). This became negative as individuals reached retirement age (i.e. the income effect became stronger).

The Beach, Boadway and Bruce study suggests why more aggregate studies do not pick up a significant effect of interest rates on consumption and saving. The average over the life-cycle is made up of income and substitution effects for each age group cancelling one another out.

The tax system of a country is often designed to influence savings via incentives: for example, if the tax system allows deductions for savings earmarked for specific purposes (e.g. life insurance, real estate, etc.), then this could have a positive impact on the *level* of savings in addition to changing the composition of savings as between choice of asset. Deductibility of interest, for tax purposes, on certain items of borrowing (e.g. mortgages) reduces the cost of borrowing for consumption, especially at high marginal tax rates. This will also suggest a reduction in savings. When inflation is high it also implies negative real rates of interest.

What empirical evidence exists to inform us about the impact of tax incentives on the level and composition of savings? Again the results will depend upon the interest elasticity of savings. Byrne (1976) using German data found no effect of tax incentives on the total level of household savings. Carroll and Summers (1987) found a positive (though weak) effect of tax incentives on savings (Venti and Wise, 1987, did also). Studies of the effect of granting interest income on savings' tax-exemption status was found to have a very small positive effect by Shibuya (1987, 1988), Makin (1986) and Horioka (1986). Generally, however, it is difficult to find empirical evidence to support one way or the other the impact of interest deductibility on savings.

Reviewing the evidence of tax incentives on housing, Smith, Rosen and Fallis (1988) concluded that the studies overwhelmingly show that it has encouraged home ownership and has transferred substantial resources from heavily subsidised owner-occupiers to less subsidised renters. It has also directed resources into home ownership away from other forms of capital.

Another fiscal impact on savings arises form the interaction between savings and the social security system, in particular pensions. Again the theoretical foundations are straightforward but since they involve the relative impacts of income and substitution effects the question can only be answered empirically. Financing public pensions via taxes (or public debt) will have an impact upon consumption. There are wealth effects which need to be taken into consideration. If individuals are assumed to be rational they will form expectations about the value of their future pension benefits (income) which will affect current savings decisions, i.e. the higher the future pension income the less pressure there will be to save as much in the current period for their old age. However, pensions can also affect the decision about the age at which to retire. If individuals decide to retire early they will increase their current period savings. Which of these two effects is the stronger?

Feldstein's (1974a) study found that, in the absence of social security, savings in the US would have been 50 per cent higher, which implied that the wealth effect was stronger than the retirement decision effect. Munnell (1974, 1976 and 1982) found no net effect suggesting that the two effects balanced one another.

Follow-up studies by Feldstein (1977a, 1978, 1980, 1982, 1983a) and Feldstein and Pellechio (1979) confirmed his earlier conclusions. Other studies have also supported Feldstein's results (Diamond and Hausman, 1984; Hubbard, 1986; Henderschott and Peck, 1985; Gultekin and Logue, 1979; Shibuya, 1988; Yamada and Yamada, 1988).

While there is evidence demonstrating a dominant wealth effect of social security on private savings there is also a substantial amount of evidence which disputes this: e.g. Barro and McDonald (1979); Kopits and Gotur (1980); Modigliani and Sterling (1983); Koskela and Viren (1983); Horioka (1986); Browning (1982). These studies used US data. Other studies using data from other countries include Boyle and Murray (1979), Canada; Markowski and Palmer (1979), Sweden; Denny and Rea (1979) and Pfaff, Hurler and Dennerlein (1979), Germany; Ouder (1979), France; and Ando and Kennickell (1987), Italy.

Aaron (1982) concluded his review, 'the evidence falls grossly short of establishing the size, or even the direction, of the effects of social security on capital formation'. This conclusion still remains valid.

2.6 NORMATIVE PUBLIC FINANCE THEORY

Much of public finance analysis is directed towards normative issues. To many this is regarded as abstract theorising which has little relevance for policy analysis. Such a view is, however, mistaken. The purpose of normative analysis is to give insight into the structure of arguments; to establish relationships between variables given specific constraints and objectives (usually in the context of perfect competition). These models can be thought of as laboratories within which the consequences of arguments are explored. There is nothing quite so practical as a good theory (Jackson, 1990). Such theorising is not, however, an exercise in explaining the political and decision processes which generate public policies – this is the province of public choice theory.

One major strand to the normative theory of public finance is that which is frequently referred to as optimal taxation. The optimal taxation literature searches for those tax systems which will minimise the efficiency costs of taxation (i.e. the amount of distortion to relative prices). In complex models efficiency costs are traded off against the effect of the tax upon the distribution of welfare. The typical analysis of optimal taxation assumes that a government has to raise a fixed amount of tax revenue with a limited set of tax instruments that should be administered cost-lessly. Lump-sum taxes which are now distortionary are ruled out. The criterion used to rank tax systems is usually the level of utility of the representative individual. In models of individuals with diverse preferences a utilitarian social welfare function is used to aggregate individual preferences. Concern for 'fairness' of the tax system is usually incorporated in the concavity assumptions of the social welfare function. Thorough surveys of the optimal tax litera-ture are found in Auerbach (1985), Stern (1987) and Slemrod (1990).

The basic idea of optimal taxation can be illustrated by means of Figure 2.1, in which total tax revenues (T) are related to the tax rate (t). The dotted line (AB) assumes no relative price distortions arising from the imposition of the tax, i.e. no supply response. On the other hand, AC does involve distortion (efficiency cost) and a supply-side response – this has been emphasised by Arthur Laffer (1982), but the rather basic idea goes back to Jules Dupuit, 1844.

If taxes distort relative prices then the introduction of the tax will have a profound impact upon individuals' welfare levels: this is the origin of the supply-side (or demand-side) response as indi-viduals reorganise their demand and supply decisions in order to avoid paying taxes. The policy problem which faces a government is to choose that tax rate which maximises welfare and tax re-venues. In terms of Figure 2.1, interest lies in locating the turning point at D.

Harberger (1959, 1964, 1966), in his classic studies of the US tax system's efficiency, especially the corporation tax, estimated that the efficiency costs of the corporation tax imposed on the US economy were about one-half to three-quarters of 1 per cent of GDP. In his 1964 paper he concluded that the combined efficiency costs of all taxes was 1 per cent of GDP. Harberger argued that there was a great need for tax reform to reduce these welfare costs, which, while they might be small in percentage terms, are, never-theless, large in terms of lost dollars.

Some try to balance this by arguing that these welfare losses are acceptable because they are set against greater welfare gains via

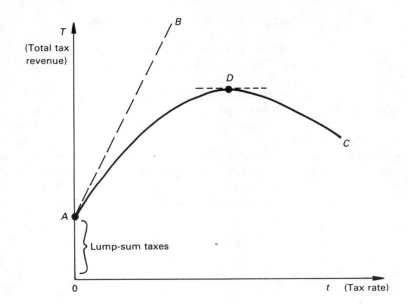

FIGURE 2.1   Optimal taxes

redistribution. There is, however, little evidence to support this view that the tax system does much to redistribute incomes. Pechman and Okner (1974) in their study suggest that the progression of the income tax is offset by the regression of sales takes, excise and payroll taxes.

To illustrate the problem the example of labour supply responses to taxation will be given (see Slemrod, 1990, for a more detailed discussion of optimal commodity taxes). The problem of income (welfare) redistribution arises because individuals are not identical in all respects. In particular they are different with respect to their earning power which in turn depends on their own personal endowments. They also differ in terms of their capital income and wealth. It is assumed that all individuals with the same wage rate supply the same amount of labour (L), i.e. there are no differences in preferences across the set of individuals. A perfectly elastic demand for labour is also assumed at the specific wage rate. The labour supply function is written as:

$$L = L_0 \left[w \left(1 - t \right) \right]^E$$

where E is the elasticity of labour supply with respect to the net wage $w (1 - t)$. The distribution of wage rates is lognormal with a coefficient of variation h.

The social value of an additional unit of income to a person with wage rate w is proportional to w^{-c}. For very right-wing economists $c = 0$ which implies distributional indifference. As $c \to \infty$ this implies that attention is devoted to the least well-off person in society (i.e. a Rawlsian maximum). If $c = \frac{1}{2}$ then if a rich man has a wage which is nine times that of a poor person then we attach $c = \frac{1}{3}$ of the weight to an increase in his income.

In this type of model the optimal tax rate (t^*) is given by:

$$\frac{t^*}{1 - t^*} = \frac{1}{E} \left[1 - (1 - h^2)^{-c(1-E)} \right]$$

The term $1/E$ is the efficiency component and is obviously related to the elasticity of the labour supply. The greater the value of E then the greater the distortion and the smaller is the value of t^*.

The expression contained within the brackets is the equity component and depends upon the degree of inequality in wage rates as measured by h. The greater the inequality the smaller is the value of h and hence the closer the expression in brackets is to unity. The greater the inequity then the higher should t^* be. The larger the elasticity (E) the faster gross earnings rise with (w) and hence the more effective is the income tax as a redistributive instrument.

Distributional values are embodied in c. If someone has no concern with distribution then $c = 0$ and $t^* = 0$.

Can empirical evidence give any insights to the trade-off between equity and efficiency? Browning and Johnson (1984) make an attempt. What is found is that the optimal tax rate formula is very sensitive to values of the key parameters. For example:

(a) when $c = \frac{1}{2}$; $h = 0.6$ and $E = 0.5$ then $t^* = 29$ per cent;

(b) when $c = \frac{1}{2}$; $h = 0.6$ and $E = 0.1$ then $t^* = 61$ per cent.

Browning and Johnson used best estimates for some of the

parameter values for the USA and compared the welfare costs of redistribution with the welfare gains. On a set of plausible estimates they found that the costs are $3\frac{1}{2}$ times the gains. Thus they conclude, 'the marginal cost of less income inequality is surprisingly high even when labour supply elasticities are relatively low' (p. 201). To counter this conclusion it is necessary to assume that the rich have a very strong preference for redistribution, i.e. that $c \rightarrow \infty$.

Recent work also confirms that the welfare costs of taxes are greater than supposed. Piggott and Whalley (1985) in their study of the UK estimated that the annual welfare loss due to taxation was between 6 per cent and 9 per cent of GNP in the early 1970s. Ballard, Fullerton, Shoven and Whalley's (1985) estimates for the USA gave a central point estimate of 8 per cent of GDP. The efficiency costs are even greater at the margin: they estimate it to be 35 cents per extra dollar of tax revenue collected. (See also Keller, 1980; Piggott, 1980; Slemrod, 1983; Daly *et al.*, 1985; and Fullerton and Henderson, 1986.)

However, while this is a demonstration of how economic theory can be used to give insight to policy issues it is also important that the limits of our knowledge be recognised and conveyed to those who have to draw policy conclusions. First, the optimal tax literature needs to look beyond the labour supply responses and take other responses into account, such as those related to savings and portfolio composition. Second, labour supply is much more complex than the simple model outlined above suggests. There are many dimensions to the supply that have not been measured – e.g. effort, morale, willingness to take responsibility, and investment in training and human capital. Furthermore, labour supply studies generally do not include the behaviour of the self-employed. Finally, there are wide confidence intervals around the point estimates for E.

These qualifications severely constrain the utility of Browning and Johnson's conclusions for policy purposes.

More generally the optimal tax literature and normative public finance have to address themselves to some of the more fundamental criticisms of the standard neoclassical model upon which their analysis is predicted. The assumption of perfect competition in the Arrow/Debreu general equilibrium model is a strong one.

Markets do not clear with infinite velocity. Information is not perfectly and costlessly distributed over all individuals, rather it is impacted (asymmetrical) and costly to collect and interpret. The standard neoclassical model frequently assumes complete certainty and yet public policy is often designed to cope with uncertainty and the contingencies that perfect markets fail to cope with.

In a second-best world (i.e. a non-Arrow/Debreu world) the welfare costs of taxation are not of the Harberger type, which are calculated assuming that perfect competition prevails. In a world of incomplete markets taxes might not distort the allocative mechanism. Indeed, in many cases the allocative process is improved by tax interventions. This does not just apply to specific taxes, such as pollution taxes; it applies to general taxes also (see Greenwald and Stiglitz, 1988).

Throughout all branches of economics there is much discussion about the nature of the objective function. Just what is it that individuals seek to maximise? Many (e.g. Sen, 1982) argue that economists need to go beyond considering pure welfare objectives (i.e. those based upon conventional notions of individual welfare): non-welfarist goals such as liberty and freedom should be included. This will have important implications for public sector economics. Within this new approach a basic principle which a fiscal constitution might embody is a principle of liberty along the lines proposed by Rawls: 'each person is to have equal right to the most extensive basic liberty compatible with a similar liberty for others' (1971, p. 60). Any proposition of this kind is, however, open to alternative interpretations, as Buchanan (1984) has shown. Buchanan believes that Rawls is arguing that there is a maximum permissible amount of redistribution that can be made via taxation.

The rich can, however, play games that threaten the welfare and the liberty of the poor. Employing Berlin's (1958) notion of positive and negative freedom, Dasgupta (1985) has made an effective riposte to the libertarians' narrow focus on negative freedom, and the work of Marshall (1964) has extended rights to include ideas such as citizenship rights which provide the foundations of an active interventionist role for government to balance these freedoms and rights (see Jackson, 1989). If individuals are to reach an effective (acceptable) level of liberty then they do not only require basic rights – they also require a certain level of economic resources. These resources can only be found from the rich. As always the problem is striking a balance so that incentives are not completely destroyed: an issue which was recognised by the founding fathers of economics (Schumpeter, 1918) and which remains today clouded in uncertainty.

2.7 INTERNATIONAL ASPECTS OF TAX ANALYSIS

International capital markets have become increasingly integrated. If a country places too great an emphasis upon corporate or equity taxes then it runs a high risk of capital flight. Fiscal policies have a strategic element: by reducing tax rates relative to other countries they can induce a capital inflow.

This issue has been studied by Hamada (1966) and Feldstein and Hartman (1979). They use a game theoretic model to study the Nash and cooperative strategies of capital exporting and capital importing countries. It is a static analysis in which the efficiency criteria are that post-tax rates of return should be equalised across countries. Others have found that investment location is very sensitive to tax policies: see Boskin and Gale (1986) and Frisch and Hartman (1983). Given this then there is a strong case for fiscal coordination: i.e. if governments agree not to compete against each other on taxes then they can set tax rates which optimise their objectives.

If taxes are not coordinated then there will be an inappropriate provision of public goods for each region or each nation state. In particular there is likely to be an under-provision. This arises because governments fearing capital flight will set taxes at a very low level, if they act in an uncoordinated way. Tax revenues will be too low to finance public good levels which would be regarded as optimal in the absence of capital flight. The scope of income redistribution via public goods will be affected (see also, McLure, 1967; Wilson, 1986, 1987; Wildasin, 1987b; Gordon, 1983; Mintz and Tulkens, 1986; and Jun, 1989).

The growth of the importance of multinational corporations in the international economy has also caused fiscal economists to consider the international dimensions to taxation. For example, deferred repatriation of funds is of importance when a multinational corporation seeks to avoid paying taxes (see Slemrod and

Razin, 1990). Multinational corporations are able to engage in tax arbitrage by, for example, shifting profits to the country with the lowest capital income tax. This can be done via a series of transfer pricing transfers (without the need to relocate physical capital) (see Tanzi, 1987b).

The liberalisation and integration of the market for goods, services and capital in the European Community will probably require a coordination of capital income taxation. A survey of 173 large UK companies found that 80 per cent of the companies were influenced by tax factors when deciding where to locate a production plant (Devereux and Pearson, 1989).

Tax harmonisation, however, presents a number of problems. First, what is meant by tax harmonisation? At the simplest level it means the alignment of the tax systems of different countries within an economic union such as the EC, such that tax does not influence the location of factors of production. This usually means the alignment of tax rates. But such an alignment is a complex issue. Does it mean the imposition of one tax system (its structure) on all other countries? This would include tax expenditures. Second, there is a need to recognise that the tax system *de jure* differs from the actual system *de facto* because of differences in tax enforcements. How could a uniform *fiscal structure* be imposed?

2.8   GENERAL EQUILIBRIUM TAX POLICY MODELS

It is accepted that general equilibrium models are superior to partial equilibrium models. They capture a wider set of relevant influences upon a policy problem; result in more accurate parameter estimates when studied empirically; and give a better understanding of the long-run consequences of policy changes. A general equilibrium approach is particularly useful when examining the incidence of the tax burden which involves tracing the backward and forward shifting of taxes. Moreover, the responses of relative prices arising from tax changes are greater in the long run than in the short run. Thus, the welfare losses due to taxes are more likely to be larger in the long run than in the short run.

Analytical general equilibrium models were pioneered by Harberger (1962 and 1966) who used a Walrasian general equilibrium model to examine the equilibrium changes caused by small tax changes transmitted via changes in relative prices. The Harberger model (explained in Brown, and Jackson, 1990) demonstrated that the elimination of the corporate income tax, with the lost revenue being found from lump-sum taxes, would yield welfare gains from between 0.3 and 0.6 per cent of CNP or between 6 and 15 per cent of the revenue raised by the corporation tax. These estimates were analytical rather than purely empirical.

Advancements is computing power and the development of computable solution algorithms (Scarf, 1984) gave a boost to the construction of disaggregated applied general equilibrium models. Whereas the Harberger model had assumed fixed aggregate supplies of factors of production and had employed a two-factor/two-product closed economy with linear homogenous production functions, the new applied general equilibrium models are more adventurous; Piggott and Whalley (1985) assumed 33 industrial groups. Households can also be disaggregated according to income, age, occupation, etc.

Disaggregation, which is a feature of the general equilibrium models, gives greater insight into how different sectors of the economy are affected by tax changes. The demand effects of taxes vary between income groups. Thus, a model which distinguishes between a greater number of income groups provides greater understanding of the differential impact of taxes. A similar argument applies to portfolio composition which also varies across income groups. As Fullerton, Shoven and Whalley (1983) have demonstrated, calculation of the size of the welfare losses from taxation is sensitive to the level of disaggregation which is being used.

General equilibrium tax models have also been used to simulate the consequences, in terms of welfare loss, of substituting one combination of taxes with another. This is an improvement on comparing the deadweight loss of one tax with a lump-sum tax (see Ballard, Fullerton, Shoven and Whalley, 1985; Slemrod, 1983; Serra-Puche, 1984; Borges, 1986).

While general equilibrium models are static in character and are not well suited to deal with dynamic questions, some recent attempts have been made to incorporate dynamic elements. A dynamic specification using overlapping generation life-cycle structures is found in Auerbach, Kotlikoff and Skinner (1983) and Summers (1981). This approach allows simulation of the effects of changing from an income tax to a consumption tax to find the inter-temporal effects on savings capital accumulation. The welfare effects of changing from one tax regime to another are assessed by comparing the different consumption profiles and assigning welfare values to them. Fullerton, Henderson and Shoven (1984) demonstrate that the estimated welfare gains due to integration of the corporate and personal income taxes in the USA are almost five times greater in the dynamic model case compared to those estimated from a static model. Moreover, these welfare gains increase with the degree of disaggregation in the model (dynamic and static).

While the general equilibrium models described above have extended understanding about complex tax systems and for measuring the effects of alternative tax regimes there are nevertheless a number of limitations that must be recognised (Borges, 1986). Such models are simple in their treatment of time, market structure, and public spending. The specifications used in the models are not tested. Simulations are often based upon imperfect and sometimes unreliable data. A great deal of subjective judgement goes into the construction of these models and these judgements need to be challenged given that the results will be sensitive to them. The functional forms which are usually chosen are the CES, Cobb-Douglas and linear expenditure systems because this simplifies calculation but at the same time constrains the results. Strong assumptions are also made when calibrating the models. For example, it is assumed that with the existing tax structure and tax rates the economy is in equilibrium. Also, tax revenues depend on the parameters of the demand function but demand depends on how tax revenues are assigned.

The results of general equilibrium tax models are not verifiable empirically; they usually tend to be static; they refer to the long run rather than the short run; and they are for closed rather than open economics. Despite these limitations and weaknesses the general equilibrium approach is useful. The models have much to offer the policy debate because the insights which they provide challenge existing perceptions about the way in which tax policies impact on an economy. They do not, nor are they intended to, give precise numerical measures of the impact of taxes on the various sectors of an economy. There are few alternatives to discussing meaningfully in a policy context the effects of tax changes on the economy. Several equilibrium models can be used to challenge and to put into perspective the folklore and beliefs about the economy generally, and the tax system in particular, which are often firmly held by those who advise governments.

2.9 PUBLIC CHOICE

Public choice theory should not be confused with the more abstract topic of social or collective choice which develops the ideas set out by Arrow (1963) and which examined the conditions under which a set of individual preferences can be aggregated into a consistent social preference ordering. While the two subjects are closely related – public choice drawing upon the theoretical propositions of social choice theory – nevertheless public choice is wider in its scope and significantly different in the methodology which is employed. Public choice emphasises the importance of the social institutions within which political, including fiscal, choices are made.

While there has been a primitive public choice literature for many years it is generally agreed that public choice was launched as a subject in its own right with the seminal and systematic contribution of Buchanan and Tullock's (1962) *The Calculus of Consent: Logical Foundations of Constitutional Democracy.* In that book Buchanan and Tullock introduced the central idea of the 'fiscal constitution', which was developed later by Brennan and Buchanan (1980, 1985).

The simplifying assumption of normative public finance is that government is ruled by a benevolent dictator who maximises social welfare or the 'public interest'. This is the essence of the Pigovian approach to modelling fiscal decisions which lies at the heart of most general equilibrium tax analysis and public expenditure decision-making. Buchanan, however, building upon the Swedish tradition of Wicksell and Lindahl preferred an alternative methodology. In his *Fiscal Theory and Political Economy*, Buchanan (1960) had written:

> Governmental decisions are no more exogenous than are those made by the private economy . . . Any approach to a complete or satisfactory treatment of the public sector must examine as a

central feature the way in which collective decisions are made.
(p. 3)

In other words, governments do not compute optimal solutions
to social welfare functions. Instead, the institutions of government
are peopled by individuals who occupy roles in other social institutions and who, therefore, bring to their roles in government institutions their self-interests. By making politicians and bureaucrats endogenous to the situational analysis Buchanan established,
for public sector analysis, a methodological individualism in which
the principal actors (politicians, bureaucrats, voters, pressure
groups, etc.) would play complex interactive games. Public policies, tax decisions and public expenditure decisions could only be
understood as the outcome of the games.

The public choice school has developed a number of models
which arch the terrain between economics and political science:
the political business cycle; the political popularity function; the
Downsian (Downs, 1957) vote-maximising politician and the Niskanen (1971) budget-maximising bureaucrat (see also, Frey, 1978;
Mueller, 1989; Jackson, 1982).

Buchanan, however, has gone further than simply endogenising
political decision-makers. He also argues that a failure to join up
knowledge of taxation with that of public expenditure will result in
the production of unsatisfactory fiscal rules. This is especially true
in incidence studies which usually focus on tax incidence only.

These ideas were developed in the *Calculus of Consent*. In that
book the problem of choosing a 'fiscal constitution' is given central
place. A fiscal constitution can be thought of as a set of policy
rules: but a set which is bounded by an appeal to notions of justice,
liberty and freedom. These also place the bounds on government
action, a theme which was developed in Buchanan's (1975) *The
Limits of Liberty: Between Anarchy and Leviathan*.

When choosing the rules that define a fiscal constitution decisions are being made under conditions of uncertainty, in the sense
that the rules need to be capable of dealing with contexts and
issues that are as yet unknown (and unknowable). These rules
need to be impersonal (Harsanyi, 1955). In many important respects Buchanan's work was a precursor to that of Rawls – both
were searching for the rules that will structure a society in a just
way in which decisions that will affect the future are made behind a

'veil of ignorance'. Differences, however, arise in the choice of what constitutes justice and hence there remains the intractable problem of choosing between constitutions without a set of clear criteria to guide such a choice. In practice, however, when faced with rules that apply to an uncertain future individuals are most likely to accept the most general rules which will minimise their risks.

Once the constitution is chosen fiscal decisions are made within the political process defined by the constitution. The constitution helps to constrain the political processes.

Buchanan's early work has spawned a new school of thought within economics and has helped to forge some links between economic and political science. Public choice and the new political economy have developed alongside one another; though political economy is wider than public choice and incorporates the insights of social choice theory and game theory. Central to the study of public choice are notions such as the 'median voter' in which vote maximising politicians need to seek out and satisfy the preferences of the voter who occupies the median and hence dominant position in the distribution. Niskanen (1971) by endogenising bureaucratic decisions extended the public choice model and stimulated a whole new area of research. Endogenising politicians into macro-economic fiscal decisions resulted in the literature of the 'political business cycle'.

The public choice model has not gone without criticism. The median voter model is a very crude first approximation to political behaviour and decision-making. It does not capture the essence of representative democracy and complex voting systems in which the median voter is not dominant. Moreover, once two or three dimensions are added to the voting space then the existence of majority voting equilibrium is doubtful. Niskanen's model of bureaucracy is too crude. Bureaucrats serve the public interest, as in the Weberian model, just as much as they serve their own interests (see Musgrave, 1985). Evidence for the existence of political business cycles is not conclusive.

Proponents of the public choice school such as Buchanan have at times been over-zealous in their criticism of the neoclassical approach to modelling tax and public expenditure problems. Standard economic analysis helps to structure policy problems and helps to provide insight to what is and is not of importance. The public choice school complements the neoclassical approach through its emphasis on the importance of institutions' political processes and fiscal behavior.

Criticism of public choice models has come from marxist or neo-marxist models. These models are more macro, holistic (i.e. general) and comparative than the public choice models, which focus more on rational choice theory. The distinction between these classes of models is more than just one of ideology. There are methodological differences. Neo-marxist models are structural whereas public choice models are more micro (see Barry, 1970; Wallerstein, 1979; Szentes, 1983; Lijphart, 1977, 1984; Lindbeck, 1977).

2.10 PUBLIC EXPENDITURE

Following the work of Samuelson on public goods and Arrow on social choice, economists have spent a good deal of time analysing the conditions for the efficient provision of public goods or near public goods – see Oakland (1987) for a review. Another dimension to this analysis has been the study of group decision-making and the translation of individual preferences into a social preference ordering: see Inman (1987a) and Mueller (1989) for reviews of this work.

At the level of empirical analysis economists still hunt the snark of the median voter. Following Duncan Black's (1958) earlier work the median voter was thought to be decisive when it comes to making decisions about public spending. However, as Romer and Rosenthal (1978; 1979a; 1979b; 1982) have argued, given the strict conditions under which the median voter could be decisive, it is not too surprising to discover that any empirical support for the proposition is weak and is confined to specific political institutional settings such as that of Switzerland (Pommerehne and Schneider, 1983).

Many of the earlier empirical studies of the determinants of public spending were based on the assumption that the demand side of the equation was adequately modelled using the median voter assumption (Barr and Davies, 1966; Bergstrom and Goodman, 1973; Borcherding and Deacon, 1972). Recent surveys are

.

found in Inman (1979, 1987a), Rubinfeld (1987) and Wildasin (1986, 1987b).

The standard model that is estimated is:

$$Z = b \, p_i^d \, Y_{im}^g \, e_i$$

where b is a constant term; e is the error term; d is the price elasticity of the public goods; Z is public spending on public goods in locality i; p_i is the price variable; g is the income elasticity of demand; Y_{im} is the income of the median voter in locality i.

This type of model is estimated using cross-section data. The price variable is usually calculated on the basis of some tax-sharing assumption. Thus, in the case of a property tax and where the local jurisdiction is in receipt of grants-in-aid from the state and/or central (federal) level of government then, if x_{im} is the median house value and X_i is the total value of housing in the locality then x_{im}/X_i is the median voter's share of the tax. If G_i is the proportion of local public spending financed by grants then the effective price faced by the median voter in locality i is assumed to be $\frac{x_{im}}{X_i} \cdot (1 - G_i)$.

There are, however, a number of problems with this model (Wildasin 1989). First, the demand estimates calculated from models of this kind will be biased because public goods are in reality financed from distortionary taxes – the effective marginal cost of public goods includes not just the direct cost but also the cost of tax distortions. Second, there is the problem of identifying the median voter. Third, the Tiebout hypothesis can result in heterogeneous populations rending in a jurisdiction which will bias cross-section estimates of the income elasticities of demand. Fourth, when measuring the price of public goods it is assured that matching grants will affect relative prices but that lump-sum grants will not. However, as Oates (1979), Hamilton (1983) and Barnett (in this volume) argue, lump-sum grants might affect relative prices (the 'flypaper effect') which will bias the price elasticities. Finally, to the extent that tax shifting exists it will affect the perceived price and hence the value of the price elasticity.

Similar models to that set out above have been used to study the growth of public spending. In the case of time-series models it is either the growth of the absolute size of public spending or some relative measure such as per capital public spending or public spending as a percentage of GDP. Borcherding's (1985) study is representative of this class. He computes the actual percentage changes in p and Y_m over time. Using the price and income elasticities of demand for public goods calculated from separate econometric studies Borcherding then calculates by how much public expenditure would have changed as a result of changes in price and changes in income. When this is compared with the actual change in public spending he finds that only about 38 per cent of the growth in US public spending can be explained by price and income changes. In other words, there is more to public spending growth than the demand-side explanation of the median voter.

Borcherding's study suffers from the problems of bias that have been described already (though not the Tiebout problem). But leaving these issues aside it is clear that as yet economists do not have an adequate model of the public expenditure process. More care has to be given to the institutional details of the supply side of the public expenditure model.

3 Income Taxation, Income Support Policies and Work Incentives in the UK

IAN WALKER

3.1 INTRODUCTION

One of the oldest, yet currently most topical, issues in the economics of public policy is the question of the disincentive effects associated with income taxation (and income support schemes). Recent concern over work disincentive effects has motivated quite drastic reforms to tax (and, in some cases, social security) systems in the USA, UK, Australia, and elsewhere. Even Scandinavian countries with socialist governments and a long tradition of steeply progressive income tax systems and extensive social security provisions, such as Denmark and Sweden, have tax reforms to promote work incentives under consideration.

Thus this chapter is concerned with the effects of income taxation and income support policies on the incentive to work, with emphasis on the UK tax and social security systems and UK econometric evidence. The chapter is largely a guide to the voluminous literature on taxation and incentives for those interested in evaluating UK policy rather than an exhaustive survey of the econometric evidence in the field.[1]

In section 3.2 the conventional theory of labour supply is outlined. Conventional neoclassical theory argues that it is *marginal* rates that are important for *incentives* while average tax rates are important for tax revenue. The effect of the structure of marginal rates on work incentives will depend on the nature of individual

31

preferences. Thus, to get a feel for the effects of taxes and social security on work incentives we need to know about *both* the effective marginal tax rate faced and the sensitivity of labour supply to (compensated) wage changes. In section 3.3 we consider the relevant taxes and benefits, explain their interaction and consider their implications for the effective marginal tax rates faced in the UK, especially by *women*. This section also compares the nature of the tax system with that reigning prior to April 1988 when the tax system was *flattened* somewhat; explains the reforms to social security that took place in 1988; and explains the changes in the taxation of the incomes of husbands and wives that came into effect in April 1990. Section 3.4 gives a brief survey of the UK econometric analyses of the determinants of labour market decisions. The UK results are consistent with the vast majority of findings elsewhere which show that women are much more sensitive to the economic constraints that they face than are men. The implication of this is that more attention should be paid to the consequences of tax and income support measures for the marginal rates faced by women even if that means that men have to face higher effective rates.

In the UK two groups of women face extreme effective marginal rates induced by the nature of the welfare system: lone mothers, and the wives of unemployed men; and the conclusions in section 3.5 contain some policy suggestions for improving the incentives for these women to work. The most compelling conclusion, however, is that since it has been demonstrated repeatedly in econometric studies that the labour market behaviour of women is much more sensitive to the structure of taxes and benefits than are men, tax and transfer policy needs to change its focus away from the high tax rates associated with the rich and towards the extremely high tax faced by *women* in poor households. The only argument against this strong conclusion is that the literature has not investigated very thoroughly other dimensions of labour supply apart from hours of work. In particular little is known about retirement, entrepreneurship and educational choices.

3.2 THE DETERMINANTS OF LABOUR SUPPLY AND TAX POLICY

Labour supply can be defined quite broadly to cover not just hours of work and labour force participation but to embrace the longer-run choices that individuals make concerning their schooling, occupation, migration and retirement. Economists have given most attention to the rather narrow view of labour supply when it comes to considering the impact of taxation on work incentives. The reason is clearly that this is the area where data are typically most informative. Moreover our analysis concentrates on the *economic* determinants of hours of work since it is the economic variables that are subject to policy control; but this does not imply that these variables are the *only* or even the most important variables in determining labour supply.

(i) Basic neoclassical theory

The simplest model of the theory of labour supply is a direct application of standard consumer choice theory so that it is assumed that the individual does the best he or she can under the constraints that he or she faces. That is, it is assumed that individuals maximise a well-defined utility function $U(c, h)$, where c is consumption expenditure and h is hours of paid work, with $U_c < 0$,[2] and $U_h > 0$, subject to the constraint that expenditure equals income, both earned (wh, where w is the wage per hour and h is the number of hours worked) and unearned (μ, assumed to be exogenously determined). Thus the individual's problem is to maximise $U(c, h)$ subject to $c = \mu + wh$. Thus, the optimum labour supply is $h^* = h(w, \mu)$ where $h(w, \mu)$ is the labour supply equation.

The dependence of labour supply on w and μ can be seen easily in the comparative static exercise in Figure 3.1. A decrease in the wage from w_0 to w_1 causes the optimum to change from h_0^* to h_1^*. It is common to disaggregate this total change in hours into an income effect and a substitution effect by constructuring a new budget constraint, parallel to the original one (i.e. with slope w_0) but tangential to the highest indifference curve attainable under the new wage w_1. This is given by the dashed constraint. *If* the individual faced this constraint the optimum hours of work would be h_c^*, where the c subscript refers to *compensated* hours since this is the hours of work the individual would supply if he were compensated for the change in utility induced by the wage decrease. The total hours effect, $h_1^* - h_0^*$, is made up of the *substitution* effect, $h_1^* - h_c^*$, which arises from the wage change holding utility constant, plus the *income* effect, $h_c^* - h_0^*$, which shows how much an extra $\mu_0 - \mu_c$ of unearned income would have on hours of work. Notice that the substitution effect of this wage *fall* is unambiguously negative ($h_1^* < h_c^*$) so that wage decreases (tax rate increases) give rise to a *reduced* incentive to work. The income effect is, however, *positive* since $h_0^* < h_c^*$. Thus the overall total effect of the wage fall on hours is ambiguous – in Figure 3.1, for example, the total effect of the wage *fall* is to *increase* hours of work ($h_1^* > h_0^*$).

Thus it is perfectly consistent for a tax rate rise (net wage cut) to decrease work incentives (i.e. decrease *compensated* hours) and yet increase hours of work. The reason why attention is usually given to compensated hours of work is its importance for welfare analysis. In order to address the question of welfare we need to move away from the use of the utility function and employ the consumer *expenditure* function. The expenditure function has been used extensively in microeconomics and is extremely useful for welfare analysis. The expenditure function[3] is defined as the *minimum* (unearned) income required to attain some level of utility, say U^1, at a wage of w: that is $E(w, U^1) = \min [\mu \mid w, U = U^1]$. Thus, the expenditure function shows the minimum unearned income needed to attain a particular level of utility at a particular wage. In Figure 3.1 μ_0 is the minimum μ required to attain U^1 at a wage w_1. At the higher wage, w_0, a lower level of unearned income, μ_c, is required to attain U^1. Thus $\mu_0 - \mu_c$ is the additional unearned income required to compensate for the reduction in wage.

In Figure 3.1 the tax would raise revenue equal to $(w_0 - w_1)h_1^*$ at the post-tax level of hours h_1^* which is given by the distance AB. The welfare loss that this tax imposes on the individual is $\mu_c - \mu_0$ so that the loss to the individual exceeds the revenue gain to the government by the amount BE; an amount known either as the *deadweight loss* or *excess burden* of the tax. A more conventional way of looking at deadweight loss is *via* the compensated (leisure) demand equation. Thus, in the bottom panel of Figure 3.1 the compen-

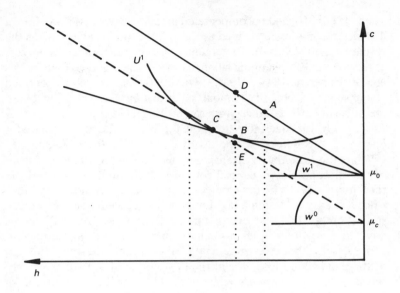

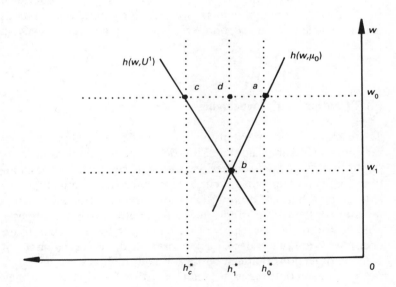

FIGURE 3.1 Labour supply, welfare and taxation

sated, at $U = U^1$, and uncompensated labour supply curves are drawn. The deadweight loss is defined as the welfare loss (bcw^0w^1) minus the revenue raised (bdw^0w^1). The argument for measuring the welfare loss as the area to the right of the labour supply function goes as follows: this area is defined as $\int h^c(w, U^1) \, dw$, where $h^c(w, U^1)$ is the compensated labour supply. Shephard's Lemma[4] states that $h^c(w, U^1) = E_w(w, U^1)$ so this area is $\int E_w(w, U^1) \, dw$, which can be integrated to give $E(w^0, U^1) - E(w^1, U^1)$ which equals $\mu^0 - \mu^c$ in the top panel. The revenue raised is $h_1(w^1 - w^0)$ as before, so the deadweight loss is the triangle bcd.

Thus, the reason why attention focuses on the *compensated* level of labour supply is its central role in welfare analysis. Indeed the total hours effect of a tax change is irrelevant (except for revenue) since it is easy to design a tax that encourages long hours of work – simply make sure that *average* rates are high so that individuals have to work long hours to achieve a reasonable take-home income. Notice that the two crucial elements that determine the size of the deadweight loss, *abc* in the bottom panel of Figure 3.1, are the slope of the *compensated* labour supply function and therefore its wage elasticity, and the marginal tax rate. The marginal rate is a feature of the tax and income support systems and the nature of the UK system is explored in section 3.3. The compensated labour supply elasticity is an econometric issue and this is surveyed in section 3.4.

(ii) Extensions and shortcomings

There are a number of extensions to the basic model that add to its realism considerably: nonlinearities in the budget constraint (arising from a number of sources – taxation, social security contributions, limits on the ability to choose the numbers of hours to work, and the possibility of non-participation) and modelling the determination of the labour supply decisions together with other household decisions (labour supply of husbands and wives, expenditure decisions, and savings decisions). Moreover there are a number of genuine objections that can be raised[5] and the literature has, thus far, given each of these issues scant attention largely because they are extremely difficult questions to answer.

The difficulties associated with nonlinear budget constraints are well known and covered in Moffit (1986) and Fallon and Verry (1989), for example. Considerable effort has gone into the application of estimation techniques suitable for nonlinear budget constraints and there exists many examples for the US although relatively few for the UK.[6]

The second set of extensions relates to the assumption, that is traditionally made, that labour supply depends only on the wage and exogenous unearned income (as well as individual characteristics), but not on other prices. There are a number of aspects to this problem but they all relate to the concept of *separability* of preferences. Separability[7] implies that individuals make decisions in stages. For example, individuals may decide on their labour supply on the basis of their real wage which then determines their earnings and income which is then, in the second stage, treated as predetermined when it is decided how to allocate that income between different commodities on the basis of relative commodity prices. Thus, labour supply decisions are independent of relative commodity prices and commodity demands are independent of the wage. This assumption has important implications for optimal tax theory[8] and has been rejected in tests in Blundell and Walker (1982) and elsewhere. Similarly, separability can be applied to *intertemporal* preferences, so that at the first stage lifecycle wealth is allocated across periods which determines savings decisions in each period (and thereby the level of unearned income in each period), and at the second stage current labour supply is determined on the basis of the wage in that period and the level of unearned income. Such a model is estimated in Blundell and Walker (1986) but the maintained hypothesis of intertemporal separability has not so far been empirically tested.

A third aspect of the separability issue arises in the context of the labour supply of married couples. Thus far we have considered *individual* decision-making which neglects the fact that individuals may live in households where (at least, husbands and wives) may make decisions jointly to maximise some collective household welfare function. The simplest way to incorporate the labour supply decisions of husbands and wives is to appeal to separability again: if the two labour supplies are separable then we can model the labour supply of one individual by treating the earnings of the other person as unearned income. Analysis of models of the labour supplies of husbands and wives typically rejects this assumption.[9] However, there is a small literature that questions the assumption that couples act in this cooperative manner.[10] Instead, they suggest that couples may behave in a game theoretic fashion. Little empirical work exists on this important issue though what does exist[11] seems to suggest that strategic behaviour between husband and wife could be important. This would have serious implications for tax and welfare policy since it suggests that intra-household distributional considerations could be important. Thus, transfer payments to the wife would have different effects than the same cash paid to husbands. Similarly, a redistribution of tax liabilities within households, as would occur in a move from a joint to an individual tax system, would have behavioural implications that would not arise in a model where household resources were pooled.

A second objection is that individuals may not know their true budget constraints because they do not perceive the impact of the tax and welfare systems on the possibilities open to them, or because they do not know at what wage they could work, if they currently do not work, and at what wage they could work further hours of work, if they do work. Brown *et al.* (1976) investigated the extent to which individuals knew the marginal tax rate which they faced and found that only a small proportion responded correctly when asked about their marginal tax rate.[12] In subsequent survey work Brown *et al.* (1986) found that the tax system was not the only problem, since individuals appeared to face much more complex budget constraints than conventional econometric approaches allowed for: bonus payments, piece rates, and overtime rates that varied across the week make modelling the budget constraint and individual responses to it fraught with difficulty. Moreover they found that many men (and a fair proportion of women) felt that they could not vary their hours of work freely.[13] A limited amount of work has been conducted that attempts to address some of these issues: for example Rosen (1976) attempts to estimate a model that allows for individuals not making decisions according to their true after-tax wage; Moffit (1986) estimates a model where the welfare system causes *stigma* so that some individuals may behave according to a budget constraint which does not incorporate the welfare system.

A third shortcoming relates to the nature of the preference specification being assumed. Much of the literature that attempts to deal with the difficult econometric issues, for example Hausman (1985), assumes particularly simple functional forms – a linear labour supply function, or a CES utility function, say. There is a suspicion that the use of such simple functional forms naturally leads to a tendency to overstate the size of the labour supply elasticities. This suspicion is confirmed in Blundell *et al.* (1988) in simulation results for alternative functional forms.

A final deficiency arises from the literature's concentration on *hours of work* as a measure of labour supply. There are clearly other dimensions to labour supply, such as effort per hour, entrepreneurship and risk-taking, and long-run decisions over the timing of joining and leaving the labour market. Research on these alternative dimensions is clearly limited by the availability of data, and empirical results are therefore thin on the ground. Work by Zabalza, Pissarides and Barton (1980) on retirement decisions in the UK suggests that such decisions are relatively sensitive to the structure of budget constraints. Similarly research by Willis and Rosen (1981) suggests that the tax schedule could affect educational choices.

Thus, despite the extensive literature to date there remains many research avenues to explore further and the availability of better data sets will be a crucial factor in determining the course of the future literature. The availability of panel data in the early 1980s onwards has given labour supply research new impetus and it seems likely that further innovations in data availability could have equally significant effects that would allow many of the shortcomings of the existing literature to be overcome.

3.3 INCOME TAXATION AND INCOME SUPPORT MEASURES

Economic theory suggests that the tax and income support systems have two effects on labour supply decisions: high *marginal* rates discourage work through the *substitution effect*, while high *average* rates encourage work through the *income effect*. Marginal and average rates are closely related in such a way that the average rate at a particular level of income is determined by the pattern of marginal rates at income levels below that. However, as far as work *incentives* are concerned it is *only* the marginal rates that matter since these relate to *compensated* changes in labour supply. The average rate is only of relevance in that it determines the tax revenue. Thus, below we emphasise the effective *marginal* rates implied by the UK tax and transfer system.

Subsections (i) to (iii) below consider the nature of the welfare and tax systems in the UK as of April 1989. In each case the discussion focuses on the relevance for women and their incentive to work. Thus our discussion will paint a rather different picture from the official view which concentrates exclusively on the effective marginal rates of male heads of households[14] with non-working wives.

(i) Income taxation and social security contributions

The UK income tax base is income in excess of allowances and deductions. The main allowances[15] are the *single allowance* (SA = £2785) for unmarried individuals and the *married man's allowance* (MMA = £4375). The tax base is generally the *couple's income*[16] but the *earned income* of wives attracts an allowance known as the *wife's earned income allowance* (WEIA = SA but only applicable to *earned income*).[17] Clearly the WEIA encourages married women to work, at least part-time. Indeed it was originally introduced in 1941 to encourage married women to work during the Second World War. There are no child tax allowances. The main deductions are for contributions to an occupational pension scheme and for interest on house purchase loans.[18] There are no deductions for travel-to-work costs or for childcare.[19] Child maintenance payments are not deductible but maintenance receipts are not taxable.[20]

There are only two rates of tax: the basic rate of 25 per cent on taxable incomes up to £20 700 and 40 per cent higher rate tax on taxable incomes above this threshold. The fact that the basic tax band covers the vast majority of the population and that the SA and WEIA are the same implies that the UK tax system is effectively an *independent tax system* as far as earned income is concerned. The presence of the MMA is, however, still something of an anachronism.

The UK tax system is largely one of pay-as-you-earn (PAYE) and, since the system is so simple for the vast majority of the

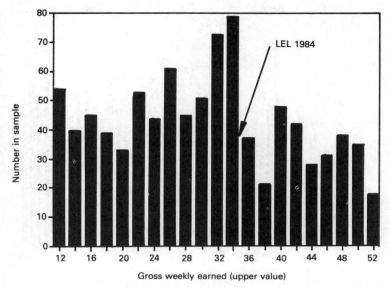

FIGURE 3.2   1984 earnings and the NI LEL

population, most individuals will pay the correct amount of tax week by week even though their earnings may vary and end-of-year assessments are typically not required. Thus, it seems likely that the great majority of individuals correctly perceive their marginal tax rate.

Social security payments (called National Insurance (NI) contributions) are based solely on current weekly earnings of individuals. Earnings below the *lower earnings limit* (LEL = £43 per week) are free from NI. If earnings are above the LEL then *all* earnings are subject to NI at 5 per cent if weekly earnings are less than £75, at 7 per cent if earnings are above £75 and less than £115, and at 9 per cent if earnings are greater than £115 but less than the *upper earnings limit* (UEL = £325). If earnings exceed UEL then NI is 9 per cent of UEL. That is, the marginal NI rate falls to zero above UEL. Notice also that at weekly earnings of £43, £75 and £115 the marginal rate is essentially infinite and this clearly gives an incentive for individuals to choose to earn up to these critical values.[21] In addition to these *employee* contributions there are *employer* contributions which are at least as great as employee contributions and for which there is no UEL.[22]

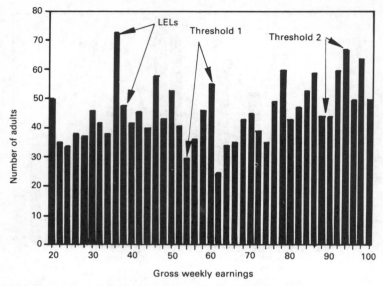

FIGURE 3.3   1986 earnings and the NI LEL and thresholds

Figure 3.2 shows the potential distortionary effect of NI. There is a clear tendency (in the 1984 FES data) for (married) women to earn just less than the LEL to avoid any NI liability. Similarly Figure 3.3 shows that in 1986, when two further jumps in NI liability had been introduced in addition to the LEL, there was some tendency for the earnings distribution to peak just to the left of these critical thresholds.[23]

(ii) Income support measures

Family Credit (FC) is the principal cash benefit for *families* with low earnings. Households containing non-working mothers married to very-low-income men will typically be entitled, and so too will many lone parents with low earnings.

At least one member of the family must be working full-time[24] and the family *after-tax* incomes (including child benefit) must be below a level that depends on the number and ages of children.[25] The level of entitlement is 70 per cent of the difference between this level and family income.[26] Thus, if the parents pay tax at 25 per cent and receive FC then their effective marginal rate is 80 per cent.[27]

The purpose of FC is to encourage individuals to take low-paid jobs which would otherwise be unattractive to someone receiving unemployment benefit or income support – that is, it encourages people to work. On the other hand, it discourages those with low incomes from earning more. Thus, it acts as a disincentive to work long hours. However, its most serious shortcoming is that it acts as a disincentive for women married to low-income husbands to work at all since there is no disregard (or free area) for FC so that the first £1 of earnings would be taxed at 70 per cent. Thus FC is effectively a policy that encourages unemployed men to take low-paid work and discourage their wives from working.

However, the take-up rate[28] for FC is thought to be very low[29] and its effectiveness both as an income support measure and as a labour market policy is open to some doubt. The reason for the low take-up rate is not known but since it is paid to the mother rather than the father it cannot easily be administered by employers. Thus mothers have to physically claim their entitlement by demonstrating that their husbands have low incomes, and it seems likely that this process may contribute to the low take-up rate.

Housing Benefit (HB) is a payment towards the housing costs of low-income individuals. Entitlement depends on the level of housing costs and the level of *after-tax* income relative to an allowance which depends on the household's demographic characteristics. Entitlement falls as after-tax and NI income (including FC) rises at a rate of 65 per cent for rent rebate and 20 per cent for rate rebate. Thus the effective marginal rate for a basic rate taxpayer receiving FC and both rent and rate rebates is 97 per cent.[30] The effective rate for a non-taxpaying wife in a household in receipt of FC and rent and rate rebates would be 96 per cent[31] but the first £5 is disregarded. There is an upper limit on entitlement of 80 per cent of housing costs.[32]

Unemployment Benefit (UB) is an insurance-related benefit where entitlement is contingent on employment status (i.e. being unemployed) and having paid NI contributions for some appropriate period in the past. While UB is a purely employment status contingent benefit for the recipient, it is affected by spouse's earnings. UB for a married man is paid at a married man's rate

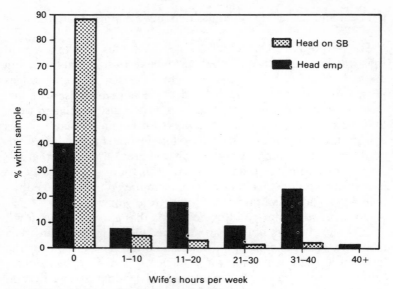

FIGURE 3.4   Hours distribution for UB wives

providing the wife's earnings are less than the difference between the married rate and the single persons rate whereupon the single rate would apply.

Thus the UB system acts as a disincentive for low-wage wives of unemployed men to work at all, while we would expect high-wage wives who would otherwise want to work part-time to have an incentive to work full-time. Given the nature of the stock of unemployed it seems likely that the first effect dominates the second.[33]

The two groups who are able to make labour supply decisions (i.e. excluding the retired, disabled and permanently sick) and that are affected by IS are lone parents and the wives of the long-term unemployed.

Figure 3.4 shows the distribution of hours of work for the wives of men in receipt of UB compared to the distribution for the wives of the employed, and shows that such wives are a little less likely to work than those with employed husbands, but if they do work they are much more likely to work full-time. Income Support (IS) is a benefit for those whose incomes (net of housing costs) fall below some *poverty* level defined as a function of household demographic characteristics and is intended to bring households' incomes up to the *poverty* level.[34] The main groups affected by IS are those pensioners who have only a state pension, unemployed youths with no entitlement to UB, the long-term unemployed who have exhausted their entitlement to UB, and lone parents with little or no income. The most important feature about IS as far as work incentives are concerned is that it carries with it a 100 per cent withdrawal rate, apart from a £4 per week *earnings* disregard.[35] Comparing Figure 3.5 with Figure 3.6 we see that lone mothers are much less likely to work than married mothers, although if they do work they are more likely to work part-time. This is consistent with the idea that IS discourages many low-wage lone mothers from working at all, and those not on low wages find that part-time work is not economic since the loss in IS involved can be large relative to part-time earnings. Thus, lone mothers are less likely to work part-time by virtue of their IS entitlement.

(iii) Recent policy reforms

There has been a widespread movement towards reforms which are aimed at improving work incentives through *flattening* tax schedules and reducing the severity of poverty traps.[36]

In April 1988 the UK income support system was reformed. The motivation for the reforms was largely the fear that the existing system of income support measures led to a *poverty trap* that resulted in very high effective marginal tax rates that had a detrimental effect on work incentives for the very poor. The main change, as far as work incentives were concerned, was to base income and support payments on after-tax (and NI) income rather than gross income. Family Credit (FC) with a 70 per cent taper on *net* income replaced Family Income Supplement (FIS), a benefit that helped the low income *workers* with families, and which carried with it a 50 per cent taper on *gross* income. Similarly the HB tapers were rationalised. Supplementary Benefit (SB), which provided income for those whose incomes were below some level, became Income Support (IS).

Table 3.1 shows the conventional view that the 1988 Social Security Reforms reduced the *poverty trap* problem. Figure 3.7 shows the relationship between gross and net incomes for a couple

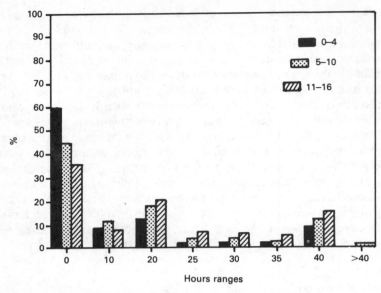

FIGURE 3.5   Hours of married mothers

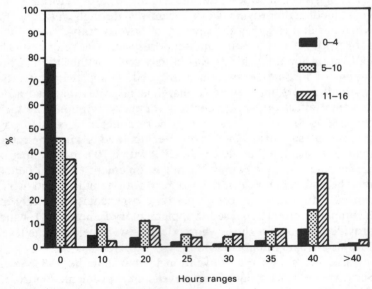

FIGURE 3.6   Hours of lone mothers

TABLE 3.1   Marginal rates and the 1988 social security reforms

Pre April 1988		Post April 1988	
Tax + NI	32	Tax + NI	32
FIS	50	FC	48
HB	23	HB	17
Total	105	Total	97

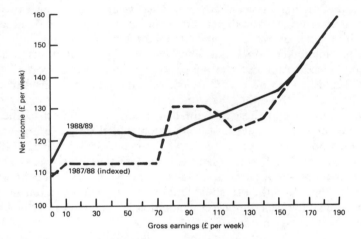

FIGURE 3.7   Pre and post social security reform poverty trap

with two children under the new and old systems. Note that the *depth* of the poverty trap has been reduced at the cost of making it *wider*, and it is not at all clear that there is any evidence that a wide shallow trap is better than a narrow deep one. Note that the *drop* in net income that occurred in net income at around £110 per week, due to the loss of *passported* benefits such as free school meals, no longer occurs since these additional benefits have been abolished.

However, Figure 3.7 tells only half of the story: the effective marginal rate facing a non-taxpaying wife in a household in receipt of old HB and FIS was 73 per cent[37] while it is 96 per cent under the new system. Thus the reform may well have encouraged low-income men to work, but at the cost of discouraging their wives from working. Moreover the 100 per cent withdrawal rate on SB remained a feature of IS.[38] However, SB had allowed reasonable childcare expenses to be disregarded while the new IS system does not.

In April 1988 the higher rates of tax which ranged from 40 per cent to 60 per cent were collapsed into a single higher rate of 40 per cent. Note that since the higher-rate tax threshold is close to the NI system's UEL and the SA is close to the LEL this implies that the UK has an essentially linear tax system: those that pay tax do so at a rate of 39 or 40 per cent, except for those few individuals with incomes above UEL and below the higher rate threshold.

In November 1989 the *employees'* NI contributions were rationalised to remove the jumps in liability that occurred at the LEL and at £75 and £115[39] which were thought to act as a work disincentive. However, the same critical levels affect *employers'* contributions and these remained in place. In addition to these jumps there is a further threshold which applies only to employers at £165 per week. Figure 3.8 shows the male earnings distribution from the 1986 FES data when the employer threshold was £130.[40] Again there seems a clear tendency for bunching to occur immediately before the threshold and there seems no good reason to distinguish between employee and employer schedules in the way that the NI system now does.

The tax treatment of married couples has been the subject of much debate both in the academic literature and in policy circles. In the UK a number of policy options were explored in a Green Paper published in 1980. One of these options was the subject of a further Green Paper in 1986. These proposals were heavily criticised at the time,[41] and in April 1988 it was announced that the present system was to be reformed along lines that had *not* been the subject of a Green Paper. This 1990 reform replaced the *joint* tax system which aggregated a couple's incomes by an independent tax system where tax liability depends only on the individual's income. However, since the tax system has such a long standard tax band and a tax allowance for the wife, the new system is unlikely to have had a dramatic impact. The wife receives an SA instead of a WEIA and so can set this against *unearned* income as well as earnings. A few wives who paid tax at 40 per cent by virtue

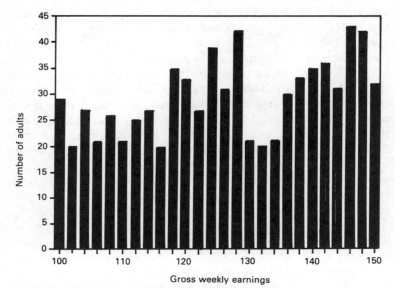

Gross weekly earnings

FIGURE 3.8   Employer NI contributions

of their high combined household incomes now face only 25 per cent. However, the major anachronism of the old joint tax system, the MMA, effectively remains. The MMA has formally been replaced with an SA plus a Married Couples Allowance (MCA) equal to the difference between the MMA and SA. The MCA is *transferable* between spouses. Nevertheless the new independent tax system retains the subsidy to marriage.

3.4   EMPIRICAL EVIDENCE FOR THE UK

Surveys and assessments of previous empirical work on male labour supply can be found in Pencavel (1986), and on female labour supply in Killingsworth (1983). Much of the available evidence is concerned with the USA, though work by Blundell and Walker (1982, 1986), Ashworth and Ulph (1981), Brown *et al.* (1976, 1986), Layard, Barton and Zabalza (1980), and Zabalza and Arrufat (1988) is concerned with the UK.[42]

There are a number of ways of investigating the effect of the tax and transfer systems on labour supply decisions: interview studies, experimental studies, time-series analysis of aggregate trends, and the analysis of cross-section and/or panel data. Interview studies are generally felt to have little value since, even if they elicit the truth, they cannot distinguish between income and substitution effects. Experimental studies have been used quite extensively in the USA where individuals have been offered an experimental tax/transfer system (temporarily) and their behaviour is monitored relative to a control group. Such experiments are expensive and the US studies are generally felt to be inconclusive, since it is difficult to infer what the permanent effects are of a permanent unanticipated change to the tax system from a temporary experiment. There is some evidence that the experimentals engaged in some *intertemporal substitution* to take advantage of the temporary offer that would not take place under a permanent change. Time-series evidence also cannot discriminate between income and substitution effects since aggregation conditions when agents face different prices (i.e. wages) are invariably not satisfied, and one cannot therefore infer how individuals behave from estimates of aggregate behaviour. Cross-section and/or panel data offer the best prospect for inferring what the effects of tax and transfer policies might be. Since there is no aggregation issue, there is the possibility of controlling for intertemporal substitution, and, if the estimates are consistent with underlying economic theory, then they can give separate income and substitution effects.

The available UK estimates for men are given in Table 3.2. Notice that the uncompensated wage elasticities are negative (i.e. backward-bending labour supply), with the exception of Minford and Ashton,[43] and the income elasticities are small, so that the compensated elasticities are fairly small at sample means and run into the danger of becoming negative at some data points.[44] Thus the UK empirical evidence on men suggests that male labour supply is relatively unresponsive to changes in the nature of budget constraints and especially unresponsive to *compensated* changes in wages.

These rather inconsequential results for men suggest that much of the variance in their hours of work may be determined by other forces, and further work on analysing the demand side of the market is clearly merited. Moreover, the small compensated labour supply effects suggest that disincentive effects may be relatively small for men.

TABLE 3.2 Male labour supply estimates

Study	Uncompensated wage	Compensated wage	Total income
Brown *et al.* (1976)	−0.13	0.22	−0.35
Blundell and Walker (1982)	−0.23	0.13	−0.36
Brown *et al.* (1986)	−0.14	0.30	−0.44
Ashworth and Ulph (1981)	−0.13	0.23	−0.36
Minford and Ashton (1989)	0.36	0.00	−0.36

TABLE 3.3 Female labour supply elasticities

Study	Uncompensated wage	Compensated wage	Total income
Blundell and Walker (1982)	0.10	0.32	−0.22
Blundell and Walker (1986)	0.19	0.35	−0.16
Ashworth and Ulph (1981)	0.32	0.55	−0.23
Layard *et al.* (1980)	0.22	0.11	−0.34
Zabalza (1983)	1.59	1.82	−0.23

In the UK there seem to be five studies of female labour supply that offer estimates that can be used to construct income and substitution effects: Ashworth and Ulph (1981), Layard *et al.* (1980), Blundell and Walker (1982 and 1986), and Zabalza (1983). The uncompensated wage, compensated wage, and total income elasticities are given in Table 3.3 for the samples of married women in these studies.

It is apparent that all the available estimates suggest that female labour supply is relatively responsive to the economic determinants of the constraints that they face, and especially to *compensated* wage changes. The most noticeable difference between male and female estimates is that female labour supply is increasing in the wage. Relative to US evidence there is a surprising amount of agreement between the estimates and they tend to be a little more conservative than US compensated elasticities.

There are considerable difficulties associated with obtaining un-biased econometric estimates of labour supply models. The main complications relate to the nonlinearity of the budget constraints which causes individuals with unobservable characteristics (whose effect on hours is, therefore, captured by the *error* term) that are correlated with high (low) hours to work long (short) hours, and they are therefore more likely to face a higher tax rate and lower marginal wage. Thus there is a natural tendency for the marginal wage (an explanatory variable) to be correlated with the error term. The techniques developed for dealing with such nonlinear budget sets are explained in Moffit (1986).

However, they cannot be used directly to infer the effects of specific policy changes. First, they cannot be used directly for policy analysis since policy changes do not take the form of 1 per cent changes in wages or incomes. Second, the estimates themselves are not necessarily consistent with the underlying economic theory and cannot therefore be used to predict behavioural changes that are generated by that theory. Third, the estimated models available in the literature tend not to produce very good statistical *fits*: in particular, they fail to capture the peaks in the hours distributions that occur around full-time hours and around part-time hours. Rather they tend to produce a predicted hours distribution that is smooth. Finally, there are a large number of technical statistical issues associated with estimating labour supply models, and no one study deals with all these issues in the most appropriate manner. The major difficulties relate to the nonlinearities in budget constraints induced by taxes and benefits. Very few studies in the literature deal adequately with the complexities associated with *non-convexities* in budget constraints induced by the interaction of the welfare system with the tax system.[45] Nevertheless, given the extent of agreement among the UK estimates it seems likely that changes in methodology may make little difference to the results. However, each of these studies use samples of married women with employed husbands, and caution should be exercised before they are applied to other populations such as lone mothers. Thus, there is considerable further work to be done in the UK on the groups in the most sensitive positions: lone mothers and the wives of the unemployed.

While considerable effort has been put into the econometric estimation of labour supply elasticities these estimates have not typically been used to demonstrate the precise impact of policy changes. Rather they have merely been used to argue that work

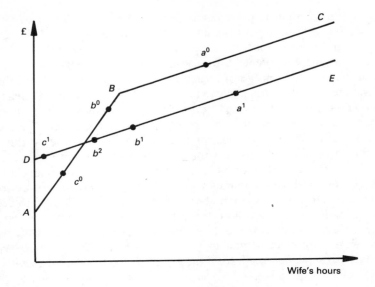

FIGURE 3.9   Transferable allowances reform

incentives are (or are not) a serious policy concern. The issues surrounding the use of econometric estimates in policy analysis have been considered in Blundell *et al.* (1988), and the estimates therein have been embedded in a microcomputer-based policy simulation package SPAIN.[46] A simple illustration of this package is considered below.

One of the original proposals for the taxation of husbands and wives in the UK suggested that the MMA be reduced to the level of an SA, the WEIA be replaced with an SA, and the additional tax revenue be used to allow spouses to transfer their SAs – the transferable allowances (TA) reform. In practice only in very few households would there be a financial advantage to the wife using both spouses' SAs, and thus the TA reform *effectively* increased the MMA (to the level of two SAs) and reduced the WEIA to zero.

Figure 3.9 shows an example of what the pre- and post-reform budget constraints might look like for a wife: *ABC* is the pre-reform constraint that reflects the WEIA, while the post-reform constraint, *DE*, has a higher intercept since the husband now has 2

SAs (rather than approximately 1.6 SAs) but is parallel to *BC* since the wife now pays tax on all of her earnings.

Clearly a pre-reform taxpayer (Type 1 individuals) only experiences an income effect (a_0 to a_1) increasing hours of work. Those non-taxpayers earning more than the break-even point where the two constraints cross (Type 2 individuals) experience a higher marginal rate that reduces hours through the substitution effect but a lower income that increases hours, and the net effect is ambiguous (b_0 to b_1 is possible, as is b_0 to b_2). Those working non-taxpayers who earn less that the break-even point (Type 3's) suffer the disincentive of a higher marginal rate but are financially better off, and the income effect reinforces the tendency for hours to fall (c_0 to c_1) – hours could even fall to zero. Finally, there are non-participants (Type 4's): these face a higher marginal tax rate and a higher net income and, for both reasons, are even less likely to work post-reform than they are pre-reform. While there are clear *theoretical* predictions of the effects of the reform, to *quantify* the magnitudes involved requires estimates of the sensitivity of labour supply to changes in the structure of the budget constraints that each individual faces. In Symons and Walker (1988) an estimated labour supply model was used to evaluate the magnitudes of these theoretical responses for a large sample of married women surveyed in the 1981 Family Expenditure Survey, and the findings are reproduced in Table 3.4.[47]

The majority of working women work longer hours since they are taxpayers (Type 1) and experience only an income effect: the average effect is one extra hour per week, which is a not insignificant percentage increase. The non-participants (Type 4) remain non-participants and are better off by £5.92 per week. The type 2's who are worse off under the reform but face a higher tax rate reduce their hours by −0.5 on average, since here the income affect (+0.64 hours) dominates the substitution effect (−1.14 hours). The type 3's who are better off and face a higher tax rate reduce their hours by 2.18 per week, of which 1.13 is due to the substitution effect and 1.05 arises from the income effect.

Thus, this proposed reform is clearly *bad* for incentives (there are no *positive* substitution effects) but at the same time manages to *increase* (uncompensated) hours of work on average. The adverse incentive effects associated with this proposal has led to the implementation (in April 1990) of an alternative scheme where

TABLE 3.4 Simulation results for transferable allowances

Person type	Uncompensated hours	Compensated hours
1 Taxpayers	+1.00	0
2 Worse-off non-taxpayers	−0.50	−1.14
3 Better-off non-taxpayers	−2.18	−1.13
4 Non-participants	−	0

individuals receive an SA and the MMA is abandoned (as in the TA reform), but an additional allowance is introduced for married couples (the MCA = MMA − SA) which is transferable between spouses. This has a relatively modest *beneficial* effect on work incentives for married women – most will find that the tax rate they face remains unchanged, a few high earner couples will find that the wife now faces the basic rate rather than the higher rate, and a few women with low-paid husbands will find that it is beneficial for the MCA to be used by the wife and this may reduce her marginal rate. Thus while the UK tax system become an independent one it retains its major anachronism: a large subsidy to marriage.

3.5 CONCLUSION

This chapter has considered the impact of the structure of the tax/benefit systems on labour supply decisions with special emphasis on their impact on the labour market decisions of women. The empirical evidence suggested that women have relatively large compensated labour supply elasticities while the evidence for men is, at this stage, largely inconsistent with economic theory.

Despite the MCA the tax system from 1990 will treat men and women equally. However, if the possibility of work disincentives were of great concern then a more progressive tax structure could *improve* matters, since it would impose higher marginal rates higher up the income distribution where women are less frequently found (because of labour market discrimination, say). This would allow lower marginal rates to be imposed at lower levels of earnings which would particularly encourage part-time work. Whether it is appropriate to encourage part-time work at the expense of full-time work is a difficult question. To the extent that labour market skills deteriorate during periods of non-participation (arising from the presence of young children, say) then encouraging part-time work may indirectly contribute to a higher probability of return to full-time work *in the future*. However, it may be that an allowance/deduction for childcare expenses may be a more appropriate way of dealing with this issue of interrupted careers.[48]

The FC system is deficient in two important respects. First it has a low take-up rate *even among those who have an entitlement on the basis of their observed earnings*. FC *potentially* serves the purpose of encouraging people to take low-wage jobs. However, it only achieves this if those that are *potentially* entitled to it if they took a low-paid job are aware of its existence and not stigmatised by it. The second problem with FC is that there are no income disregards associated with it, so that it imposes a 70 per cent effective tax rate on non-participating married women which clearly strongly discourages participation.

The IS and UB systems have disregards but they are so small that they can really only be rationalised as administrative conveniences. The fact that the IS disregard for lone mothers is an *earnings* disregard means that it cannot be used against maintenance payments. Greater disregards for the earnings of spouses would act against the current tendency for low-wage wives to stop working when their husbands become unemployed. The problem that a growing proportion of lone mothers are reliant on IS is a significant one, and the IS system contributes to it not only because the disregard is small but also because it cannot be set against maintenance payments. Encouraging maintenance payments would not only reduce the cost of the IS scheme by an equivalent amount, it would also encourage maintenance recipients to work, since they would only benefit from them if they worked and earned sufficient to exhaust their entitlement to IS. However, it seems likely that at least part of the reason for low maintenance payments among IS recipients is that recipients have little incentive to pursue absent fathers, and absent fathers who are concerned about the welfare of their children have little incentive to contribute towards it. Disregarding at least some of such payments would be a major contribution to increasing their importance.[49]

Finally, the most important observation about the UK tax/benefit system is that it appears to have been constructed to avoid imposing very high marginal rates on *men* without much concern about the implications for the marginal rates facing *women*. Indeed, if the reason for wanting to avoid high marginal rates were potential disincentive effects, then policy ought to pay much more attention to the rates they impose on women and relatively little weight ought to be given to the rates that are imposed on men. However, at this stage the existing empirical literature is deficient as far as policy usefulness is concerned in its the lack of attention to alternative dimensions of labour supply: particularly retirement, education, effort and entrepreneurship and risk-taking. Until concrete evidence on these aspects of behaviour is available, tax policy based on existing estimates of hours of work equations could have serious unintended effects.

4 The Economics of Taxpayer Compliance

D. J. PYLE

4.1 INTRODUCTION

There is now a great deal of evidence suggesting that tax evasion is fairly widespread throughout European and North American economies. Estimates of the so-called 'black economy' indicate that perhaps 10 per cent of economic activity in these countries has been driven underground in the attempt to evade payment of tax (for a detailed survey, see Pyle, 1989, chs 2–4).

Tax evasion, it has been claimed, has potentially damaging economic consequences, of which the loss of the tax revenue itself is probably the least important. More important may be the impact of evasion upon (i) the reliability of macroeconomic indicators such as GDP and unemployment; (ii) the distribution of post-tax incomes; and (iii) the allocation of resources. Of these perhaps the most important of all is the effect which evasion has upon the efficiency with which resources are allocated. The simultaneous existence of a taxed (regular) sector and an untaxed (black) sector drives a wedge between net returns in the two sectors. If resources are mobile they will move from the taxed to the untaxed sector until net returns are brought into line. However, then the gross rates of return (reflecting the social productivity of the factors) will be different and resources will be misallocated. Alm (1985) has estimated that the welfare cost of tax evasion in the USA in 1980 may have been between 5 and 10 per cent of GNP. (For a full discussion of the economic consequences of tax evasion, see Pyle, 1989, ch. 7.)

The problems of the size of the black economy and its economic consequences, fascinating though they are, will not concern us in

58

this chapter. We will examine three other issues relating to tax evasion. First, what are the compliance costs of the tax system? Second, why do people try to evade their tax obligations? Third, what policies should the tax authorities pursue in attempting to enforce compliance?

In section 4.2 we consider the nature of compliance costs and review several studies which have attempted to measure such costs for the UK and US tax systems. It is clear both that relatively little work has been done in this area and that the costs to individuals of complying with their tax obligations are not insubstantial. This may be one reason why individuals decide not to declare all or part of their income to the Inland Revenue.

In section 4.3 we examine one simple economic model of income tax evasion. Economists working in this area have largely ignored compliance costs as a motive for engaging in tax evasion. Instead they have adapted a model from the economics of crime literature which focuses on the benefits (reduced taxes) and costs (punishment) associated with such activity. In section 4.4 we review the empirical evidence concerning the relationship between tax evasion and tax rates, detection rates and penalties for evasion.

In section 4.5 we discuss a number of policy issues relating to tax compliance. For example, is total compliance a desirable goal of the tax authorities? If it is, then what is the most efficient policy to achieve such a goal? If it isn't, then what is the optimal amount of evasion?

The subject-matter of this chapter is tax *evasion*, which is the failure to disclose all or part of one's income to the tax authority. As such, evasion is an illegal activity, although the *economic* activity which generated the income in the first place need not be illegal. Tax evasion should be distinguished from tax *avoidance*, which is the entirely legitimate use of tax loopholes in order to reduce one's tax liability. For example, if an author fails to declare to the Inland Revenue the royalties she earns from writing a book, then she is guilty of tax evasion and if caught may be subjected to a heavy fine. On the other hand, if our successful author tries to claim tax relief for the costs she has incurred in writing her best-seller, e.g. typing costs, then she has merely tried to avoid her tax liability. In the literature of tax compliance, some writers define non-compliance to include both evasion *and* avoidance. This seems to put unusual strain on the definition of compliance. We have chosen to follow the more usual treatment and equate non-compliance with evasion only.[1]

4.2   COMPLIANCE COSTS

Compliance costs are those costs incurred by taxpayers or third parties (e.g. employers, financial institutions, etc.) in meeting the requirements of the tax system. By convention compliance costs exclude the costs incurred by the Inland Revenue and other tax authorities in collecting taxes. These are termed administration costs.

It might help us to understand what is meant by compliance costs if we take a few examples. They all relate to income taxes but can easily be applied to other forms of tax. The most obvious example, at least in the UK, is the cost to employers of operating the Pay As You Earn (PAYE) income tax system. Employers have a duty to deduct income tax from employees' wages and salaries and to pass on the revenue so collected to the Inland Revenue. As a result, firms have to operate a rather more sophisticated and costly wages and salaries system than they would otherwise need.

Another form of compliance cost is the amount of time which taxpayers must spend in keeping records of their income receipts (for wages and salaries much of this work is done for them by employers – see above) and in completing their tax returns. Some taxpayers, especially those who have several, different kinds of income, may have to employ accountants and/or lawyers to help them to complete their tax returns. These costs are, of course, another form of compliance cost. Finally, taxpayers may experience certain psychic costs in complying with their tax obligations – for example, the sheer anxiety they suffer when that ominous brown envelope drops through the letter-box!

All taxes, whether income tax, corporation tax, VAT, inheritance tax and so on, have associated compliance costs. Of course, these costs may vary from one kind of tax to another. In what follows we shall be particularly concerned with the compliance costs of the income tax system. The compliance costs incurred by some groups, e.g. employees, may be substantially different from those borne by other groups, e.g. the self-employed (for employees a large part of the cost falls on the employer). If these cost differences are substantial, they may have some influence on occupational choice. More important from our point of view (but perhaps not unrelated), high compliance costs may lead people to try to avoid them by, for example, failing to declare their income to the tax authority.

There has been remarkably little empirical work aimed at estimating the compliance costs of tax systems. For the UK the only study is that by Sandford (1973), which has been recently updated (Sandford, 1989). For the USA there have been two more recent studies by Slemrod and Sorum (1984) and Dubin, Graetz and Wilde (1989).

Sandford's original study was based on a survey of some 2700 potential taxpayers. The questions related to income tax, surtax, capital gains tax and estate duty, i.e. *all* personal taxes. Respondents were asked to estimate how much time they had spent attending to their tax affairs in the last twelve months, how much money they had spent on hiring tax advisers and how much time had been spent on their tax affairs by unpaid advisers, e.g. relatives. In order to convert the time costs to a monetary figure, Sandford made what appear to be quite arbitrary assumptions about the value of time. In addition, he added some 50 per cent to the costs of paid tax advice to allow for underestimation by respondents and a further 10 per cent to allow for what he claimed were uneconomic fees charged by advisers.

To the above costs, Sandford added estimates of the postage and travelling costs incurred by taxpayers in dealing with tax matters and a pure 'guesstimate' of the costs to employers of operating the PAYE scheme. A summary of Sandford's estimates are reported in Table 4.1.

Slemrod and Sorum (1984) analysed returns from a survey of some 600 residents of Minnesota carried out in 1982. On the basis of this rather small sample, they concluded that the aggregate compliance cost of the US federal and state individual income tax was between $17 billion and $27 billion per year, or between 5 per cent and 7 per cent of the revenue raised by the two taxes. It is important to note that they did not include third-party costs, e.g. the costs to employers of operating a tax withholding system. Slemrod and Sorum's estimates, if accurate, suggest that the American income tax system imposes rather higher compliance costs upon the individual taxpayer than does the UK system. One

TABLE 4.1   Compliance costs of the UK personal tax system, 1973 (as percentage of tax revenue)

	Minimum estimate	Maximum estimate
Fees paid to advisers	0.9 (+ 1.4)*	1.5 (+ 3.9)*
Value of time spent by taxpayers	0.5	1.2
Postage and travel expenses	0.4	0.7
Costs to firms of operating PAYE scheme	0.6	1.0
Value of time spent by unpaid advisers	negligible	negligible
Total	2.4 (+ 1.4)	4.4 (+ 3.9)

* The figures in brackets relate to fees paid for tax-related work which is not billed as such.

reason for this is that in the UK a significant part of the cost is borne by the employer. However, in view of the rather small samples and the sometimes arbitrary assumptions made, we should perhaps refrain from attempting to make comparisons between the two systems.

Dubin, Graetz and Wilde (1989) report a number of other recent studies of compliance costs undertaken in the USA, the most important of which is an investigation by the Arthur D. Little Corporation for the Internal Revenue Service. The objective of this study was to measure 'the paperwork burden' of the federal income tax only. To this end they carried out three surveys of individual taxpayers and employers. The 'Little' results are reported in hours only, but approximate closely to those produced by Slemrod and Sorum, despite the fact that the latter's results include state income taxes.

It seems reasonable to conclude that the costs of tax compliance may be large, although we must admit that the estimates so far obtained are rather rough and ready. If one adds to them the administrative costs of the tax authorities, then it is plain that the costs of collecting taxes are not an insignificant proportion of the total revenue collected. However, for our concerns, it is the compliance costs that matter.

4.3 ECONOMIC ANALYSIS OF TAX EVASION

(i) A simple model of taxpayer non-compliance

The first rigorous theoretical analysis of an individual's decision to evade tax was due to Allingham and Sandmo (1972). The impetus for this work came from two related literatures – first, the newly emerging work on the economics of crime (Becker, 1968), and second, work on the economics of risk and uncertainty (Arrow, 1970). Deliberate under-reporting of income to the tax authority is inherently risky and also illegal. It seems natural, therefore, to apply the analytical tools developed in these other fields to answer the question 'how much of my income should I declare to the tax authority, given that I might get caught and punished?'

In this approach individuals are assumed to be rational, amoral and risk averse. It is further assumed that they attempt to maximise expected utility which is dependent solely upon their income. In other words they neither derive pleasure from beating the tax man nor suffer pangs of remorse from cheating on their tax obligations. (We consider briefly how some of these factors can be built into the individual's decision framework.)

In the model developed below we analyse an individual's decision whether or not to evade in one time period. This is clearly unrealistic. If I decide to evade this year, then that would affect my decision next year and in future years. An erratic time stream of declared income is likely to arouse the suspicion of the tax authority. A life-cycle model would seem more appropriate. Unfortunately such a model is rather complicated mathematically and so will not be considered here.

Each individual's actual income (I) in the time period is assumed to be fixed. A constant tax rate (t) is paid on declared income (D). The probability of being investigated by the tax authority is given by p, which is also assumed to be constant. Finally, if a taxpayer is caught evading, she must pay a penalty on her undeclared income (i.e. $I-D$) of F per unit of undeclared income. The penalty is assumed to be greater than the tax rate. If she is not caught then her net income after tax will be given by

$$W = I - t \cdot D$$

However, if she is caught her net income after taxes and penalties will be given by

$$Z = I - t \cdot D - F[I - D]$$

Of course, if $D = I$, then $Z = W = (1 - t)I$.

The individual's 'budget constraint' is shown in Figure 4.1 by the line AB. At point A, all income is declared to the tax authority, i.e. $D = I$, so that net income will be the same in both states of the world. At B, no income is declared, so that, if unsuccessful, income falls to $I(1 - F)$. However, if she gets away with it then net income will be I. Clearly the slope of AB is given by $1 - F/t$. How far our taxpayer moves along AB indicates the extent of her involvement in tax evasion.

The taxpayer's expected utility is simply a weighted average of her utility in the two situations which can arise, i.e. caught or not caught for evasion, the weights being given by p and $1-p$ respectively, i.e.

$$EU = (1 - p) U(W) + pU(Z)$$

If she can increase her expected utility by not declaring some income, then the economic approach suggests that she will evade. It is fairly easy to show that she will decide to evade if the expected penalty on undeclared income (pF) is less than the tax rate payable on declared income (t).[2] If the individual is risk averse then she will have indifference curves in Z, W space that are convex to the origin (see Pyle, 1983, p. 19). Assuming an interior optimum, the individual would be maximising expected utility at point like C in Figure 4.1.

An interior optimum (i.e. some undeclared income) will be given by

$$\frac{dEU}{dD} = -t(1 - p) U'(W) - (t - F) pU'(Z) = 0 \qquad (4.1)$$

where $U'(\ )$ is the first derivative of the utility function.

The second order condition for a maximum is automatically satisfied by the assumption that individuals are risk averse.

It is possible to predict what will happen to the optimal declara-

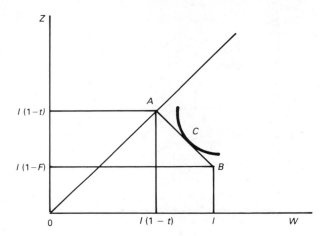

FIGURE 4.1   Optimal tax evasion

tion of income (D^*) when the tax rate (t), the penalty (F) and the probability of detection (p) change by differentiating equation (4.1) above with respect to t, F and p in turn and solving for

$$\frac{\partial D^*}{\partial t}, \frac{\partial D^*}{\partial F} \quad \text{and} \quad \frac{\partial D^*}{\partial p} \quad \text{respectively.}$$

The results of this exercise are as follows:

$$\frac{\partial D^*}{\partial t} \qquad ? \qquad \text{cannot be signed unambiguously} \qquad (4.2)$$

$$\frac{\partial D^*}{\partial F} > 0 \qquad (4.3)$$

$$\frac{\partial D^*}{\partial p} > 0 \qquad (4.4)$$

Unfortunately it is not possible to say what will happen to declared income as the tax rate changes and so it is impossible to confirm the common assertion that evasion is encouraged by increasing tax rates (result (4.2)). Results (4.3) and (4.4) confirm

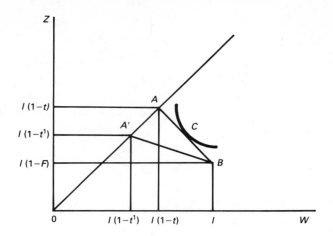

FIGURE 4.2   A change in the income tax rate

that both harsher penalties and increased auditing will enforce greater taxpayer compliance. We shall return to these results and the 'entry condition' when we examine policy issues.

Fortunately, while mathematically complicated, these results can all be shown fairly easily diagrammatically. Consider, first, the effect of an increase in the tax rate (t). This is shown in Figure 4.2.

An increase in the tax rate, say from t to t^1, merely slides the point A along the certainty line to A^1. The new 'budget constraint' becomes A^1B. The change from AB to A^1B clearly involves both an income (or wealth) effect and a substitution effect. Unfortunately, they work in opposite directions and so we cannot be sure what the overall outcome will be. The substitution effect tends to increase risk-taking, but, if we assume decreasing absolute risk aversion, the income effect will tend to reduce it.

The effect of a change in the penal rate of tax (F) can be analysed in a similar fashion. Examination of Figure 4.3 shows that increasing F moves point B down vertically to B^1. The effect is again to change both the slope and position of the budget constraint. However, in this case the income and substitution effects work in the same direction, i.e. discouraging risk and moving C^1 closer to A.

Finally, an increase in the probability of detection (p) will not affect the 'budget constraint', but will alter the slope of the indif-

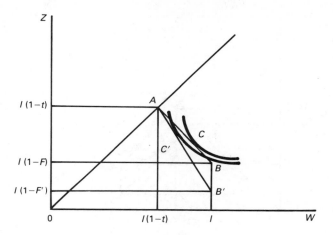

FIGURE 4.3   A change in the penal rate of tax

ference curves. Recall that the slope of an indifference curve is given by

$$\frac{dZ}{dW}\bigg|_{u} = \frac{-(1-p)}{p} \cdot \frac{U^{1}(W)}{U^{1}(Z)}$$

As W and Z are independent of p, an increase in p will flatten the indifference curves. Consider the old optimum at C. The new indifference curve passing through C will cut the budget constraint AB. The optimum must, therefore, move to the left and the individual declares more of her income.

Yitzhaki (1974) has tried to remove the ambiguity concerning the effect of a change in the tax rate. He argues that under many countries' tax laws penalties are levied on evaded tax, i.e. $t(I-D)$, and not on evaded income, i.e. $(I-D)$. Under this formulation of the penalty it is possible to show that

$$\frac{\partial D^{*}}{\partial t} > 0$$

i.e. an increase in the tax rate will encourage individuals to declare more income for tax purposes. This result looks distinctly odd and

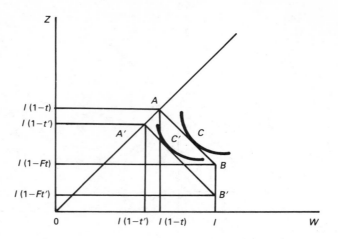

FIGURE 4.4 An increase in the income tax rate: Yitzhaki case

certainly does not accord with 'common sense'. It happens because the penalty paid on undeclared income (Ft) and the tax rate (t) are now proportional to each other, so that there is no substitution effect if the tax rate is changed. A rise in the tax rate now produces a pure income effect. It reduces the taxpayer's income and, if we assume decreasing absolute risk aversion, she will declare more of her income in order to reduce risk. This can be seen more clearly in Figure 4.4.

The slope of the budget constraint is clearly $- (Ft - t)/t = 1 - F$ and is independent of t. An increase in the tax rate will then simply shift AB inwards and paralled to itself, say to A^1B^1. If we assume decreasing absolute risk aversion, falling income will mean that C^1 (the new optimum) involves declaring more income than does C.

(ii) Some criticisms and developments of the economic model

Obviously the model outlined above is very simple. It could be, and in some cases has been, developed considerably. In this section we briefly outline some of these developments.

The first and most obvious change is to relax the assumption of a constant tax rate by incorporating a progressive income tax schedule (Srinivasan, 1973; Witte and Woodbury, 1985).[3] At the same time we could adopt a rather less restrictive set of assumptions about the enforcement strategy of the Inland Revenue. The consequence of these changes is that a progressive income tax system acts as a disincentive to the declaration of income unless there is a counteracting incentive effect caused by an increased likelihood of punishment. As a taxpayer's income rises, whether she declares more or less of her income depends on the relative strengths of these two countervailing forces. If the effect of a rising marginal tax rate is stronger, she will declare less, but if the increase in expected penalties is stronger, she will declare more.

Second, individuals are assumed to be amoral utility maximisers. They will evade if they think they can get away with it. Casual observation suggests that not all individuals think quite like that. Indeed, it seems that while the odds are heavily in favour of evaders getting away with it, the vast majority of taxpayers behave honestly. Such behaviour requires us to believe either that taxpayers exhibit a remarkable degree of risk aversion or that they attach a considerable disutility to dishonesty (Skinner and Slemrod, 1985). Recently, a number of authors have shown that by incorporating psychic or stigma costs into the utility function, the behaviour of the honest taxpayer can be explained perfectly well by the expected utility approach (Benjamini and Maital, 1985). In simple terms, it is no longer sufficient that the net expected financial gain $(t-pF)$ be positive before an individual would start to lie to the tax authority about her income. The financial rewards must be large enough to overcome the stigma of being possibly labelled as an evader. This modification of the simple model means that many individuals will refuse to evade, but as the tax rate rises it becomes increasingly worthwhile for some of these honest taxpayers to contemplate evasion. If the majority of taxpayers behave like this, then in the aggregate we would expect evasion to increase as tax rates rise. (Compare this result with that outlined earlier.)

A third development is to consider another avenue available to the disaffected taxpayer. She does not have to behave illegally in order to reduce her tax liability. She could instead try to *avoid* her tax liabilities by using various legal loopholes in the tax law. The simple model outlined earlier is justifiable if one believes that evaders and avoiders are two entirely different groups of people. Certainly, it has been usually accepted that evaders come from lower income groups, while avoiders live in the richer echelons of society. The justification for this view is that the rich could not afford the risk of being convicted for evasion, but can afford to employ accountants and lawyers to reduce their tax bills.

Recently economists have begun to examine joint evasion–avoidance decisions (Cross and Shaw, 1982; Alm, 1988; Waud, 1988). Individuals are seen as being free to switch between evasion and avoidance in response to changes in tax rates and deterrence variables (audit rates and penalties). As a result, for example, an increase in the detection rate for evasion might discourage evasion but does not necessarily increase the tax base if it merely encourages individuals to switch to tax avoidance. In other respects evasion and avoidance could be complementary activities: for example, if a justifiable claim for expenses (avoidance) facilitates an inflated claim (evasion). The moral of this particular literature is that predicting the effects of policy proposals may be difficult if individuals can switch between these alternative means of reducing their tax liabilities. However, it does seem to assume that switching between these kinds of activity is a costless exercise. At the very least, switching between evasion and avoidance will mean declaring an erratic time profile of income. That in itself is a risky business and must cast some doubt on the usefulness of assuming such behaviour by taxpayers.

Fourth, the model examined in section 4.3(i) ignores compliance costs. In fact the whole literature concerning tax evasion generally has given scant regard to compliance costs. This seems to be an unfortunate oversight. How might such costs affect individuals' behaviour? The answer to that question depends upon the nature of the cost itself. If compliance costs take the form of a fixed cost which is incurred whether one declares £1 or £50 000 of income to the Inland Revenue, then they will act as a deterrent to declaring anything at all. In other words compliance costs will tend to loosen the entry condition outlined earlier. If, on the other hand, compliance costs rise with income (perhaps because the number of sources of income rises with income level), then compliance costs will be akin to a tax on income. Without further information or heroic assumptions little more can be said about their role at this stage.

One development of the model which has been popular with economists has been to transform the decision about tax evasion into one about labour supply. In the model of section 4.3(i) the individual decides, in filling in her income-tax form, whether to declare all her income. That is not what most people have in mind when they think of tax evasion. Instead they recall 'The Boys from the Blackstuff', who cheated the government by taking one or more different jobs in the black economy. There, wages were paid in cash without income tax being deducted. Individuals then have to decide whether or not to work in the black economy, and if they do then they have to decide how many hours to spend working there. (For a survey of this literature, see Pyle, 1989, ch. 5.)

While such an approach seems much more realistic, it does present certain problems. The most important one is that it is virtually impossible to generate any unambiguous predictions about the effect of changes in tax and sanctions variables upon the extent of evasion. Of course this should not come as a complete surprise. Even in the simple introductory textbook model of individual labour supply, it is impossible to predict whether a change in the wage rate or the tax rate will increase or reduce the number of hours of labour supplied. The reason for this uncertainty is that the wage (or tax) change produces both an income effect and a substitution effect and these work in opposing directions, if leisure is a normal good. The situation in the evasion–labour-supply case is, if anything, slightly more complicated, because there are now two forms of work – work in the black economy and work in the regular economy – and there is a risk element. However, the overall conclusion is that changes in tax and sanctions variables produce income, substitution and portfolio effects which compete with one another, so that we are unable to predict the overall outcome.

This has been brought home forcefully by Pencavel (1979), who has examined the effect upon declared income of various parameter changes, first when hours worked are fixed and second when they are allowed to vary. He concludes that in moving from a model with fixed working hours to one with variable working hours 'it is evident that the predominance of unambiguous sign implications . . . is converted into a predominance of ambiguities' (pp. 120–1).

In this situation economists would normally be content to accept theoretical uncertainty and seek salvation in the results of empirical analysis. Unfortunately, in the area of tax evasion satisfactory data are virtually impossible to find (see below), so that empirical analysis cannot be relied upon to furnish definitive conclusions. Instead economists have tried to modify their theoretical models in an attempt to obtain unambiguous predictions. This has usually been achieved by imposing some form of separability on the utility function.[4] While this can be made to 'work' (see Andersen, 1977, or Isachsen and Strom, 1980), it only does so by imposing the most severe restrictions on the nature of individuals' preferences. The formulation adopted by both Andersen and Isachsen and Strom, for example, implies that the marginal utility of leisure is completely independent of income. Cowell (1985 a and b) has argued that it may be possible to produce unambiguous predictions by a less drastic route if we assume some form of hierarchy of decision-making. First, individuals decide how many hours to work and then they decide how to distribute their working time between the regular sector and the black economy. However, even his approach requires further strong assumptions, e.g. about relative risk aversion.

Finally, the simple model treats individuals as 'price takers' whose decisions, taken in isolation from one another, have no impact upon their chances of being caught or the punishment they might suffer. Clearly, one can envisage situations in which an individual's behaviour could have a significant influence upon the tax authority's decision to instigate an investigation. Models of taxpayer–tax-authority interaction are examined in section 4.5, when we consider policy issues. However, recently there has been some work concerning interaction between taxpayers themselves. There is some evidence that individuals are more likely to evade if they feel that others are also evading (see section 4.4). Work by Benjamini and Maital (1985) and Schlicht (1985) and has produced models in which taxpayers' decisions to evade are interdependent. These models clearly show that growth of the black economy weakens the rule of tax law and generates a further spread of the 'disease'. Accordingly, it may be dangerous to draw conclusions from models which treat the individual taxpayer as someone whose decisions are taken in splendid isolation. Benjamini and Maital, for example, show that, in a world of interacting taxpayers, gradualist anti-evasion policies may be singularly ineffective if an 'everyone evades' norm has become established in society. Policy then requires a 'big push' to reduce the number of evaders below some critical level. However, once below this level the policy develops a momentum of its own and further expenditure is unnecessary.

Theoretical models of taxpayer (non)-compliance have been considerably developed over the last few years. No doubt further theoretical advances will be made, but it is not clear that this is all that is required. As Pencavel (1979) has argued, 'this literature requires . . . a healthy infusion of empirical work to confront these hypotheses with actual behaviour and to resolve the ambiguities' (p. 124). Alas, as we will see in the next section, empirical work is not that easy to perform.

4.4 EVIDENCE

Economic theory cannot provide totally unambiguous predictions of the effect of many of the factors thought to influence involvement in tax evasion. Even if it could do so, the design of policy towards evasion requires precise estimates of elasticities and these can only be obtained by rigorous empirical testing. Unfortunately, while there is now a relatively large literature concerned with the theoretical modelling of tax evasion, the number of empirical studies aimed at testing these models is still very few indeed.

The paucity of studies in this area merely reflects the absence of good data upon which tests can be performed. After all, tax evasion means hiding taxable income from the tax authority, so that accurate statistics on the true extent of tax evasion simply do not exist. At best all that we have to work from are indirect estimates of the so-called black economy (see Pyle, 1989, chs 2–4) and results of relatively small, possibly non-random examinations of taxpayers' affairs.

Faced by these difficulties, empirical research has followed three broad fronts: first, sample surveys concerning individuals' attitudes to taxation and involvement in tax evasion; second, experimental tax games in which participants are given information about income, tax rates, conviction rates and penalties for evasion and are then asked to file a tax return; third and finally, there has been a limited number of studies of individual income tax returns.

(i) Surveys of taxpayers' attitudes

Studies of this kind are broadly similar. They usually take the form of a questionnaire designed to discover what individuals think about the tax system, e.g. whether they consider that tax rates are too high, whether they feel that they are paying more tax than others with similar incomes, whether they feel that small- or large-scale evasion is fair and so on.

The responses to questionnaires of any kind should be treated with the utmost caution, and questionnaires relating to possible tax evasion are probably more suspect than most. For example, would tax evaders bother to respond? If they did, would they answer truthfully? Are respondents consistent? Obviously there are good reasons for treating surveys of this kind with some caution. Despite this, they do provide some interesting and possibly useful information for other, more rigorous analyses. With this cautionary note very much in mind we briefly examine several surveys of this kind.

Song and Yarbrough (1978) conducted a sample survey of 640 households in North Carolina in 1975, although only 287 questionnaires (i.e. 45 per cent) were successfully completed and returned. Respondents were asked to either agree or disagree with a list of seven statements designed to 'measure their ethical predisposition toward tax obligations' (p. 444). Typical statements were, 'Since tax dodging hurts no-one but the government, it is not a serious offence', and 'In dealing with the Internal Revenue Service (IRS) the main thing is not to get caught' (p. 444).

Analysis of the responses shows that while the vast majority of the sample (i.e. 88 per cent) regarded tax dodging as a crime, they did not feel that they had an obligation to report tax evaders to the authorities. Further, nearly one-half of respondents felt that they were under no obligation to volunteer information to the tax authority when *their own* affairs were being audited. Song and Yarbrough asked respondents to guess what proportion (most, some, a few, etc.) of individuals committed acts such as not reporting some income, padding expenses and so on. While the vast majority (90 per cent) of respondents felt that few individuals would be foolish enough not to make a tax return, nearly three-quarters felt that some or most people inflate their expenses and two-thirds felt that some or most people did not report all of their income. Respondents were generally satisfied that the tax system was fair. Three-quarters thought that taxation should be based upon ability to pay and only one in five thought they paid more tax than others in similar circumstances. Despite this there was considerable disenchantment with the federal income tax, largely it seems because the burden was felt to be borne by the middle class!

Lewis (1979) conducted a similar survey among 200 male taxpayers in Bath in the UK in 1977. The sample was somewhat unrepresentative of the population at large, containing larger proportions of old people and Conservative voters and a smaller proportion of manual workers than the population as a whole. Respondents generally disapproved of *large-scale* tax evasion and felt it should be treated harshly by the law (85+ per cent). However, responses concerning small-scale evasion were less clear-cut. High income earners, the middle class and the old generally felt that small-scale evasion should be treated fairly leniently. On the whole respondents believed that a reduction in taxation would have little effect upon the extent of evasion. Although most people in the sample regarded income taxation as a necessary means of paying for essential services, just over a half of respondents felt that their own contribution was unreasonably large. This was particularly noticeable among higher income groups who felt that progressive income taxation was unfair.

Finally, Dean, Keenan and Kenney (1980) report the results of a questionnaire completed by 424 adults in Fife, Scotland in 1977. The vast majority of respondents (93 per cent) thought that 'income tax in this country is (much/a little) too high'. In addition, many respondents felt that they were paying too much income tax compared with other people, possibly because they 'were . . . conscious of other people's tax evasions' (p. 36). The survey also included questions concerning perceptions of opportunities for evasion and it is interesting that more than a quarter of respondents thought that all or most taxpayers could get away with failing to declare a small part of their income to the tax authority. Another quarter thought that about one-half of taxpayers had such opportunities. Two-thirds of respondents thought that all or most taxpayers would exploit an opportunity for small-scale evasion if they thought that they could get away with it, while nearly a quarter of respondents thought that all or most taxpayers would attempt large-scale evasion if they felt that it would go undetected.

Rather like the groups surveyed in Carolina and Bath, this group did not appear to exhibit strong moral objections to small-scale evasion. Less than 37 per cent of the sample felt that failing to declare a small part of income was 'bad'. Dean *et al.* asked respondents to offer reasons why 'people decided to evade tax'. The most popular single reason (given by more than 25 per cent of the respondents) was that the general level of taxation was considered too high. A further 10 per cent of the sample thought that the tax system was generally unfair. A significant proportion (about one-third) suggested various 'economic' motives such as 'greed', 'poverty or financial hardship' or 'other financial pressures'. The researchers concluded that 'there is a pent-up demand for safe evasions . . . and . . . moral considerations do not always weigh heavily as an inhibiting force, particularly where small amounts of tax are involved' (p. 44).

None of the studies has rigorously tested any of the specific hypotheses developed in section 4.3. Several studies, which also used sample survey methods, have gone one stage further than those we have encountered so far. They have tried to establish the reasons for 'admitted' tax evasion by relating measures of evasion to measures of certainty and severity of punishment, socio-economic and demographic characteristics, using regression analysis.

One such study, by Spicer and Lundstedt (1976), was aimed at isolating factors which affected individuals' decisions to evade tax. The sample consisted of 130 upper and middle income heads of households taken from two suburbs in Central Ohio. Spicer and Lundstedt were concerned to test whether (i) certainty and severity of punishment deterred potential evaders; (ii) taxpayers' (dis)satisfaction with the bundle of government services and taxes influenced their decision to evade; and (iii) individuals were persuaded to engage in evasion by knowing someone who had got away with tax evasion.

They used a questionnaire to measure individuals' propensities to evade taxes and to collect other socio-economic and demographic information relevant to the study. They constructed two indices – first, a measure of tax resistance, and second, an index of tax evasion. The scores of the individuals for each of these two indices were then related to a number of socio-economic variables such as age, education, employment status, certainty and severity of punishment, taxpayer satisfaction with government services and

acquaintance with tax evaders. Unfortunately, the regression results were rather mixed. Both equations had poor fits (at least
when measured by R^2) and t-statistics were often insignificant,
especially for the deterrence variables. Of these only the probability of punishment was significant and only then in the tax resistance equation. On the other hand, the variables measuring
taxpayer satisfaction with government services and acquaintance
with evaders were found to be significant.

Mason and Calvin (1984) surveyed some 800 taxpayers in Ore-
gon. The survey was undertaken originally in 1975 and repeated in
1980. They found that between the two interview dates there had
been a slight increase in the proportion of respondents who admitted some form of evasion. Also, the proportion of the sample who
said that they thought that the tax system was fair dropped from 71
per cent to 56 per cent. In addition, by 1980 respondents thought
that the chances of being caught for evasion were less than they
had been in 1975. Finally, the proportion of respondents who felt
that people cheated on their taxes because taxes are too high rose
from 48 per cent to 64 per cent.

Mason and Calvin analysed the pooled sample of approximately
1400 observations to test for the effects more rigorously. They
found that fear of apprehension exerted a statistically significant
deterrent effect and that those with larger incomes were less likely
to engage in evasion. However, views about the fairness of the tax
system seemed to have no effect upon whether an individual
evaded or not. Clearly fear of being caught was keeping the
majority of taxpayers in line. However, it was noticeable that a
vastly increased proportion of the dissatisfied but honest taxpayers
blamed too high taxes for *others'* transgressions.

(ii) Experimental tax games

In this section we discuss three tax 'games' played under experimental conditions by relatively small numbers of individuals.
The first, carried out by Friedland, Maital and Rutenberg (1978),
examined the effect on evasion of factors such as the tax rate and
the certainty and severity of punishment. The second, reported by
Spicer and Becker (1980), examined the relationship between tax
evasion and perceived inequities in the tax system. Finally, a third

game, reported by Spicer and Hero (1985), examined the link between levels of evasion and perceptions of evasion by others.

The rules of the games were basically similar. Participants were told that the game lasted a specific number of rounds. In each round every participant was told what her income was during that time period. She was also given information about (i) tax rates, (ii) the probability of being audited in any time period, (iii) the punishment if she was caught evading tax, and so on. Participants were then asked to decide what amount of their income to declare to the tax authority. To ensure that participants took the experiment reasonably seriously, small money prizes were paid to those who achieved the highest net income (i.e. net of taxes and penalties) at the end of the game.

Friedland *et al.*'s sample consisted of a mere fifteen students. They each played the game for 4 rounds of 10 months per round. At the end of each round Friedland calculated for each individual (i) the number of times (out of 10) that income was under-declared, (ii) the average fraction of income not reported for months in which under-declarations occurred, and (iii) the overall fraction of income declared. It was found that when the tax rate was increased from 25 per cent to 50 per cent the probability of under-reporting rose from about 0.5 to about 0.8, and that overall declarations fell from about 80 per cent to 60 per cent of income. When the fine was increased from three times to fifteen times the amount of tax evaded, the probability of an under-declaration fell, but only marginally.

An almost identical approach was used by Spicer and Becker (1980) to examine the link between tax evasion and perceived inequity of tax treatment. They recruited fifty-seven students to play the tax game over a period of 10 'months'. In this game participants were given erroneous information about the tax rates being levied on other individuals playing the game. All were told that they would pay tax at a rate of 40 per cent. However, one-third were told that the average tax rate was 65 per cent and another third were told that the average tax rate was 15 per cent. The remaining one-third were told the truth. As a result, those who thought that they were paying more tax than others evaded nearly 33 per cent of taxes payable, while those who thought they were paying less evaded only about 12 per cent. Those who knew the truth evaded approximately 25 per cent of tax.

Spicer and Hero (1985) report a game played by thirty-six psychology undergraduates, the main object of which was to examine the link between levels of evasion and perceptions of other people's evasion. The game was played along identical lines to those previously examined, except that individuals were now given incorrect information about levels of evasion in previous plays of the game. Twelve participants were told that in a previous playing of the game participants had revealed only 10 per cent of taxes due, twelve were told that previous participants had paid 50 per cent of taxes due and the remaining twelve were told that the previous players had paid 90 per cent of taxes. However, it seems that this information did not significantly affect the students' decisions to evade.

(iii) Studies of individuals' tax returns

The studies discussed so far have not examined the amounts of income that individuals actually declare for tax purposes. The surveys discussed in section 4.4(i) were concerned with eliciting either information about individuals' willingness to evade tax or confessions of previous acts of evasion. The danger with the experimental approach examined in section 4.4(ii) is that individuals might act quite differently in a game from the way they would in real life. After all, it is one thing to act illegally when the punishment is a 'paper fine', but quite another when the punishments is a real one. In addition, the audit probabilities and fines may be quite different in experimental situations from what they would be in reality.

For various reasons we would prefer to examine how individuals really behave. In other words we would like to analyse a sample of income tax returns. Recently a few studies of individuals' income tax returns have been published and we examine these studies below. In addition, there have emerged several analyses of aggregates of tax returns.

Clotfelter (1983) examined the relationship between marginal tax rates and undeclared income using data from the Internal Revenue Service's Taxpayer Compliance Measurement Programme (TCMP) survey for 1969. This includes tax returns for about 47 000 individuals. He measured undeclared income as the difference between the amount of income which the IRS auditors determined was due and the amount actually reported by each individual. Of course, this difference might also contain some 'honest', i.e. mistaken, under-declarations as well as deliberate evasion. However, if mistakes of under- and over-declaration of income are randomly distributed across the population, then the proportion of individuals who declare 'too high' an income would be approximately equal to the proportion who declare 'too low' an income. In practice the proportion found to have declared too low an income far exceeds those who declare too high an income (by a factor of at least five).

Clotfelter used the following explanatory variables: (i) after-tax income, (ii) the individual's marginal tax rate, (iii) wages as a proportion of true gross income, (iv) interest and dividends as a proportion of true gross income, and (v) dummy variables for marital status, age, region and those having to complete four or more tax forms.

Notable omissions from Clotfelter's list of explanatory variables are any measures of the probability of detection and severity of punishment. He argued that it was inappropriate to include such measures because their levels might themselves be affected by the extent of any evasion. However, if there *is* a simultaneous relationship between evasion and sanctions variables, it is entirely inappropriate to exclude the sanctions variables from the estimating equation. This merely introduces specification error. The correct approach is to build a simultaneous equation model, ensuring that the various equations are identified.

Clotfelter's main findings were that under-reporting increased with both after-tax income, and the marginal tax rate. The elasticity of under-reporting with respect to income varied from 0.29 to 0.66, while the elasticity with respect to the marginal tax rate ranged from 0.52 to 0.84, depending upon the type of tax return.[5] This latter finding led him to conclude that 'higher tax rates tend to stimulate tax evasion' (p. 368). Subsidiary findings were that where wages, interest and dividends formed a larger proportion of income, then under-reporting was less common. This is presumably because tax withholding at source is common for these forms of income. Greater complexity in returns is associated with lower-reporting of non-business income, but not of business income.

Witte and Woodbury (1985) attempted explicitly to test for the effects of sanctions variables on tax compliance. In order to do this they used a data set provided by the Internal Revenue Service (IRS) which relates to 1969 tax returns filed in 1970. Unlike Clotfelter's data, however, these data are aggregated to the three-digit zip code level. The dependent variable in this study is an IRS measure of voluntary compliance, calculated following a series of audits of a stratified random sample of taxpayers for the 1969 TCMP. It is measured by the ratio of total taxes paid to the sum of total taxes paid and the absolute value of both tax overpayments and underpayments. A large selection of independent variables was used, including income, measures of the probability and severity of punishment, a measure of return complexity, proxies for knowledge of tax laws, awareness of the IRS and attitude to government, various demographic variables such as age, education, race, ethnic origin, mobility, marital status and indices of unemployment, poverty, drop-outs and urbanisation.

Witte and Woodbury examined seven separate audit classes and their principal results are as follows. First, higher overall probabilities of audit are associated with higher compliance rates, except for low-income non-business taxpayers. However, the effects of increased probability of civil and criminal sanctions are not as expected. Where these variables are significant (which is not often) they are generally associated with lower compliance rates. It is possible that these variables have been poorly specified but more likely that there is some simultaneous equation bias present. In other words, groups with low compliance rates are being put under closer scrutiny and this leads to an increased likelihood of detection and punishment (Dubin, Graetz and Wilde, 1987).

Second, increased average severity of prison sentences for criminal fraud generally increased compliance, although in only three cases is its coefficient significant. Third, *fear* of detection (measured by the proportion of taxpayers receiving warning notices) usually increased compliance, with its coefficient being significant for five of the seven audit classes. Fourth, compliance rates are found to increase with income, up to incomes of approximately $30 000 per year, but beyond that compliance rates begin to go down. Fifth, taxpayers with higher proportions of labour income in their total income are more likely to comply with tax regulations than those with higher proportions of non-labour income, confirming that withholding increases compliance.

Crane and Nourzad (1986) report a significant impact of tax rates upon the extent of evasion, using a macro measure of the extent of unreported income. The tax rate is measured by a weighted average of marginal tax rates in each year's tax schedule, the weights being given by the percentage of total income in each tax bracket. Other explanatory variables are the audit rate, the fine rate, true income, the inflation rate, the share of wages and salaries in national income, and a time trend.

Two equations are estimated. The dependent variable in the first equation is the absolute amount of under-reported income and in the second it is the proportion of income that is under-reported. All coefficients are statistically significant, except for the audit rate in the second equation. The sanctions variables exert their expected deterrent effects, while both the tax rate and the inflation rate are positively related to evasion. Again, a larger share of wages and salaries in income is associated with reduced evasion. The absolute amount of evasion increases with income, but the proportion of income not reported falls as income rises.

We have queried the assumption that enforcement activity can be treated as an exogenous variable. If it cannot, then empirical work based on the assumption that such activity is exogenously fixed must be seriously flawed and a simultaneous equations model must be estimated instead. Dubin, Graetz and Wilde (1987) have used state-level data for the USA to estimate just such a model. The data comes from the Annual Reports of the Commissioner of Internal Revenue from 1977 to 1985. The arguments in favour of a simultaneous relationship between evasion and sanctions variables seem intuitively more appealing when aggregate data are being used. The measure of 'evasion' used by Dubin *et al.* is the additional tax and penalties resulting from audits as a percentage of total tax collections. This measure is regressed on the lagged (one year) value of the audit rate and a whole host of socio-economic and demographic variables, such as per capita income, the unemployment rate and the percentage of the population with high-school education. A separate equation models the determination of the audit rate. Dubin *et al.*'s estimates suggest that '(1) the audit rate *is* an endogenous (variable) . . . (2) there *is* a deterrent effect associated with increases in the audit rate . . . and (3) compliance increases with per capita income, but at a decreasing rate, peaking below the maximum income. In addition, there is a significant negative time trend in the audit rate and in compliance' (pp. 243–4, my emphases).

What can we conclude about the determinants of tax evasion? It is difficult to make sweeping generalisations because the amount of solid evidence is quite small and much empirical work still needs to be done. Also, some of the studies examined above are based on relatively small and/or possibly biased samples. Furthermore, they sometimes offer conflicting evidence.

Survey evidence would indicate that while the majority of taxpayers regard evasion as a crime, they do not feel that small-scale evasion should be treated harshly. In addition, there is a substantial number of taxpayers who are now somewhat disenchanted with the income tax system. This is particularly true of middle income groups, who seem to feel that a disproportionate share of the tax burden falls on them. It would appear that at least some taxpayers see evasion as a 'legitimate' means of reducing what they consider to be the excessive demands of taxation. Evasion helps to offset some of the costs of a progressive tax system, and in a world in which others are seen to be evading it offers a means of preserving both vertical and horizontal equity. Certainly there is some econometric evidence to support the view that those on higher incomes and those paying higher marginal rates of income tax are less likely to comply with the tax laws than others.

Evidence of the impact of certainty and severity of punishment upon the extent of evasion is rather less clear-cut. While the majority of evidence points to a significant deterrent effect of increases in the probability of detection/auditing, there is less evidence that more severe penalties act in the same way. This may be explained in some cases by mis-specification of relationships and in others by possible measurement error. Finally, there is strong evidence that tax withholding has a substantial impact upon the extent of tax evasion.

4.5 POLICY ISSUES

The case against tax evasion is that on balance it is thought to produce more harm than good. For example, there is now some evidence that it biases macroeconomic indicators and leads to a misallocation of resources (see Pyle, 1989, ch. 7). The question, then, is 'what should governments do about tax evasion?' In this section we consider a number of policy options. We begin by considering a policy aimed at completely eliminating evasion. However, it becomes clear that such a policy may be costly and so we are forced to consider how much evasion can be tolerated and what an optimal policy towards evasion might be. In what follows we will only sketch some rather simple proposals and leave the interested reader to follow up the rather more sophisticated developments that have been recently suggested.

(i) Elimination

If the tax authority's objective is to enforce complete tax compliance, how might it achieve this? To make the discussion a little more concrete, suppose that we live in a world characterised by the model of section 4.3(i). That is, taxpayers are all amoral, risk averse expected utility maximisers, who are faced by a given probability of being audited, a constant income tax rate and a fixed penalty per unit of evaded income. In such a world, a rational individual would only evade if the expected penalty per unit of evaded income is less than the rate of income tax, i.e. $pF < t$.[6]

If the tax authority wishes to enforce compliance then it must choose p and F such that the expected penalty exceeds the rate of income tax. This can be seen perhaps more clearly from Figure 4.5, which plots the rectangular hyperbola $pF = t$.

The set of values of p and F which satisfy the policy rule clearly lie in the area above and to the right of the curve. Figure 4.5 also indicates that there is an infinite set of combinations of p and F which satisfy the policy rule. Furthermore, there is a clearly identifiable trade-off between certainty of punishment (p) and its severity (F). The question then arises, which of these combinations should the tax authority choose? There is a fallacious argument in the economics of crime literature which suggests that the enforcement agency should set F at very high levels indeed and so p would be close to zero. In other words one should have a system of very severe penalties, which are rarely applied. The argument behind this proposal is simply that increasing the probability of detection is costly (employing more tax inspectors) whereas increasing the penalty, if it is a fine, is relatively cheap. Fines are

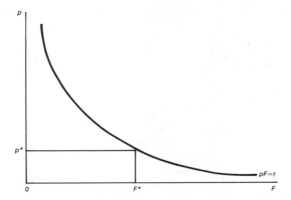

FIGURE 4.5 **The trade-off between certainty and severity of punishment**

merely transfer payments, and so increasing their size does not impose a cost upon society, except perhaps for fine administration and imprisonment of fine defaulters! If the penalty is one of imprisonment the above argument does not hold, of course.

At first glance this policy seems appealing. It fails for two reasons. First, economists working in the area of criminal law enforcement (e.g. Stigler, 1970) have pointed to the need to preserve an element of marginal deterrence in the structure of penalties. For example, suppose that the penalty for tax evasion was life imprisonment. As the penalty for murder is also life imprisonment, any tax evader has an incentive to murder anyone who might know about her tax irregularities. After all, the penalty they might suffer is no worse if they behave in this way. Clearly, then, a sensible criminal justice policy has to design a set of penalties which does not produce perverted signals to potential criminals. In other words the punishment must, in some sense, fit the crime. Second, severe penalties applied relatively infrequently would mean that detected and undetected evaders would be treated very differently. This would produce a further inequity into the distribution of income. It is perhaps the recognition that on occasions taxpayers can make genuine mistakes that has caused penalties for evasion to be held down (Skinner and Slemrod, 1985; Keith Report, 1983).

It seems, then, that the tax authority must accept an upper limit

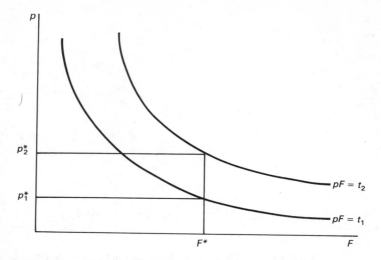

FIGURE 4.6   Differential audit probabilities by income tax group

on the level of punishment that can be imposed upon tax evaders, say F^* in Figure 4.5. In that case, elimination requires setting p slightly above p^*. Once we accept that complete elimination of tax evasion requires setting non-negligible levels of p, then we must ask whether it is sensible to aim for completely eliminating such activity. To do so might entail incurring costs far in excess of the benefits such a programme might generate. Before considering this argument, we need to examine one further aspect of a policy aimed at eliminating evasion.

In the model examined so far there is only one income tax rate. However, in practice different individuals are often faced by different marginal tax rates. If society is divided into two groups, say 'the rich' who are faced by a marginal tax rate of t_2 and 'the poor' who pay tax at a lower rate, t_1, then the logic of our argument should be that the rich should be faced by higher expected penalties. If the maximum size of the fine is independent of income this amounts to saying that higher-rate taxpayers should be confronted by a higher probability of being audited. This is depicted in Figure 4.6.

Clearly such a policy is superior to one of setting a uniform audit probability. With a uniform probability, it would have to be set slightly above p_2^* for both groups. This would be more expensive than setting different rates for the two groups. Alternatively, if the uniform rate is set below p_2^* tax revenues would decline, because some evasion would exist among higher-rate taxpayers. A similar policy has been suggested by Landsberger and Meilijson (1982) and Greenberg (1984), although they advocate allocating individuals to different groups quite arbitrarily rather than on the basis of the tax rate they face.[7] In this policy the punishment for a detected evader in the group with the lower audit rate is to be transferred to the group with the higher audit rate, while the reward for honesty is to be transferred to the group with the lower probability of being audited. These policies are discussed in more detail in Pyle (1989, ch. 8).

(ii) The optimal level of evasion

So far, it has been assumed that society's objective is to eliminate evasion altogether. However, such a policy requires the use of resources which have alternative uses and so we need to question whether it is economically efficient. It would only be so if the cost of eliminating evasion were outweighed by the benefits such a policy would produce. Consider the situation depicted in Figure 4.7.

The curves labelled *MC* and *MB* represent the marginal cost and the marginal benefit of reducing evasion respectively. They are drawn on the assumptions that (i) when there is a great deal of evasion then the cost of reducing it by a small amount is relatively small and the marginal benefit is high, and (ii) that as evasion is reduced the marginal cost of reducing it still further rises while the marginal benefit declines. These arguments have a certain intuitive appeal; at least in relationship to the marginal cost curve. When everyone evades, it doesn't take very much in the way of extra enforcement to achieve some degree of compliance (however, recall the arguments of section 4.3(ii) concerning taxpayer interaction). Presumably, too, the tax authority chooses the easiest (i.e. cheapest) options first. Later on, the forms of evasion are more difficult to uncover and so become more expensive to eliminate. Likewise, when there is a great deal of evasion the gains from reducing it in terms of improved efficiency of resource allocation

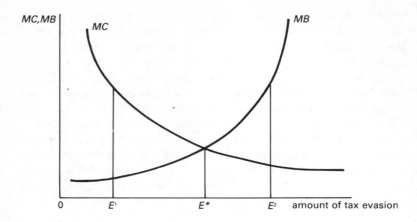

FIGURE 4.7   The optimal level of tax evasion

or enhanced reliability of economic indicators may be quite substantial. However, when there is anyway very little evasion the extra benefit to be gained from reducing evasion still further is probably not much.

While measuring the cost of reducing evasion is fairly straightforward, it is not immediately apparent how one can measure the benefits. It would clearly be wrong to measure them by, for example, the extra tax revenue generated.[8]

Consider, then, the case depicted in Figure 4.7. An 'optimal' policy towards evasion would be to spend resources on detecting it up to the point at which $MC = MB$. If one were to enforce compliance beyond that point, say to E^1, then the cost of doing so would exceed the benefit generated and welfare would be reduced. If the tax authority wishes to reduce evasion below E^* it must think of ways of reducing the cost of detecting evaders. If it could find a method which lowers marginal costs at all levels of evasion then clearly the optimum level of evasion would fall below E^*.

The moral of this little section is simply that a policy aimed at completely eliminating evasion may be inefficient. As we can see from Figure 4.7, when evasion is reduced to zero we have gone way beyond the optimal level of evasion. Indeed it is possible that when evasion has been eliminated we are worse off than if we had done nothing at all and left evasion at its pre-intervention level, say E^2.

Unfortunately, because of the difficulties involved in measuring the benefits to be derived from reducing evasion, tax authorities will tend to set other objectives, such as elimination or spending on enforcement up to the point at which the marginal cost of evasion reduction equals marginal tax revenue. Both policies produce sub-optimal levels of evasion.

There may be another reason why the socially optimal level of evasion may be non-zero. If society's welfare function is simply the sum of individuals' utility functions and the representative individual chooses to be a tax evader, then increasing compliance not only reduces the individual tax evaders' utilities, but also reduces social welfare (Cowell, 1987). Of course, this assumes that tax evaders' dishonesty does not adversely affect the utility of the honest taxpayers.

(iii) Alternative strategies

Consider Figure 4.5 again. We have so far argued that if we change p and/or F we can deter individuals from becoming involved in income tax evasion. Another option suggests itself. Suppose instead we reduce the income tax rate until the expected penalty exceeds the tax rate. Again, entry into the evasion 'business' is no longer financially desirable and the tax base will be expanded.[9]

Of course tax rate changes are not normally the preserve of the tax authority. Tax rates are set by government ministers with largely other considerations in mind, e.g. income redistribution, incentives effects on labour supply, saving and risk-taking and so on. The Inland Revenue is then charged with the responsibility of raising the revenue by use of its enforcement powers. However, it would be a rather narrow view of policy to ignore the effect that a change in the tax rate has upon the extent of evasion. Indeed one of the motives behind the reduction in the top rates of income tax in the UK, USA, Australia, etc. has been a realisation that such rates are hardly ever paid. They have been either avoided or evaded.

Empirical support for a policy of tax-cutting is difficult to find (see section 4.4). Graetz and Wilde (1985) have found that under-reporting of capital gains is a large share of all under-reporting despite the fact that rates of tax on capital gains are considerably below those on other forms of income. They argue, therefore, that 'where there is an opportunity for under-reporting of income people will understate such income even if the unreported income would be taxed at a low rate' (p. 360). They conclude that 'there is little reason . . . to believe lower rates alone are likely to inhibit non-compliance' (p. 360).

There is another reason for treating a tax-cutting policy with some caution. Even if it did encourage greater compliance, this in itself is insufficient to generate additional tax revenue, for while the tax base is expanded the take per unit of declared income is reduced. If the government is faced by a revenue constraint a cut in the tax rate might cause revenue to fall. (Consider, for example, what would happen if the tax rate were cut to zero.)

A much less contentious policy, at least in terms of its effect, is the widening of withholding legislation. Empirical work quite clearly shows that where income tax is deducted at source compliance is much less of a problem. Improvements in third-party reporting and the matching of third-party information with individual returns will encourage compliance. However, both of these policies entail costs, about which very little is known. In the circumstances it is difficult to decide whether they are economically efficient policies.

4.6　CONCLUSIONS

In this chapter I have surveyed the literature on two main issues. First, what are the 'incentives', broadly defined, that cause individuals to engage in tax evasion? Second, what policies should be followed in order to achieve an 'optimal' level of evasion?

The theoretical modelling of individuals' decisions to engage in tax evasion has basically followed the approach suggested by Becker (1968) for analysing criminal behaviour. While the degree of sophistication of these models has been considerably improved in the last few years this has brought its own problems. For example, as models have become more complicated, their comparative-static predictions have become much less clear. Economists are used to this. Most 'price' changes involve income and substitution effects which often work in opposite directions. As in demand theory, so in the theory of income-tax evasion. However, this does bring into question precisely what role further theorising should play in the study of evasion and what insights one can expect from further effort along existing lines. The second strand of criticisms about existing theoretical models is that they are deficient in certain important respects. For example, Skinner and Slemrod (1985) have shown that the odds are heavily stacked in favour of evaders getting away with it, and yet, they claim, the vast majority of taxpayers declare all their income. The fact that they do so seems to require that taxpayers either are remarkably risk-averse or attach a considerable disutility to dishonesty.

On this last point there have been some interesting recent developments incorporating stigma costs into the utility function. Models of this type have been successful in explaining why some individuals prefer not to become involved in tax evasion. Further, they have proved capable of explaining why an increase in tax rates would encourage such activity. Standard expected utility models have tended to produce, at best, inconclusive 'evidence' on this point and, at worst, rather odd predictions. As yet, models including stigma costs have been rather simplistic. Further development of models of this type may prove worthwhile. This would make the economic models more realistic and may even improve their predictive power.

Further criticism of theoretical models focuses upon the failure to construct dynamic (i.e. lifetime) models and upon the treatment of enforcement policy as an exogenous factor influencing individuals' decisions. On this latter point it is interesting to note that Reinganum and Wilde (1983) claim that when a 'responsive' tax authority is incorporated into a general equilibrium model, then many of the comparative static properties of simpler, partial equilibrium models do not hold.

The solution should lie in the results of empirical studies. Alas, the current harvest of such studies is remarkably thin. The real obstacle to empirical work has been the absence of virtually any, let alone reliable, information about the extent of tax evasion at the micro level. The two studies (Clotfelter, 1983, and Witte and Woodbury, 1985) which have exploited perhaps the best data source must remain suspect, because of possible specification error

and simultaneity bias. Others have resorted to using questionnaires and game simulations. While this work is interesting, one
must remain sceptical about how far one can generalise from the
results of such work. There is an overwhelming need for a careful,
sophisticated econometric analysis of individual tax returns.

One major omission from both the theoretical and empirical
analysis of tax evader behaviour is the treatment of compliance
costs. In fact they are a much neglected area of taxation research
altogether. As we saw in section 4.2, compliance costs are not
trivial and may thus be expected to have some influence on the
decision whether or not to evade and how much income to hide
from Inland Revenue.

There have also been some considerable developments on the
policy front, although there is some disagreement about precisely
what the objectives of policy in this area should be. For example,
there are those who simply regard evasion as bad and hence
conclude that it should be eliminated or at least reduced as far as
possible, and those who argue that some evasion should be tolerated, for to remove it all would lower social welfare.

Research points to the dangers of imposing very high penalties
as a means of deterring evasion. The need to retain a proper
structure of penalties so as to maintain marginal deterrent effects
and the dangers of ex-post horizontal inequality which severe
penalties would create, mitigate against their use. The seductive
option of relatively costless, harsh penalties applied fairly infrequently does not, on closer examination, seem quite so appealing.
However, once we acknowledge that realistically evasion can only
be deterred by spending on increasing detection rates, we also
have to acknowledge that a certain amount of evasion may have to
be accepted.

There is now a growing literature examining what we have
called sophisticated strategies for tax authorities. It is clearly the
case that a more efficient use of the tax authority's resources
requires differential audit probabilities across individuals. However, precisely how rules can be formulated is rather less obvious.
Further research along these lines should be quite informative.

The case for using tax rates to deter evasion is much less clear-
cut. The theoretical and empirical analysis as yet hardly offers
convincing proof that a reduction in income-tax rates would bring
about an unequivocal increase in income declared to the tax

authorities. At this point economics and 'common sense' seem to part company. Everyone 'knows' that evasion is a consequence of high tax rates. Of course, the failure of economists to confirm this view may be their own fault. The empirical work, for instance, has not been particularly distinguished in this respect and we have earlier recommended that a substantial research commitment should be undertaken in this particular area.

One policy weapon which seems to be universally accepted as being an effective safeguard against tax evasion is the withholding of tax at source. Whilst such an option would be difficult to apply to the self-employed, there seems little to prevent its more rigourous application to employees, unless, of course, one is concerned about equity considerations. However, the wider application of withholding might give employees an incentive to move into self-employment which is not necessarily a more efficient use of their time and skills. So, even apparently non-controversial options such as withholding are not quite so obviously desirable when subjected to closer scrutiny.

A great deal of interesting and imaginative research has been undertaken. Unfortunately, the subject presents peculiar difficulties for researchers, so that while much has been learned there is still much to be done before economists can be confident in making policy proposals.

5 Preference Revelation and Public Goods

RICHARD R. BARNETT*

5.1 INTRODUCTION

The conditions that must hold if a public good is to be provided at a Pareto-efficient level are well established in the economics literature and were first set out formally by Samuelson (1954, 1955). Assuming that the public good is financed out of non-distortionary taxation, these conditions require that the good be provided up to the level at which

$$\sum_i MRS_{gx} = MRT_{gx}$$

where MRS_{gx} is the marginal rate of substitution between the public good, g, and a private good numeraire, x; MRT_{gx} is the marginal rate of transformation between the two goods; and there are i consumers of the public good.[1] This is often referred to as the Samuelson condition, and the required amendments to it to allow for finance out of distortionary taxation have been established by Stiglitz and Dasgupta (1971) and Atkinson and Stern (1974).

However, while the Pareto-efficiency conditions are well established, it has also long been recognised that it may be quite a difficult matter for the government, as provider of the public good, to ascertain information on each individual's preferences (that is, on each individual's MRS_{gx} schedule). And this information is required if the public good is to be provided at a Pareto-efficient level. This preference revelation problem arises for two fundamental reasons. First, unlike the case for private goods, an individual's preferences are not automatically revealed in the market place; the reason being, quite simply, that there is no market for public goods (as we shall see in sections 5.2 and 5.4, this statement has to be modified slightly in the case of *local* public goods – a definition of such goods is provided in section 5.2). Second, each individual will not necessarily have the incentive to voluntarily reveal their true preferences for public goods. Instead, to use Samuelson's famous phrase, each individual may have the incentive to give 'false signals'. The preference revelation problem is then an example of a wider class of problems in economics which arise due to asymmetric information. In this case each individual has information about their true preferences for public goods which is not automatically available to the government, and thus we have a type of asymmetric information problem which is known as hidden information.[2] Each individual will attempt to use this private (or hidden) information to their own advantage, and this may not involve revealing its true nature to the government.

In this chapter I review some of the main developments which have taken place in response to this preference revelation problem in the context of public goods supply. In section 5.2 I provide some background to the preference revelation problem; in particular I discuss why it arises and show how the incentive to give false information is related to the tax system that is used to finance the public good. In this section I also show that the preference revelation problem can arise in the context of the public provision of private goods. In section 5.3 I outline the main findings of a body of research which has been directed at devising tax (or payment) schemes which give individuals the incentive to reveal their true preferences. These incentive compatible tax systems are known as demand-revealing mechanisms. Then in section 5.4 I outline how individuals may in fact indirectly reveal their true preferences for local public goods, and the discussion centres on some of the main economic problems that arise when attempts are made to estimate the demand for such goods. Some of the issues have counterparts in the literature on shadow pricing non-marketed goods in cost–benefit analysis. Towards the end of section 5.4 I discuss briefly the link between capitalisation and hedonic pricing. Finally, in recent years there has been a growing use of the direct questionnaire approach to elicit individuals' preferences and I review the main aspects of this approach in section 5.5. Again there have been parallel developments in the cost–benefit literature and more generally the survey approach is known as contingent valuation.

The concluding comment, which makes up section 5.6, directs the reader to some literature which questions the importance of the preference revelation problem; also some literature not surveyed in this review is referred to.

5.2   BACKGROUND TO THE DEMAND REVELATION PROBLEM

In this section I want to put our future discussion into context by doing two things. First, I ask what it is about the characteristics of public goods that leads to the preference revelation problem. In answering this question we shall see that the same problem can also arise in the context of the public provision of private goods. Thus, on this account, the preference revelation problem is wider in scope than might initially appear to be the case. This is especially so since many of the goods that are supplied by government are private, rather than public, goods. We shall also see, however, that to the extent that public goods are local goods (and/or the level of provision of publicly provided private goods varies between localities), then the preference revelation problem may be more limited in scope. The second aim of this section is to show how an individual's incentive to reveal their true preference is related to the form of the tax system that is used to finance the publicly provided good.

Public goods have two defining characteristics. First the consumption of these goods is non-rival; that is, the goods can be jointly consumed and one individual's consumption of the good does not diminish the amount that is available for others to consume. Second, public goods are non-excludable: once a public good is provided to one individual it is impossible, or at least prohibitively costly, to prevent other individuals from consuming the good. It should be noted that these two characteristics are quite independent of one another and hence it is possible for goods to possess one of the characteristics without possessing the other. For a good to be a public good, however, it must possess both characteristics. It should also be noted that the two characteristics have different implications for the achievement of a Pareto-efficient level of supply of the good. If a good possesses the first characteristic, quite independently of whether it also possesses the second, then the Samuelson condition for the Pareto-efficient level of provision applies. Sometimes the term 'collective consumption good' is used to define goods for which the Samuelson condition is relevant. (Thus collective consumption goods include public goods and non-rival goods for which exclusion is possible – for example, theatre performances and soccer matches.) If a good is non-rival but exclusion is possible it means that a price can be collected and thus the private sector may be able to provide such goods. But it is quite a different matter as to whether the private sector will provide such goods at a Pareto-efficient level;[3] for example, if the good is truly non-rival then the cost of providing the good to an additional individual is zero and thus the marginal price charged should be zero.

If a good is non-excludable then a price cannot be collected for the good since non-payers of the price cannot be excluded from consuming the good. And clearly this is the case whether or not the good is non-rival. Non-excludability can arise for a variety of reasons and I want to distinguish between three main causes here. First, non-excludability may arise due to the technological nature of the good; and national defence (or at least deterrence) is an example of such a good. Second, the lack of enforceable private property rights may give rise to non-excludability; an example here could be common resources such as ocean fisheries. And third, non-excludability may arise as a consequence of government (or judicial) policy; for example, it may be government policy that everybody has the right to a free state education. The second of these causes of non-excludability is not of central concern to us in this chapter and the interested reader is referred to a text on common resources issues, an excellent example of which is Hart-wick and Olewiler (1986).[4] We are, however, concerned with the other two causes on non-excludability and what I want to show is that both can give rise to the preference revelation problem.

Non-excludability which arises due to the technological nature of the good coupled with non-rivalness in consumption defines the classic case of a public good, and it is clear that the preference revelation problem can arise in this context. Once any given quantity of such a good is provided everybody *can automatically consume* the total amount provided irrespective of how much, if anything, they have contributed towards the finance of the good. And exactly the same state of affairs exists when the good is technically excludable, as is the case for education (apart from any externalities associated with education), but the government has legislated that everybody has the right to free access to whatever level is provided: everybody *has the right to consume* the good irrespective of how much, if anything, they have contributed towards its financing. Thus non-excludability alone is sufficient to generate the preference revelation problem. The important implication of this is that the preference revelation problem can arise in the context of both public goods and publicly provided private goods.[5] When it is not important to distinguish between these two types of good I shall refer to publicly provided goods.

The fact that the preference revelation problem can arise in the context of both public goods and publicly provided private goods widens the scope of our analysis, and from an empirical perspective this is especially the case since many goods that governments actually provide are private goods. (Some goods, of course, are part private and part public: such goods – and education is perhaps one of these – are sometimes called mixed goods.) However, there is another consideration which may work in the opposite direction and narrow the scope of the preference revelation problem. This further consideration relates to the spatial (or geographical) area over which the benefits of a public good extend. The benefits from some public goods can be enjoyed by everybody in a nation, and national defence is an example of such a good. But the benefit area of some public goods is more spatially limited. In the development of the economics literature on public goods a commonly cited example has been a lighthouse. The benefits of a lighthouse are spatially limited: a lighthouse provides guidance to shipping passing particular hazards, but it does not provide guidance to all shipping attempting to pass all hazards. Similarly, at a more parochial level, the benefits from a streetlight are spatially limited. Thus, it is possible to classify public goods according to the spatial area over which their benefits extend. Public goods with benefits which do not extend to everybody in the nation as a whole can be defined as local public goods. (In addition there are public goods whose benefit area extends beyond the boundaries of a single nation and these might be termed supranational public goods. These will not be of direct interest to us in this chapter.)

Another way of considering local public goods is to say that the non-excludability property extends only to people who are present in a specified geographical area. Individuals outside this area are excluded from consuming the public good due to the simple fact that its benefits do not extend to them. Thus, we can say that local public goods are non-excludable within the area over which their benefits extend, but excludable between areas. Of course, the Samuelson condition applies to all public goods, be they national, local or supranational, but this does not mean that local public goods which supply different areas should all be provided at the same level. In terms of local public goods we can think of different localities each being provided with a Pareto-efficient level of the good, but with the level of provision in each locality being different, due, for example, to different preferences (i.e. different MRS_{gx} schedules).

Just as the level of provision of local public goods can vary between different geographical areas so also can the level of provision of locally provided private goods. For example, the level of education provision which each individual has a right to consume might vary between areas, again perhaps due to different preferences. Now, to the extent that such geographic variability in the level of provision does occur, individuals do, in part at least, reveal their preferences for these goods by their choice of where to live. This is the insight of the seminal paper by Tiebout (1956) which was written in response to Samuelson's comments about the preference revelation problem and the difficulty of achieving a Pareto-efficient level of provision of public goods.[6] Tiebout referred to each individual's ability to go 'fiscal shopping' and to 'vote with their feet' for their most preferred bundle of publicly provided goods. And to the extent that individuals do go fiscal shopping they are revealing their preferences for these goods. In Tiebout's original paper the opportunities for fiscal shopping are maximised since his assumed world was populated by people living off unearned income and thus nobody was tied to a particular location due to workplace requirements. But the ability to go fiscal shopping does exist especially in the larger urban areas where an individual often has the choice of living in many different localities without changing their job. Also some Tiebout-moves may take place within a given local government area: for example, to get within a given school catchment area. And some sectors of the population do approximate to Tiebout's rentier class: for example, the growing number of retired people. Thus individuals may, in part at least, reveal their preferences for locally provided goods, and in section 5.4 we shall examine how use has been made of this information in research which seeks to measure demand curves for such goods.

We turn now to the second set of issues to be discussed in this section, namely the link between the incentive that an individual has to reveal his[7] true preference and the tax system that is being used to finance the provision of the publicly provided good. I consider the three types of taxation which are most commonly cited in discussions of the preference revelation problem; these are a benefit tax, a lump-sum tax, and a tax base under which an individual faces a given tax price for publicly provided goods.[8] Under a benefit tax an individual's tax payments are related to benefits received. But the value of such benefits received is of course private (or hidden) information to the individual, and thus each individual has the incentive to understate their true benefits thereby reducing their tax payments. This incentive to understate true preferences, and to *free-ride* on the provision by others of the publicly provided good, has long been recognised in the economics literature and is at its greatest when the individual is one of many consumers of the good. For example, Wicksell (1896) writes:

> If an individual is to spend his money for private and public uses so that his satisfaction is maximized, he will obviously pay nothing for public purposes (at least if we disregard fees and similar charges). Whether he pays much or little will affect the scope of public sources so slightly, that for all practical purposes, he himself will not notice it at all. Of course, if everyone were to do the same, the State would cease to function. (p. 81)

And it *is* the dominant strategy for each individual to free-ride in this way. If, however, the individual is one of a few people consuming the good then he will realise that his stated preference is likely to have a significant impact on the overall quantity of the good provided and the incentive to free-ride may be modified.[8] Thus, in sharp contrast to the analysis of private goods where larger numbers of economic agents leads to a competitive (and socially more favourable) outcome, in the case of publicly provided goods under benefit taxation larger numbers exacerbate the free-rider problem.

By lump-sum taxation I mean a tax system under which each individual pays a fixed amount of taxation quite irrespective of both his stated preference for the publicly provided good and how much of the good is actually supplied.[9] In this case the marginal price of a publicly provided good is equal to zero, and thus the individual will wish to have the good provided up to the level at which $MRS_{gx} = 0$. It is generally argued that under a lump-sum tax the individual has the incentive to *over*state his true preferences. The reason for this is that the individual wishes to make sure that the good is provided up to at least the level at which his $MRS_{gx} = 0$, and one way to make this more likely is to overstate his true preference. Such overstatement of true preferences has no tax consequences for the individual since his tax payments are fixed. Again we have an example of free-riding, but this time an individual is free-riding on other people's financing of the good (i.e. other people's tax payments). The only slight modification that we need to make to the above line of reasoning is if the publicly provided good is non-rejectable, in the sense that an individual *has* to consume the total amount of the good provided. In this case there is a cost to the individual of provision beyond the level at which his $MRS_{gx} = 0$ in the form of the disutility that he gets from having to consume, what are to him, excessive units of the publicly provided good. Thus the characteristic of non-rejectability may serve to modify the incentive that an individual would otherwise have to overstate his true preference when finance is by means of lump-sum taxation.

The third type of tax system that I want to consider is one in which an individual pays a fixed tax price for each unit of the publicly provided good. This type of tax system is common in analyses of the demand for locally provided goods. To illustrate how such a tax system works, assume that a publicly provided good can be provided at a constant cost c and that the good is to be financed by means of a poll tax. Then if there are n poll-tax payers, the price of a unit of the good to each individual is $(1/n)c$. Similarly if finance is by means of a proportional income tax then the price of a unit of the good to individual i is $(y_i/\Sigma_i y)c$, where y_i is individual i's income. Thus under a fixed tax price system of finance each individual pays a share s_i of the total tax bill and the price of a unit of the publicly provided good to each individual is $s_i c$. As in the case of the lump-sum tax considered above, each individual will have a desired level of provision of the publicly provided good, and in this case it occurs at the level of which $MRS_{gx} = s_i c$. But will the individual have the incentive to reveal this true preference? It will depend on where he believes his utility maximising level of provision lies relative to the Pareto-efficient level of provision. If an individual believes that the Pareto-efficient level of provision exceeds his most preferred level of provision then he will attempt to bias the government's decision downwards by understating his true preference. The objective behind this understatement of true preferences is to avoid paying the fixed tax share for units of the good for which $MRS_{gx} < s_i c$. Similarly, if, given his fixed tax price, an individual's utility maximising level of the good exceeds the Pareto-efficient level an individual will have an incentive to overstate his true preference. Under a system of fixed tax shares, the only time when no individual has an incentive to mis-state his true preference is when $MRS_{gx} = s_i c$ for all individuals at the Pareto-efficient level of provision. In such a case the fixed tax shares are Lindahl prices: an outcome that must be considered fortuitous and unlikely. Thus Lindahl prices aside, we have considered three commonly studied tax systems each of which has given at least some individuals the incentive to mis-state their true preference. This is disturbing news for a government interested in achieving a Pareto-efficient level of supply of publicly provided goods. It should be noted that there are simple public decision rules (or public choice rules) that the government could follow and which would induce individuals to reveal their true preferences; the problem with these rules is that they are unlikely to result in a Pareto-efficient level of provision of publicly provided goods. For example, the government might use a fixed tax price means of finance and decide to provide a good at the level preferred by the voter with the median preference. The reason that each individual has the incentive to reveal their true preference under such a decision rule is because by mis-stating their preference they can change the level of provision of the good only in a direction which is unfavourable to themselves. An individual whose true preference exceeds that of the median voter would ideally like to bias the government's decision in an upward direction, but any overstatement of true preference by this individual will not affect the position of the median preference. The only way in which this individual could affect the outcome is by understating his true preference (i.e. by stating a preference below that of the existing median voter, thereby making an individual with a lower preference the median voter), but such an action moves the government decision further away from his own utility maximising level of provision. It is unlikely, however, that the preference of the median voter will equal the Pareto-efficient level of provision. For example, in the case of a public good and a fixed tax price system of financing, it is the mean preference which equals the Pareto-efficient level, and only if preferences are symmetric about the mean will the median preference equal the mean preference.[10]

5.3 DEMAND-REVEALING TAXATION

As we noted in the introduction to this chapter, the preference revelation problem is an example of a class of problems which arises due to asymmetric information. In this case each individual has information on their true preference for publicly provided goods which is not automatically available to the government. The central idea behind the programme of research which I outline in this section has been to design a tax (or payments) system which gives each individual the incentive to reveal their true preference for such goods. An alternative way to describe the objective of this research is to say that the aim has been to devise a tax system under which telling the truth is the dominant strategy for each individual; that is, such tax systems are (individual) incentive compatible. More prosaically we might say if such a tax system can be devised then 'honesty is the best policy' for each individual.

The work in this area builds on some early work by Vickrey (1961) and I begin this section by briefly reviewing the salient aspects of his analysis. The situation analysed by Vickrey is one in which there are many potential buyers of a single (indivisible) commodity which is being offered for sale by auction. It can readily be shown that each potential buyer has the incentive to reveal their true valuation of the commodity if the following procedure is used. Each potential buyer is required to place his bid in a sealed envelope and is told that the commodity will be sold to the individual who makes the highest bid, and the price paid will equal the value of the second highest bid. Vickrey calls this the 'second price' method. To see why this procedure encourages the revelation of true preferences, consider any potential bidder i, then we need to distinguish between two cases:

(i) i's true valuation is greater than any other individual's true valuation;
(ii) i's true valuation is less than at least one other individual's true valuation;

Let $v_1, v_2, \ldots, v_i, \ldots, v_n$ be the true valuations of the n potential buyers ordered from the highest downwards, and let $b_1, \ldots,$ $b_2, \ldots, b_i, \ldots, b_n$ be the bids of these potential buyers again arranged in descending order. Then in case (i) we need to show that it is a dominant strategy for the individual to bid v_1 and to pay b_2. As long as $b_1 > b_2$ the individual will receive the commodity which he values at v_1 and will pay b_2 thereby making a net gain of $v_1 - b_2$. Clearly there is no point in overstating his preference since he will still gain the commodity and pay b_2 for it. Thus there is no gain from overstatement of true preference. However, if the individual understates his true preference then either this also will have no effect because $b_1 > b_2$, or the individual will no longer be the highest bidder. In the latter case he loses the net gain of $v_1 - b_2$ which he would have achieved had he revealed his true preference. Thus in case (i) there is no gain to be had from overstatement, and a potential loss of $v_1 - b_2$ to be had from understatement. In case (ii) there is nothing to be gained from understatement of true preference since by definition it is already the case that $v_i < b_1$. If the individual overstates his true preference then either this has no impact because $b_i < b_1$, or the individual buys the commodity. In the latter case the individual pays b_1 for a commodity which he values at v_i thereby making a net loss of $b_1 - v_i$.

What we have just shown is that a potential buyer confronted with a Vickrey second-price auction can reason prior to the auction that he must be in one of the two situations described by cases (i) and (ii) above. And in both of these situations there are no gains to be had from the mis-statement of true preferences. Indeed there are only potential losses to be had. Thus the dominant strategy for all potential buyers is to make a bid equal to their true valuation: that is $b_i = v_i$ for all individuals.[11] While the Vickrey second-price auction is individual incentive compatible – that is, acting independently it is a dominant strategy for each individual to reveal their true valuation – the procedure is not necessarily group incentive compatible. If individuals can form coalitions there may be a gain to be had from the mis-statement of true preferences. This problem will be analysed in more detail below since it carries over to the demand-revealing taxes which build on the ideas developed by Vickrey.

The central idea that carries over from this Vickrey second-price auction to demand-revealing taxes is that each individual pays a price (or tax) equal to the opportunity cost of the individual's action and is sometimes referred to as an externality tax.[12] (It might be noted that the same principle is used in establishing shadow prices in cost–benefit analysis.) Thus, in the above example, if the individual is not the highest bidder he does not buy the commodity, does not impose a cost on the rest of society and hence pays no price. However, if the individual is the highest bidder he succeeds in buying a commodity which is of value to the rest of society. The opportunity cost of his action is the value placed on the commodity by the second highest bidder and this is the price that is paid.

The idea of this externality tax as a means of inducing individuals to reveal their true preferences has been used in the context of public goods supply by Clarke (1971, 1972) and Groves (1973) and is now often referred to as Clarke–Groves taxation. It should be noted that the Clarke–Groves tax is required to induce individuals to reveal their true preference and thus is in addition to any tax that is required to finance the provision of the good. We can demonstrate the key features of Clarke–Groves taxation in a context in which the relevant public good is assumed to be provided at zero cost. By making this assumption we can concentrate on the demand-revealing tax without worrying about other taxes. In fact, the assumption is not too unrealistic when a regulatory policy constitutes the public good under consideration. For example, the policy under consideration might be the appropriate speed level to set on a given stretch of road. We shall also assume that a discrete choice is to be made: for example, should the speed limit be 40 mph or 50 mph? All of the salient features of a Clarke–Groves tax can be analysed in the context of this simplified example, but readers who wish to see an analysis of a continuous choice problem with positive costs of providing the public good are referred to a highly readable paper by Tideman and Tullock (1976) and the review in Mueller (1989). It should be noted, however, that some of the analysis, for example the benefits of coalition formation, are obscured in the Tideman and Tullock type setting.

Analysis of Clarke–Groves taxation builds on two key simplifying assumptions. First, it is assumed that individuals cannot get together to form coalitions. We shall relax this assumption below and show how coalitions may be able to defeat the Clarke–Groves mechanism. Second, each individual, i, is assumed to have a utility function which is defined over the public good, g, and the private good numeraire, x_i, and which is quasi-linear (i.e. is linear in x_i). Thus, it is assumed that the utility function can be written in the form:

$$u_i(x_i, g) = x_i + v_i(g)$$

The reason for this assumption about the form of the utility function is that the Clarke–Groves mechanism requires each individual to state his preference for the public good before he knows what his tax bill will be and hence how much x_i he will be able to buy. In order for an individual to be able to answer such a question we require the utility that he gets from the public good to be independent of x_i, and quasi-linearity guarantees this.

Consider now a society which comprises just three individuals, a, b and c, and in which there is a choice between the status quo S_0 (for example, a speed limit of 50 m.p.h.) and policy S_1 (for example, a speed limit of 40 m.p.h.). Each individual is asked how much they would be willing to pay to see the policy change from S_0 to S_1 be implemented. This is equivalent to asking each individual how much they value the policy change, and some individuals may prefer S_0 over S_1 and thus have a negative valuation. In being asked to state their preference each individual is told that if as a result of their stated preference society's choice between S_0 and S_1 is changed, then the individual will pay a tax equal to the net cost that this change of outcome imposes on the rest of society. And if as a result of an individual's stated preference society's choice between S_0 and S_1 does not change, then no (Clarke–Groves) tax is payable. It can readily be seen how this tax relates to Vickrey's second-price auction procedure in that each individual pays a tax equal to the net cost that his stated preference imposes on the rest of society. To see that the Clarke–Groves tax induces true prefer-

TABLE 5.1 Clarke–Groves tax

	Valuation of S_1 over S_0	Clarke–Groves tax
a	40	30
b	50	40
c	−80	0
Sum	10	

ence revelation, assume that the true preference of each of the individuals is as set out in the first column of Table 5.1. Individuals *a* and *b* prefer S_1 over S_0 and are willing to pay 40 and 50 respectively to see the policy changed; individual *c* prefers S_0 over S_1 and the minimum compensation that he would accept to see the policy change from S_0 to S_1 is 80. Since the sum of the valuations is greater than zero the policy change would be undertaken (the policy change from S_0 to S_1 constitutes a potential Pareto improvement).

The second column in Table 5.1 gives the size of the Clarke–Groves tax that each individual will pay. If individual *a* had not taken part in the social decision-making process the proposed policy change, S_0 to S_1, would have been defeated: although individual *b* values the policy change at 50, individual *c* has a negative valuation of the proposed change of −80. Thus individual *a*'s stated preference has affected society's decision, since with his stated preference the policy change goes ahead, and individual *a* is described as a pivotal (or decisive) voter. The Clarke–Groves tax that individual *a* pays is 30, this being the net cost that he imposes on the rest of society (by causing the change in policy from S_0 to S_1 he makes individual *b* better off by 50 and makes individual *c* worse off by 80). In a similar way, individual *b* is also a pivotal voter, and his stated preference imposes a net cost of 40 on the rest of society and hence this is the Clarke–Groves tax that he is required to pay. Individual *c*, however, is not a pivotal voter. If he did not take part in the social decision-making process the policy change, S_0 to S_1, would go ahead, and it still goes ahead when he registers his preference. Since he is not a pivotal voter, he imposes no net cost on the rest of society and pays no Clarke–Groves tax. Before moving on to show why such a procedure induces true preference revelation, it should be noted that the Clarke–Groves tax that an individual pays (and hence the income that he will have left to spend on other goods as summarised in the private good numeraire) is dependent on both his own and everybody else's stated preference. Hence the size of this Clarke–Groves tax, if any, is not known to the individual when he is asked to state his preference, and this is why the second assumption outlined above plays a key role.[13]

The demonstration of why the above procedure induces each individual to reveal their true preference follows the same line of reasoning that we used when discussing the Vickrey second-price auction.[14] Consider initially individual a. There is clearly no advantage to this individual in overstating his true preference since any overstatement would not change the social decision and thus would not change his Clarke–Groves tax of 30. No matter how much he overstates his true preference he is going to pay a tax of 30 and receive a *true* benefit of 40. Is there any advantage to this individual from understating his true preference? As long as he continues to state a preference of 31 or above such an understatement of true preferences would not affect the social decision; thus he would continue to pay a tax of 30 and receive a true benefit of 40. But what if he states a preference of below 30? In this case he is no longer a pivotal voter since without him the proposed change S_0 to S_1 would be defeated, and with his stated preference it continues to be defeated. Since he is no longer a pivotal voter he will not have to pay a Clarke–Groves tax, and on this account benefits by 30. But in order to make this saving of 30 a proposed policy change which he valued at 40 has been defeated. Clearly he has made himself worse off. Thus in the case of individual a, overstatement of preferences cannot make him better off, and with the understatement of preferences he chances making himself worse off: honesty is the best policy. Exactly the same argument applies in the case of individual b. For individual c it can be seen that the understatement of compensation required will not change anything, and while he can 'succeed' in blocking the policy change by overstatement of compensation required, if he achieves this he will end up paying a Clarke–Groves tax in excess of the amount by which he values S_0 over S_1 (to block the policy change, individual c

TABLE 5.2 Clarke–Groves taxes and incentives

	True valuation of S_1 over S_0	Clarke–Groves tax	Mis-stated valuation of S_0 over S_1	Manipulated Clarke–Groves tax
a	40	0	200	0
b	50	0	200	0
c	−100	90	−100	0
Sum	−10		300	

must state a figure for compensation required in excess of 90, but he will then pay a Clarke–Groves tax of 90 – the net cost imposed on individuals *a* and *b* – and receive *true* benefits of 80). Thus any individual confronted by a Clarke–Groves tax system can reason in the way that we have analysed the decisions facing the three hypothetical individuals above and will come to the conclusion that the dominant strategy is to reveal his true preference.

While the Clarke–Groves tax is an ingenious, yet relatively straightforward, mechanism for encouraging individuals to reveal their true preferences for public goods, it does contain some weaknesses and I now want to outline some of these. There are perhaps four main problems associated with the Clarke–Groves tax. The first two of these relate to the two simplifying assumptions on which the analysis rests and which we outlined above. One of these assumptions rules out individuals getting together and forming a coalition; if we allow for the possibility of individuals forming a coalition then it can be shown that they may be able to change the social decision in a direction which is favourable to themselves. In view of this, the Clarke–Groves tax can be said to be *individual* incentive compatible but it is not necessarily *group* incentive compatible. To see this, consider the example illustrated in Table 5.2.

The example is similar to that depicted in Table 5.1 except that individual *c* now has a relatively stronger preference for S_0 over S_1, and as a consequence of this stronger preference the social decision is now not to go ahead with the policy change. In this situation only individual *c* is a pivotal voter and he pays a Clarke–Groves tax of 90. Using the type of reasoning that we employed above, it can be seen that there is no mis-statement of their true preferences which individuals *a* and *b* could make which *acting alone* would make them better off. The only way that they could change the outcome is by overstating their true preference by a sufficient amount, and in such a case they would end up paying a Clarke–Groves tax in excess of their true valuation of the policy change S_0 to S_1. However, things are different if they get together and form a coalition. Now it is unlikely that they will know the value of individual c's preference, but they will know that if they both register a very large valuation of the policy change S_0 to S_1, then the policy will go ahead and neither will pay a Clarke–Groves tax. For example, assume that they both agree to register an overstated preference of 200;[15] in this case the policy change goes ahead yet neither of the individuals is a pivotal voter and thus neither has to pay a Clarke–Groves tax. Individuals a and b receive a net benefit of 40 and 50 respectively (their true valuations) from forming the coalition.

The above simple example shows how the Clarke–Groves tax is not necessarily *group* incentive compatible. While this weakness has been widely recognised, some writers have argued that in large heterogeneous populations it is difficult to form effective coalitions. This, of course, is an empirical matter, but at a theoretical level, at least, the possibility that coalitions can manipulate the system to their own advantage is a serious weakness of the Clarke–Groves tax mechanism. The second weakness of the mechanism relates to the assumed nature of each individual's utility function, and this can be quickly dealt with. A quasi-linear utility function implies that the income elasticity of demand for the public good is zero: this is not, in general, found to be the case in empirical studies of the demand for public goods.

The third problem with the Clarke–Groves tax mechanism is that it might drive some individuals into bankruptcy. In the case illustrated in Table 5.2 (assuming the true revelation of preferences), individual c is required to pay a Clarke–Groves tax of 90, and this may exceed individual c's income. Other things equal, an individual who feels strongly about a policy issue is more likely to face a sizeable Clarke–Groves tax, and face the possibility of bankruptcy. The final weakness of the Clarke–Groves tax mechanism is that it does not actually achieve a Pareto-efficient outcome. It will be recalled that the objective behind this line of research has been to devise a tax mechanism which will induce each individual to reveal their true preference for a public good, thereby enabling a government to provide a Pareto-efficient level of the good and achieve an overall Pareto-efficient outcome. The reason that the Clarke–Groves tax mechanism fails in this direction is because the yield of the Clarke–Groves tax itself represents a surplus to the government and must be wasted. The Clarke–Groves tax itself is not required to finance the provision of the public good (in our example the cost of provision was zero in any case); instead it is levied to induce individuals to reveal their true preference. Thus it represents a surplus to the government. However, it cannot be returned to the individuals because this would remove the incentive to reveal true preferences. Also it cannot be spent on other government programmes because some individuals might like to see more money spent in these areas (for example, on overseas aid), and thus mis-state their preference to encourage the government to do this.

It has been argued that the surplus generated by the Clarke–Groves tax becomes very small as the number of individuals in the society increases.[16] Thus as society increases in size the economy tends to a state of Pareto-efficiency. However, there is something of a numbers dilemma here. As society increases in size it is less likely that any one individual will have a significant impact on the final decision and thus there is less incentive for each individual to register their true (or indeed any) preference. In the small numbers case it is more likely that an individual will have an impact on society's decision, but in these cases the Clarke–Groves tax mechanism falls short of Pareto-efficiency. And we have a precise measure of the extent to which it falls short of Pareto-efficiency as given by the yield of the Clarke–Groves tax.

It might finally be noted that there have been attempts to devise demand-revealing mechanisms which result in a budget balance for the government but the general finding is that mechanisms which are individual incentive compatible generate a budget surplus, and those which yield a budget equilibrium are not necessarily individual incentive compatible.[17]

5.4 INDIRECT PREFERENCE REVELATION: THE DEMAND FOR LOCALLY PROVIDED GOODS

In section 5.2 we saw that a key characteristic of some public goods is that their benefit area is spatially limited, and we defined such spatially limited public goods as local public goods. Similarly, publicly provided private goods can be supplied at different levels in different geographic areas. The existence of such spatial variability in the level of provision of publicly provided goods gives the economist the opportunity to estimate a demand function for these goods. This is clearly not possible when publicly provided goods are supplied at a uniform level throughout the nation, since by definition there is no variability in the dependent variable in the demand equation. (The level of provision might vary across time or across countries thereby permitting time-series analysis or inter-country cross-section analysis, but there is a difficulty in such studies of controlling for differing cultural, institutional and other exogenous influences.) In this section I review some of the main issues that have arisen when economists have attempted to esti-mate the demand functions for locally provided goods. The em-phasis here is on the economic issues, and readers interested in the econometric issues are referred to Blundell (1988) and Rubinfeld, Shapiro and Roberts (1987). However, there is one econometric issue that we must note, and this arises due to what has become known as 'Tiebout bias'. In section 5.2 we saw that by 'fiscal shopping' or 'voting with their feet' individuals indirectly reveal their preferences for locally provided goods, but such 'fiscal shop-ping' means that, to some extent at least, individuals sort them-selves into localities. This can cause a selection bias problem in the demand estimation.[18] Given the central role that Tiebout's analy-sis has played in local public economics, it is somewhat surprising that the selection bias problem that Tiebout-moves might give rise to was not noted earlier.

In carrying out a study of the demand for locally provided goods there are perhaps two essential ingredients to the analysis. First, there is the question of whose preferences it is that count in determining how much of the goods are provided in each locality. And second, there is the question of the nature of the constraints faced by these individuals or groups of individuals. Or to put this slightly differently, we need to know the nature of the relevant objective function and the nature of the constraints against which it is maximised. There is also the issue of whether the perceived constraints are the same as the actual constraints.

To date the most commonly used model is one in which it is assumed that the level of provision in each locality reflects the utility maximising level of the voter with the median preference.

The reason for such a choice is that in a direct vote the median voter's preference would defeat any other level of provision and a government interested in re-election will have an incentive to take note of the median voter's preference.[19] Thus the political process is assumed to be demand-driven with supply responding to the demand of the median voter. In this section I concentrate on a median voter representation of the demand estimation although much of the analysis is of direct relevance to models which build on different behavioural assumptions. I also initially assume that the median voter correctly perceives his budget constraint. There is a growing body of literature which assumes that the constraint is misperceived (or misrepresented) and later I spend some time analysing these models.

Using the above framework, a demand equation of the following general form is often estimated:

$$D_i = D(y_i, p_i, z)$$

where D_i represents the demand of the median voter, y_i is the median voter's income, p_i is the price to the median voter of a unit of the publicly provided good and z is a vector of variables reflecting such things as the socio-economic and political composition of the locality. Given this general form of the demand equation several questions arise:

  (i) Who is the median voter?
 (ii) How is the output of the publicly provided good measured?
(iii) How do intergovernmental grants affect the values of y_i and p_i?
(iv) How does the deadweight cost of taxation and capitalisation (to be defined later) affect the value of p_i?

In this review I want to concentrate on the issues raised by the last two questions since it is in these areas that most of the research has been taking place in recent years. But initially I consider briefly the issues raised by the first two questions. It is generally assumed that the individual with the median income in a locality is the median voter. This assumption is sometimes made without any explicit justification, in which case the individual who owns the house which has median value, or some other assumption, could equally be used. But the use of the median income is supported by the early pioneering work of Bergstrom and Goodman (1973) which shows that given certain assumptions the median voter's preferred level of provision will be a function of the median income in the locality. Bergstrom and Goodman's assumptions include the log-linearity of the demand function for the locally publicly provided good, and, to some extent at least, this may explain why this is a favoured functional form in applied work. It should be noted that given Bergstrom and Goodman's result the actual identity of the median voter is an irrelevancy, since we know that, whoever he is, his demand for the publicly provided good is a function of median income. Inman (1978) does, however, find some evidence to suggest that the median voter is the individual (or household) with median income.

A problem which all studies of the demand for publicly provided goods must face is how we measure (or define even) the output of these goods. What, for example, is the output of education, and how is it measured? Many studies side-step this issue by assuming that public expenditure on the good is a satisfactory proxy measure for the output of the good. And to some extent this assumption is inevitable when the study concerns the demand for a bundle of publicly provided goods, although ideally in this case a demand system comprising demand equations for each of the goods should be attempted. Also sometimes the objective of the study is more modest and is to explain variations in expenditure levels between different localities. The use of public expenditures as a proxy measure for output is, however, fraught with difficulties since public expenditure is often only one of the inputs into a production process which produces the public output. Consider again the example of education; it is likely to be the case that there are private (family) inputs into a child's education. To some extent these private inputs are likely to be either substitutes or complements for public inputs, and thus variability in public inputs across localities may not be a very good proxy measure for the variation in output. These issues are taken up by Hamilton (1983), and it is sufficient for us to note here that the definition and measurement of the output of many publicly provided goods raise some thorny conceptual issues. One final point should be mentioned here. Demand estimation studies have been used widely in the context of both public goods and publicly provided private goods. Indeed since in practice it is not always clear what form particular goods take, the demand studies have sometimes been used to determine the precise nature of a good in a particular context. A common way of doing this is to incorporate into the study the following equation (for details of how this is done, see, for example, Blundell, 1988).

$$g_i = g/N^\alpha$$

where g_i is the amount of the publicly provided good consumed by each individual, g is the total amount of the good provided, N is the size of the population (or client group), and α is a crowding parameter, $0 \leq \alpha \leq 1$, which is estimated within the study. If $\alpha = 0$ the good is a public good with $g_i = g$ (i.e. each individual consumes the total amount provided); if $\alpha = 1$ the good is a private good with $g_i = g/N$; and if $0 < \alpha < 1$, the good is a mixed good, partially public and partially private.

I turn now to the measurement of the income and price terms within the demand equation. The main conceptual issues that arise here concern the impact that intergovernmental grants have on these two terms, but as an introduction to the analysis I shall initially assume that there are no intergovernmental grants. Also, so that we can concentrate on the central issues at hand I shall assume throughout the rest of this section that expenditure is a good proxy measure for the output of the publicly provided good, that the publicly provided good is a public good, and that just one public good is being provided by the local government. Thus the median voter maximises a utility function of the general form

$$u_i = u(g, x_i)$$

subject to a budget constraint

$$y_i = x_i + t_i$$

where, as before, g is the public good, x_i is a private good numeraire, y_i is income, and (the new term) t_i represents the individual's tax payments to local government. The local government's budget constraint is also of relevance and in this case it is simply given by

$$p\,g = t$$

where p is the price per unit of the public good (assumed constant) and t represents total tax payments. The price per unit of the public good paid by the median voter depends on the form of the local government tax base, and as we saw in section 5.2 for each type of tax base we can calculate the median voter's tax share. Recall that we defined this as s_i, where under a local poll tax $s_i = 1/n$ (n is the number of poll-tax payers) and under a proportional local income tax $s_i = (y_i/\Sigma_i y)$. Thus the price of a unit of the public good to the median voter is given by $s_i p$ and his budget constraint can be rewritten as

$$y_i = x_i + (s_i p)g$$

where $s_i p = p_i$. Now since we are assuming that expenditure is a good proxy measure of output, $p = 1$, but it is useful to retain the p term in the formulations since the introduction of intergovernmental grants often changes the price term and it will aid the exposition if the price term is retained in explicit form. Maximising the utility function (which for estimation purposes will need to be given an explicit functional form) subject to the rewritten budget constraint gives the demand equation to be estimated, which, as we have seen, has the general form

$$D_i = D(y_i, p_i, z)$$

In estimating this equation, y_i is generally taken to be exogenously determined and is measured net of taxes paid to the central (or, more generally, other levels of government); and, as we have just shown, p_i is dependent on the median voter's tax share, which in turn may depend on the form of the local tax base.

In most countries it is common for a higher level of government to contribute towards the finance of locally provided goods by means of intergovernmental grants. There are various justifications for such grants: for example, to correct for horizontal inequities, to correct for externalities (or spillovers), to plug any fiscal gap between a local government's expenditure responsibilities and its ability to raise revenue. In this chapter, the rationale for the payment of grants is not our central concern, but rather we are interested in how we might incorporate such grants into the demand estimation.[20] There are two main types of intergovernmental grant. First, there are lump-sum (or block) grants; these grants are equivalent to an income supplement to the local government, and a local government in receipt of such a grant has a budget constraint

$$pg = t + l$$

where l is the lump-sum grant. Second, there are matching grants, and these are equivalent to a price reduction for the public good. In this case the local government's budget constraint becomes

$$(1 - m) \, p \, g = t$$

where m represents the matching rate for the grant. Thus if, for example, $m = .3$, the price to the local government of the public good is reduced to $.7p$ with the central government paying the remaining $.3p$ in the form of matching grant. Total grant received is $.3pg$ or, more generally, mpg. I shall initially assume that only one of the above types of grant is received by the local government and, having seen the implications for the demand estimating exercise, I shall then assume that both types of grant are received simultaneously.[21]

When a lump-sum grant is received, the local government's tax demand is given by $t = pg - l$, and thus the median voter's tax bill is given by $t_i = s_i(pg - l)$. If we substitute this into the median voter's budget constraint we get

$$y_i = x_i + s_i \, (pg - l)$$

which on rearrangement gives

$$y_i + s_i l = x_i + (s_i p)g$$

Thus a lump-sum grant paid to the local government of amount l has the same impact as far as the median voter is concerned as a lump-sum increase in his personal income of amount $s_i l$, where s_i is his tax share. This important result was first noted by Bradford and Oates (1971) and is known as the equivalence theorem. The equivalence theorem states that, under plausible assumptions, a lump-sum grant paid to a local government is equivalent in its allocative and distributional consequences to a set of personalised lump-sum grants paid to the individuals who make up the local community. This result has important implications for the demand estimation exercise; it suggests that either the income term should be replaced by $y_i + s_i l$, and we might define this as the median voter's full income, or if y_i and $s_i l$ are entered separately in the demand equation there should be no significant difference between the coefficients on the two terms. Most of the empirical work in this area has been carried out in the US (for a review of the early findings, see Gramlich, 1977), and in general the empirical literature has not found support for the equivalence result. Instead of the coefficients on the income and lump-sum grant terms having approximately the same value, it has been found that the coefficient on the lump-sum grant term is generally significantly larger than is the coefficient on the income term. This finding casts doubt on the usefulness of the simple median voter model (the model makes some predictions which are not supported by the facts), and has led researchers to search for alternative models. I review some of these alternative models below, but before doing this I examine the implications of the introduction of a matching grant.

When a matching grant is received by the local government, its tax demand is given by $t = (1 - m) \, pg$, and the median voter's tax bill is given by $t_i = s_i (1 - m) \, pg$. Substituting this into the median voter's budget constraint we get

$$y_i = x_i + (1 - m)(s_i p)g$$

A matching grant reduces the price of the public good to the median voter from $s_i p$ to $(1 - m) \, s_i p$. Thus the price term in the demand equation must allow for matching grants, and p_i must be set equal to $(1 - m)s_i p$. To summarise our findings on the implications for the demand estimation of the introduction of lump-sum and matching grants: A lump-sum grant is equivalent to an income supplement for the median voter and a matching grant is equivalent to a price reduction for the public good. From these findings we can establish a further prediction of the median voter model. It is that, for each pound of grant awarded, a matching grant will lead to a greater level of provision of the public good than will a lump-sum grant. The reason for this is that a matching grant, being equivalent to a price reduction, has both an income and a substitution effect and the substitution effect must work in the direction of the increased provision of the public good. A lump-sum grant, being equivalent to an income supplement, has an income effect only. This prediction of the median voter model has found general support in the empirical literature.

Sometimes matching grants are paid up to a certain level only, after which no further grant is received. Such grants are known as closed-ended matching grants, and I now want to explore the implications of such for the demand estimation exercise. A matching grant which is not closed-ended is known as an open-ended matching grant. Exactly the same issues would arise if the rate at which the matching grant is paid varies according to the level of provision of the public good, and thus the analysis that we are about to undertake would have relevance for a study of local government in Britain up until the wholesale reform of the system of local government finance in 1990. Up until that date a matching grant was paid at varying rates depending on a local government's level of expenditure.[22] Assume that the matching grant is payable for provision of the public good up to level $g = g^*$, after which no further grant is received. The median voter will now face a piece-wise linear budget constraint with two segments. For provision of the public good up to $g = g^*$, our previous analysis of a matching grant will continue to apply, and thus we can write the first segment of the median voter's budget constraint as

$$y_i = x_i + (1 - m)(s_i p)g \quad : \quad g \leqslant g^*$$

And this is shown by line *ac* in Figure 5.1. In that figure the budget constraint faced by the median voter when no grants are received is given by *ab*, which has a slope of absolute value $s_i p$. When an open-ended matching grant is received the budget constraint is given by *ad* which has a slope of absolute value $(1 - m) s_i p$. But in the case being analysed now, no further grant is received for $g > g^*$, thus for provision beyond g^* the median voter faces a budget constraint given by *ce* which has a slope of absolute value $s_i p$. That is, once the level of provision of the public good exceeds g^* the closed-ended matching grant has the same impact as an income supplement to the median voter of value $m s_i p\, g^*$ (and thus, as lump-sum grant to the local government of value mpg^*).

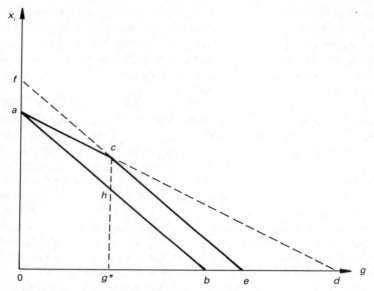

FIGURE 5.1   Closed-ended matching grants

In Figure 5.1, distance ch $(=fa)$ depicts the size of this income supplement. Point f is found by projecting line ce back to the vertical axis. Thus for provision in excess of g^* the median voter's budget constraint is given by

$$y_i + ms_i pg^* = x_i + (s_i p)g \qquad g > g^*$$

This has important implications for the demand estimation, since now the estimation technique has to allow for the fact that the median voter's full income and the price of the public good are endogenous and hence ordinary least squares estimation cannot be used.[23] In terms of our general demand equation we now have two demand equations that are of potential relevance, but only one of which holds for any given median voter.

$$D_i = D(y_i, (1 - m)s_i p, z) \qquad : \qquad g \leqslant g^*$$
$$D_i = D(y_i + ms_i pg^*, s_i pg, z) \qquad : \qquad g > g^*$$

Finally, we must note that it is often the case that local govern-

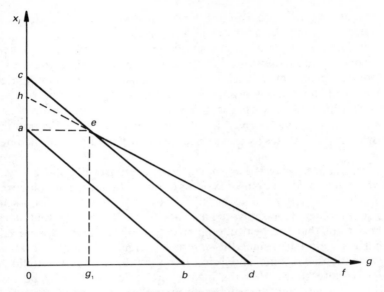

FIGURE 5.2   **Lump-sum and matching grants**

ments receive both matching and lump-sum grants.[24] In this case the median voter's budget constraint can be modelled using the principles outlined above, but it is important that the institutional detail of the grants be correctly specified: in this area of research institutional detail is important. What I want to show now is that if a matching grant is used in addition to a lump-sum grant then the equivalence theorem referred to above takes on a very specific form, and this is an issue, I think, that has not been fully appreciated in some of the empirical work which purports to test for the presence of an equivalence result. To show this I shall assume that a local government receives a lump-sum grant and that its *own* expenditure on the public good receives a matching grant. (This approximates to the system that operated in Britain until 1990.) Using the analysis developed above, assume that the lump-sum grant alone would shift the median voter's budget constraint from *ab* to *cd* in Figure 5.2 Thus the lump-sum grant is sufficient to finance g_1 of the public good (if g_1 of the public good was provided, the median voter would be at point *e* on his budget constraint, having all of his own personal income available to spend on x_i).

Now assume that provision of the public good *beyond* g_1 receives matching grant aid, thus for $g > g_1$ the median voter's budget constraint becomes *ef*. If the public good is provided at a level beyond g_1 the median voter's full income is given by $0h$, where h is found by projecting *ef* back to the vertical axis (as we did in Figure 5.1), and the price is given by the negative of the slope of the budget line *ef*. Thus what is important is that in this example for $g > g_1$ full income is given by $0h$, whereas a naive application of Bradford and Oates's equivalence theorem would set full income at $0c$.

The above analysis has shown how intergovernmental grants, which are a feature of most systems of public finance, can influence the income and price terms in the demand functions for local public goods. Hopefully, I have been able to convey that it is important that the institutional structure of the grant system be correctly modelled since this can have a significant impact on the value of the income and price terms in the demand equation. I have also shown that the income and price terms may be endogenous and that the estimation procedure must allow for this.

There are two further economic issues that are of relevance here. Both relate to the value of the price term in the demand equation. The first of these issues has been highlighted by Wildasin (1989) and in part built on the insights of Hamilton (1986) and concerns the full economic price of a public good when it is financed out of distortionary taxation.[25] Wildasin points out that if a public good is financed out of distortionary taxation then its full economic price includes the deadweight loss (or excess burden) created by the tax in addition to the price paid for the good. And in such a case the price term that we have used above underestimates the full economic price of a public good. Empirically how important this bias will be depends on the size of the deadweight loss and thus on the elasticity of demand and supply of whatever it is that constitutes the local government tax base. But the presence of such a distortion can influence some of the predictions of the standard theory as outlined above. For example, a lump-sum grant may no longer have only an income effect. If as a result of receiving a lump-sum grant a local government decides to reduce local taxation (in order that some of the real income gain may be spent on private goods), then this will reduce the deadweight loss of local taxation thereby reducing the effective price of the public good and producing a price effect in favour of the public good. It is too early for Wildasin's analysis to have yet made an impact on the empirical work, and no doubt the first line of research will be to see if any distortions are empirically significant.

The second issue relates to a complex set of problems concerned with capitalisation. In the above analysis we have followed what is the standard procedure in the literature and assumed that the full price that an individual pays for a locally provided good is reflected in his tax payments. However, an individual may also pay for publicly provided goods indirectly via the price that he pays for his house. Suppose, for example, that in a particular locality good-quality schools are in short supply, then in order to get good-quality schooling for his children an individual may attempt to buy a house in the catchment area of a good school. But as other parents attempt to do the same thing the price of houses in this locality will be bid up. Thus, those who succeed in buying a house will be paying for education (the locally provided good) not only through local tax payments but also via the higher price that has been paid for housing: the good-quality schooling, which is in short supply, is capitalised into the value of housing. This increased price of housing represents part of the price for the local good. There have been several studies of the extent to which capitalisation occurs and the first pioneering study was undertaken by Oates (1969), although Oates's methodology has since been substantially refined.[26] It should be noted, however, that capitalisation will not occur if all individuals are able to consume their desired quantity of publicly provided goods (i.e. there is a Tiebout equilibrium). Capitalisation is a sign that some publicly provided goods are in short supply, and to the extent that this is the case the full price that an individual pays for these goods is the tax price plus the differential housing costs. Ideally this full cost should be inclined in demand estimation studies.

In the introduction to this section I noted that there is a growing body of literature which builds on the assumption that the median voter either misperceives his true budget constraint or that government officials misrepresent the local government budget constraint. The main body of literature in this area is concerned with what is known as the 'flypaper effect': this is the finding that money tends to stick where it hits! And the impetus for much of this work was the failure to find empirical support for Bradford and Oates's equivalence result. As we saw above, the equivalence result suggests that lump-sum grants paid to a local government are analytically equivalent to a set of personalised lump-sum grants paid to individuals.[27] However, a general finding in the empirical literature is that lump-sum grants to local governments stimulate a greater increase in spending on locally provided goods than does an equivalent increase in personal income. Hence the conclusion that money tends to stick where it hits. It should be noted that, as we pointed out above, distortionary local taxation could produce such a non-equivalence result and this possibility was first pointed out by Hamilton (1986). But most of the literature seeks to explain this flypaper effect in terms of a misperceived or misrepresented budget constraint. While the motivations differ between misperceived and misrepresented budget constraint type arguments, the analysis is essentially the same and we concentrate here on a misperceived budget constraint.[28] The central idea is that the median voter misperceives the nature of a lump-sum grant and instead thinks of such grants as reducing the price of the public good. Assume that the median voter's budget constraint is initially given by ab in Figure 5.3 and that he is in equilibrium at point e_1 consuming g_1 and x_1. If a lump-sum grant is now paid to the local government, the standard theory predicts that this will have an income effect only and that the median voter's budget constraint will shift out in a parallel manner, say to cd. The new equilibrium is at e_2 with the median consuming g_2 and x_2 (both g and x are assumed to be normal goods though this is not necessary for the analysis). Thus the result is exactly the same as if the median voter received a lump-sum increase in his personal income of ac: once again, this is the equivalence result. Assume now, however, that the median voter misperceives the nature of the lump-sum grant and thinks (perhaps because the grant is paid to the local government) that the price of the public good is now reduced. In effect, the lump-sum grant is being thought of as a matching grant. We know that a matching grant can be depicted in terms of Figure 5.3 as causing the median voter's budget constraint to rotate outwards about point a. But clearly it is also the case that, while he may misperceive his budget constraint, the median voter's true budget constraint must balance. Thus the final equilibrium will be at a point such as e_3 in Figure 5.3, where the median voter's indifference curve is tangential to the misperceived budget constraint at a point on the true budget constraint. Given the usual convex pre-

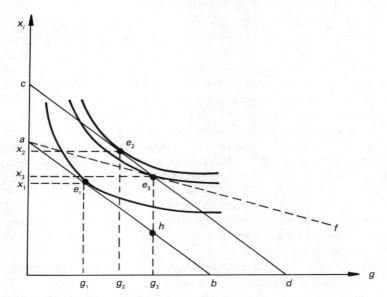

FIGURE 5.3   Flypaper effect

ferences, point e_3 must entail a higher level of expenditure on the public good than does point e_2, and hence we have a flypaper effect: a lump-sum grant which if correctly perceived would increase the median voter's full income by amount ac, stimulates a greater increase in expenditure on the public good than does an increase in the median voter's personal income by amount ac. Building on this type of analysis Barnett, Levaggi and Smith (1991a) have found that a flypaper-type model explains the expenditure levels of English local governments better than does a conventional model in which budget constraints are correctly perceived.[29]

There are, however, problems with the flypaper model: in particular, like the standard theory, it gives some predictions which are not supported by the empirical facts. From Figure 5.3 it can be seen that if the grant was given as a matching grant the median voter's true budget constraint would be given by af and total grant received would be given by e_3h ($=ac$). Thus the flypaper theory, at least in the strict form presented here, predicts that, per pound of grant received, matching grants stimulate the same increase in expenditure on public goods as do lump-sum grants. This prediction is not supported by the facts: in general it is found that matching grants stimulate a greater increase in expenditure on the public good than do lump-sum grants. Thus, perhaps the current state of the research is that we have two rival theories, each of which can explain some of the empirical findings but neither of which is universally supported by the facts.

In concluding this section I want to do two things. First I want to relate our analysis of the *demand* for locally provided services to the wider body of literature which is concerned with modelling the local public sector. And second, I want briefly to refer to some related literature in the wider public finance field. The emphasis in this section has been in exploring the issues that arise when attempts are made to estimate the demand for locally provided goods. In order to concentrate on the central economic issues we have assumed that a single public good is provided and that the median voter is the decisive individual. The analysis readily generalises to allow for the introduction of publicly provided private goods (and mixed goods) and to cases in which some other set of preferences is decisive in explaining the level of provision of the locally provided goods. But it must be emphasised that our interest here is with the *demand* for locally provided good. It may well be that the actual level of provision is also in part at least explained by supply-side influences, and there are models which emphasise these supply-side aspects (see, for example, the work on bureaucracy as surveyed in Jackson (1982) and the work on government as Leviathan by Brennan and Buchanan (1980); in the context of the flypaper theory, Romer and Rosenthal (1980) is relevant). Now it is clearly an empirical matter whether demand-side models as explored in this section do dominate in the determination of the size of local government outputs. If supply-side forces play a significant role then clearly these must be modelled in addition to the demand-side factors. If the researcher is interested in explaining the pattern of service provision across local governments then a reduced form estimating equation which includes both demand- and supply-side influences is quite acceptable. The interest here, however, is in estimating the demand equation and this becomes a much more difficult, if not impossible, exercise if supply-side influences play a significant role. After all, if supply-side factors dominate it is not clear that any individuals will be on their demand curves for locally provided goods; for example, the electorate may be offered the choice between a discrete number of fixed bundles of goods none of which represented points on their demand curves. This is a sobering thought for research which seeks to determine the demand for locally provided goods, but it is the kind of thought that we must keep in the back of our mind when reviewing demand-driven explanations such as the median voter model.

Finally in this section I want to direct the reader to some related literature in another area of public finance. It will be recalled that part of the price that an individual pays for a public good may be the indirect price that he pays in the form of differential housing costs. This idea has been generalised and used quite extensively to infer individuals' preferences for certain types of local public goods (or bads), and is known as hedonic pricing. Perhaps the most common applications have been in attempts to place a value on air quality and noise pollution. This indirect valuation exercise involves a two-stage procedure. The first stage is to estimate a hedonic price equation for housing. In doing this, housing is treated as a bundle of characteristics – for example, relating to its physical characteristics, its location, and say the ambient air quality. An equation is then estimated in which the price of the house is a function of the various characteristics. This gives an implicit, or hedonic, price for each of the characteristics, including, in this example, air quality. These hedonic prices are then used in the second stage of the analysis to infer individuals' valuations for the public good (air quality). In carrying out this second stage of the exercise, care must be taken in correctly modelling the supply side of the housing market, although often the assumption is made that the supply of housing is fixed, which may be a satisfactory assumption for short-run analysis. The seminal work in this area is Rosen (1974), and a useful exposition with illustrative examples is given in Johansson (1987).

5.5 DIRECT PREFERENCE REVELATION: SURVEYS AND CONTINGENT VALUATION

As we noted in the introduction, in recent years there has been a growing interest in the use of surveys and questionnaires as a means of eliciting individuals' preferences for publicly provided goods. In view of our discussion in section 5.2 about the incentive that individuals have to mis-state their true preferences, at first sight this seems a surprising development; and indeed the possibility that individuals do not give honest answers is one of the weaknesses of the survey approach. The main advantage of it is that the researcher can generate his own data set and design a questionnaire that will produce the information required. This method of estimating individual preferences for publicly provided goods is now generally referred to as contingent valuation,[30] the idea being that individuals are asked for a valuation (or more generally response) contingent on the occurrence of some hypothetical event as described by the researcher. In this section I am going to concentrate on the use of the survey approach to estimate the demand for a locally provided good, and in this context they are often referred to as micro-based studies. By doing this I shall be able to draw direct parallels with, what to date has been, the more traditional approach as discussed in section 5.4 above. However, in discussing the strengths and weaknesses of the survey approach I shall be drawing on a wider literature. The survey approach has been used to elicit individual preferences for such diverse goods as safety and the value of human life (Jones-Lee, Hammerton and Philips, 1985) and clean air (Brookshire *et al.*, 1982). And useful general surveys of the contingent valuation approach are given in Hanley (1989) and Mitchell and Carson (1989).

The contingent valuation approach to the estimation of the demand for locally provided goods was pioneered by Bergstrom, Rubinfeld and Shapiro (1982) who used the survey approach to estimate the demand for locally provided schooling in Michigan. The objective of the research is once again to estimate a demand function for a locally provided good and we can write such a function with the general form

$$D_i = D(y_i, p_i, z_i, z)$$

where the D_i, y_i and p_i are as defined in section 5.4, but now we have two vectors of other variables. The first of these, z_i, represents characteristics of the individual being interviewed, and the second, z, represents characteristics of the location in which he lives. Like median voter type models, the contingent valuation approach must correct for possible 'Tiebout bias', and the same issues arise in defining the y_i and p_i terms. The strength of the contingent valuation approach lies in the richness that the researcher is able to bring to the analysis in the form of the variables included in z_i and z. In median voter type models it is virtually impossible to distinguish between personal and locational characteristics, whereas in the contingent valuation approach questions on each of these can be asked in the survey. Thus, for example, in US studies of the demand for publicly provided education,[31] questions are asked on the age, religion and educational background of the interviewee as well as questions about how many children there are in the family and what age they are. A question is also generally asked about whether the interviewee is a school employee, although clearly this could be a supply-side influence. A set of questions is also asked about the location (or sometimes details on this can be fed in from other sources); for example, information may be included on the political composition of the local government and the racial make-up of the locality.

Then in order to derive the demand function, individuals are asked if they would like to see an increase in spending on the locally provided good, and if so by how much, and whether they would be willing to see an increase in the local taxes to finance the increase in spending. Given answers to these questions from samples of the population, together with the responses to questions on personal and locational characteristics, the demand function can be estimated using full-information maximum-likelihood estimation. (For a highly readable account of how this is done, see Rubinfeld and Shapiro, 1989.)

So the relative strength of the contingent valuation approach lies in the richness of the data set that it is able to generate as a basis for the demand estimation exercise. Its relative weaknesses are generally listed as various types of bias that may feature in this type of analysis. There are six main types of bias that have been mentioned at various points in the literature; not all of these are likely to apply to any one study. The first is known as strategic bias and refers to the incentive that individuals may have to mis-state their true preference (i.e. Samuelson's 'false signals' problem). There have been various attempts to frame questions in different ways to test for strategic bias, and the general conclusion seems to be that it is not a serious problem.[32] It may be that the hypothetical nature of the contingent valuation approach reduces the incentive to behave strategically: there is nothing to be gained from doing so. However, the hypothetical nature of the exercise is viewed by some authors as a potential source of bias in itself – hypothetical bias: since the exercise is hypothetical, the interviewee may not take the exercise seriously. A further type of bias is known as information bias. Responses have been found to vary according to the information that is provided to the interviewee about the nature of the local good. For example, how many of us know how much more educational output can be provided for a 5 per cent increase in local taxes? And in any case our concepts of output may differ. It has also been found that stated preferences may be sensitive to the initial level of provision of the good – this is so-called starting-point bias. The implication of starting-point bias is that the demand equation is sensitive to the initial level of provision: individuals who register a preference for a $10 increase when the starting point is, say, $100 of provision do not necessarily register a preference for a $10 decrease when the starting level is $120.[33] It has also sometimes been found that differences in responses depend on who is doing the interviewing: some interviewers seem to be able to get people to register a greater preference than do other interviewers! The final type of bias referred to in the literature is known as instrument bias. There are two aspects to this. The first refers to the fact that stated preferences have sometimes been found to be sensitive to the size of the increments in the level of provision used in framing the question. For example, a questionnaire which asks if respondents would like to see increases of (a) 2 per cent, (b) 4 per cent, (c) 6 per cent, etc., might get different stated preferences than a questionnaire that asked about increases of (a) 5 per cent, (b) 10 per cent, etc. The second form of instrument bias refers to the finding that stated preferences are sometimes sensitive to the form of finance that is being used in the provision of the good. But it is not clear that this is necessarily bias at all. The price that an individual faces may well depend on how a publicly provided good is financed: for example, an individual's tax price under an income tax may differ from his tax price under a property tax.

Contingent valuation represents a challenging approach to the estimation of preferences for publicly provided goods. As we have seen, analysis in this area must guard against, and try to avoid, various types of bias. But the rich data set on which such analysis is able to build and its wide area of application (unlike median voter type models it is not restricted to locally provided goods) will inevitably make this an exciting area of future research.

5.6 CONCLUDING COMMENT

Any review of an area so large and so active as the preference revelation problem must of necessity be selective. And in this conclusion rather than reviewing the earlier analysis I want briefly to point to two areas of omission. First, there is a body of literature which suggests that the emphasis on the preference revelation problem is misplaced, and perhaps the leading exponent of this view is Johansen (1977). Johansen writes:

> economic theory, in this as well as in some other fields, tends to suggest that people are honest only to the extent that they have economic incentives for being so. . . . the assumption can hardly be true in its most extreme form. (p. 148, quoted in Atkinson and Stiglitz, 1980)

Instead, Johansen suggests, honesty itself may be a social norm, rather than simply the outcome of utility maximising behaviour. Johansen is echoing an unease that has been expressed by several economists about the central role that self-interested utility maximising behaviour plays in conventional economic models. Some of the main contributors to this general literature are Sen (1977), Collard (1978), Margolis (1982), Sugden (1984), and Frank (1987, 1988).

The second area of omission concerns the rapidly expanding research in experimental economics some of which has sought to test for free-rider behaviour. Results in this area are highly varied. But the general pattern of the research findings seems to be that there is little evidence of free-riding behaviour in experiments which involve participants taking part in a single experiment which is played only once (i.e. a single-shot game). However, when an experiment involves repeated plays of the game (i.e. a repeated game) and/or each participant takes part in a given experiment several times, the participants do begin to free-ride. Relevant literature in this area includes Marwell and Ames (1981), Bohm (1984), Isaac, McCue and Plott (1985), and Andreoni (1988).

6 Public Choice: An Introductory Survey

VANI K. BOROOAH

6.1 INTRODUCTION

Perhaps the most difficult aspect about writing a chapter on 'Public Choice' is that of offering a definition that conveys the full flavour of the variety of topics encompassed by the subject. One definition, which has the merit of being both succinct and reasonably accurate, is that it is 'an invasion by economics of political science' (Tullock, 1988, p. 1). By this is meant that Public Choice takes as its province the application of economists' methods of a positive analysis of problems that are conventionally regarded as being those of political science, concerning events generally in the public sector.

Public Choice derives its rationale from the fact that in many areas 'political' and 'economic' behaviour interact so that a proper understanding of issues in one field requires a complementary understanding of issues in the other. Much of economic activity is carried out in a market environment where the protagonists are households on the one hand and firms on the other. Both sides, according to the rules of economic analysis, have clear objectives,[1] on the basis of which, in the goods market, households reveal their preferences to firms through their demand functions, and firms, in their supply decisions, take these preferences into account. However, a significant part of economic activity is carried out in a non-market environment in which households (or individuals) face the state (or the government).[2] The reason for the existence of such non-market activities is due to the existence of public goods: that is to say, goods which once supplied to some members of the community, cannot, or should not, be unavailable to other members. Of course the scope of non-market activities depends on how wide is the definition of a public good: in Sweden for example a large range of services – provision of creche facilities, health, education, etc. – are provided by the state whereas the same services in the USA might be provided by the market.

The existence of public goods, then, provides one reason why governments involve themselves in the economy. Another reason is that markets do not always operate efficiently and need 'guidance' from the state. At the micro-level the classic argument for government interference with markets is provided by the existence of externalities: governments institute a system of taxes and transfers, or directives, aimed at particular parts of the economy, in order to reduce imbalances between private and social welfare. This is the neoclassical interpretation of government, due to Pigou, of an agent correcting market failures. At the macro-level governments involve themselves in the economy to stabilise its performance with respect to unemployment, inflation and the balance of payments. Whatever the reason for a government's involvement in economic affairs the basic problem that it faces is of acting in a manner consistent with what its citizens desire. Failure to do so over a sufficiently long period of time, will, in one way or an other, lead to its removal. In democratic societies people express their wishes through their votes. Thus the demand/supply problem which lies at the heart of market economics has a direct analogue in non-market (or market corrective) situations.

This then leads directly to the basic issues addressed by Public Choice. On the demand side it asks: What factors influence the voting decision? What is the 'best' system of voting for ensuring a correct revelation of preferences? Can individuals' preferences be made more effective by individuals coming together in 'special interest' groups? On the supply side it investigates issues relating to the behaviour of government, the role of re-election concerns in determining the supply of economic output, the possibility of conflict between different government departments, etc. Many of these issues, relating to the demand and supply of 'government', will be discussed in the subsequent pages. The analysis of these problems will be predicated on the assumptions of economics – that is to say, the behaviour of individuals and institutions are motivated by self-interest. This mode of analysis is both a strength and a weakness of Public Choice: it is a strength because it leads to sharp, analytically clear results; it is a weakness because, by limiting its perspective to one in which self-interest is the main motive for behaviour, it is always in danger of neglecting some of the richness of political-economic behaviour.[3]

6.2   HOW VOTERS DECIDE

The most celebrated work on the theory of voting is arguably that of Downs (1957), and coincidentally, since it is a view that accords most closely with standard economic theory, it has been used by economists as a framework for much of the applied work in this area. In a Downsian world of two parties (though the analysis could be modified for a multi-party system) a voter is rational in the sense that he casts his votes for the party he believes will provide him with more benefits than any other. These benefits, which may be many and various, are reduced to a common denominator, which Downs refers to as the utility income of government activity. To discover which party he would vote for, the voter compares the utility incomes he would receive over the coming election period from each of the parties and votes for the party from which he expects the higher utility income.

It is recognised, however, that collecting information for an evaluation of the different utility income streams is a costly process, and for this reason no voter would attempt a comprehensive evaluation. Instead each voter will base his evaluation upon those areas where the differences between parties are sufficient to impress him. Thus the voter remains indifferent as to which party is in power until the difference in utility flows is large enough, that is until his party differential threshold has been crossed.

Within the framework of the Downsian world, one can distinguish between 'valence' issues on which there is essentially one body of opinion, and 'position' issues on which there may be rival bodies of opinion (cf. Butler and Stokes, 1974). Thus, for example, a government's views on nationalisation or labour relations may be regarded as 'position' issues. On the other hand, a reduction in unemployment or growth in real income could be regarded as valence issues. As will be discussed below, most empirical work in this area has regarded the economy as a valence issue, that is, one which has been based on a view of voter behaviour in which the government has been electorally rewarded or punished for the attainment or non-attainment of certain universally desired goals.

While it is true that several economic issues command a near unanimity of opinion as to their desirability or otherwise, and as such are valence issues, 'position' models of voting behaviour are important because they highlight the differences between the different voters and the different parties, differences which are undeniably important to understanding electoral outcomes. One example will suffice to illustrate this point. Converse (1958), noted that the view that different status groups in society have different interests and that these different interests are expressed in differential voting behaviour, is fairly widely accepted. Thus, for example, 'over the last 25 years, high status persons in the United States have favoured the Republican party while the less fortunately placed have subscribed instead to the Democratic party' (Converse, 1958, p. 388). The status–vote relationship was termed 'status polarisation' and the hypothesis put forward was that 'polarisation would increase in times of depression and decrease in periods of prosperity' (p. 396). Thus on this view the consequence of hard times is not a general reduction in the support for the ruling party but an increase of support for each party in the class whose interests it represents and a decline in the support for each party in the class whose interests it does not represent.

Turning to the empirical results in this area, this chapter, for reasons of economy, confines itself to the United Kingdom. The earliest study for the UK investigating the link between economic performance and political popularity was that of Goodhart and Bhansali (1970). Using Gallup poll data the first question that they asked was whether political popularity was affected significantly by economic developments, when the level of unemployment and the rate of inflation were chosen as the variables of greatest concern to the electorate.

The strongest relation between unemployment and government popularity was found to be between popularity and the lagged level of unemployment and the most successful lag structure was a simple six months' lag. The inflation rate also had a significant immediate effect on popularity. At the same time there was statistical evidence for certain regular movements in the popularity of the government of the day between elections. These suggested that immediately after an election there was a sizeable increase in the support for a newly elected government. Then there followed a period of slow but steady decline in popularity, but this unpopularity was reversed in the final few months preceding the next elections. The significance, strength and regularity of such movements ('the electoral cycle') were measured using dummy variables.

The Goodhart and Bhansali conclusions were questioned by Miller and Mackie (1973) whose objective was to test the economic influence model against an electoral cycle model – that is, a model which explained variations in popularity purely in terms of cyclical variables. The major conclusion that emerged from the Miller and Mackie study was that the link between economic performance and popularity was not so strong as had been thought. The cyclical pattern of government popularity continued over the sample period although it was not always accompanied by a similar cyclical movement in the economic variables. An alternative explanation suggested for the observed cycles in government popularity was that the nature of the response altered as time passed. When a general election was near, the nature of the response was likely to involve comparisons between the government and the opposition parties. On the other hand, away from a general election, the response was likely to be non-comparative and hence, as a consequence, the incumbent party would emerge more unpopular in mid-term than nearer elections.

Pissarides (1980) re-examined the relation between voting intentions and economic performance with a view to investigating the extent to which 'it is possible to model the relation between voting intentions and a few macroeconomic indicators in a stable and systematic fashion' (Pissarides, 1980, p. 569). Pissarides argued that if a government's popularity was indeed stable and systematically affected by its economic performance then popularity functions would contain useful information on how to manage the economy to ensure re-election. On the other hand, if a stable, systematic relationship did not exist then such functions would not influence the policy-making process.

The main conclusion of his study was that though there was evidence of a systematic relation between economic performance and government popularity over the sample period 1955–77, taking account of this relation in making out-of-sample forecasts reduced forecasting errors only marginally. Thus an excessive preoccupation by a government about the effect of its policies on its popularity would not appear to be justified. Economic conditions that favoured a faster growth in consumption, a 'stronger' pound, lower inflation and lower unemployment, had a favourable effect on lead, though quantitatively inflation and unemployment appeared to be the least important of the economic influences.

This selective list of three studies highligths some of the empirical work done in this area for the United Kingdom. The basic technique employed by these studies was regression analysis, in which movements in certain economic variables were correlated against movements in voting intentions – in the jargon, they estimated 'popularity functions' – and the majority opinion of investigators in this area was that movements in economic variables did influence voting intentions, though of course the list of relevant variables differed between investigators. However, all work in this area is characterised by two fundamental (and restrictive) assumptions. These are, first, that the reactions of respondents do not change over time, and second, that all respondents are alike in the sense of having identical reactions to changes in the economic environment.[4]

6.3 VOTING PROCEDURES

The voting problem may be defined as one of selecting, on the basis of the declared preferences of the individuals constituting the electorate, one alternative out of an available set of alternatives. Stated in this manner, the voting problem is but a particular instance of the more general problem of social choice, namely the aggregation of individual interests, judgements or well-beings into some aggregate notion of social welfare. Indeed Arrow (1987, p. 124) describes voting as 'a pure case of social choice in action . . . [in which] the social decision is made by aggregating the votes according to the voting scheme chosen'.

The best known and most celebrated result in social choice theory is Arrow's (1963) 'Impossibility Theorem' which states that there exists no social welfare function (i.e. a function which translates individual orderings over say N alternative policies into a social ordering) which simultaneously satisfies four 'reasonable' conditions. These conditions are: (*I*) independence of irrelevant alternatives, by which the social ranking of any pair of options depends only on the individual rankings of that pair and is not affected by individual rankings of either member of the pair *vis-à-vis* other alternatives; (*P*) Pareto principle by which, if everyone expressed a strict preference over a pair of alternatives, this would also be the social preference; (*U*) unrestricted domain by which the social welfare function was defined over all logically possible *N*-tuples of individual orderings; and (*N*) non-imposition by which the social ordering was not imposed on the basis of some individual's preference.

The relevance of this result to the voting problem lies in attempting (a) to identify the desirable conditions that any voting system should satisfy, and (b) to identify a voting system that satisfied these conditions. This was addressed by May (1952) who showed that when there were only two alternatives, majority voting was unambiguously the 'best' voting rule. By 'best' was meant that it satisfied – and indeed was the only voting rule that would satisfy – the following four conditions: (i) decisiveness – however people voted there would always be a clear outcome; (ii) neutrality – in deciding a pair of issues only the ordinal preferences of voters over that pair are considered; (iii) anonymity – a specific association of voters to votes was irrelevant in deciding the outcome; and (iv) positive responsiveness – if *A* ties *B* and then one voter switches from *B* to *A*, then *A* wins.

The point at issue is to extend this result to situations where there are three or more alternatives. In such situations, different voting procedures may be constructed, all of which appear fair and reasonable and all of which reduce to majority rule in the event of two alternatives, but which nevertheless yield different outcomes. One possible voting procedure is plurality ('first-past-the-post') voting, in which each voter votes for exactly one alternative and the alternative with the largest number of votes wins. The essence of this procedure – which is also its weakness – is that it is based on an incomplete revelation of preferences: a voter divides the alternatives into that which he favours and into those which he does not and there is no requirement to rank the latter set of alternatives. Thus, as shown in Table 6.1, on the basis of votes cast by 60 voters, *A* wins by plurality; yet *A* would lose against *B* alone (25 to 35) and against *C* alone (23 to 37). This then points to the second defect of plurality voting: it is subject to agenda manipulation so that the presence or absence of alternatives – even if such

TABLE 6.1   First-past-the-post voting

	23	19	16	2
		60 Voters		
1st preference	A	B	C	C
2nd preference	C	C	B	A
3rd preference	B	A	A	B

alternatives themselves cannot win – can affect the outcome.

The alternative is for each voter to rank the alternatives in order of preference, after which the appropriate voting procedure aggregates these preferences into a choice of alternative. Such a procedure is called an 'ordinal procedure'. One possible voting rule, in the context of such a procedure, is the Borda count. This rule, in the presence, say, of N alternatives, assigns N points to the alternative ranked first on a particular ballot, $N-1$ points to the alternative ranked second on that ballot, and so on, down to assigning a single point to the least preferred alternative. By aggregating over all the ballots the alternative with the largest number of points is declared the winner. The Borda count is susceptible to false preference revelation – voters could give the lowest preference to the candidate most threatening to their preferred candidate irrespective of their true preferences.[5]

Both plurality and ordinal procedures may be multi-stage voting procedures – so that the choice of alternative is only made after successive rounds of voting – by combining either of them with the procedure of elimination. Thus, for example, plurality plus run-off eliminates, in the preliminary round, all but the two strongest alternatives and then holds a simple majority vote run-off between these two in a later round. An alternative is to eliminate, at each successive round, the weakest alternative and to choose an alternative after $N-1$ successive rounds of voting. Although all these voting procedures – or variants thereof – are, by themselves, quite reasonable, they can – as in Table 6.2, taken from Miller (1987) – lead to different conclusions. Under plurality, C wins with 9 votes; under a Borda count, A wins with 50 points; with plurality and run-off B wins over C; with successive elimination of the weakest candidates, B is again selected. The interested reader

TABLE 6.2   Multi-stage voting

| | 19 Voters | | | |
	4	4	2	9
1st preference	A	B	B	C
2nd preference	B	A	D	D
3rd preference	D	D	A	A
4th preference	C	C	C	B

Source: Miller (1987).

TABLE 6.3   Paradox of voting

| | 60 Voters | | | | |
	23	17	2	10	8
1st preference	A	B	B	C	C
2nd preference	B	C	A	A	B
3rd preference	C	A	C	B	A

should consult Riker (1982) for a more detailed discussion of voting procedures.

One way out of this conundrum – first proposed by Condorcet in 1785 – is to have a pairwise comparison of the various alternatives, choosing at each comparison the alternative with majority support. An alternative that wins over all other alternatives on this basis is then called a Condorcet winner, chosen on the Condorcet criterion of pairwise dominance. Thus in Table 6.1 the Condorcet winner *C* beats *A*, 37 to 23, and also beats *B*, 41 to 19. In any given situation, a Condorcet winner need not of course exist. Table 6.3 shows an example of cyclical voting – a situation known as 'paradox of voting' – where *A* beats *B* (33 to 27), *B* beats *C* (42 to 18) and *C* beats *A* (35 to 25). Condorcet's idea of reducing everything to pairwise comparisons is central to Arrow's (1963) impossibility theorem – see condition (*I*) above. In this sense Arrow's theorem means that the paradox of voting is inevitable in any non-dictatorial voting method satisfying condition (*I*).

The question, following from the above discussion, is whether one can specify conditions under which cyclical voting will not

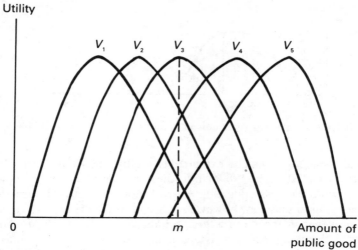

Utility

V_1 V_2 V_3 V_4 V_5

0   *m*   Amount of
                                          public good

FIGURE 6.1   The median voter decides

occur. This was addressed by Black (1948, 1958) using the concept of single peaked preferences. Suppose that the set of alternatives can be represented in one dimension, for example choice among different levels of public expenditure. Suppose for each voter there is a most preferred alternative – which may be different for different voters – such that preferences drop steadily for alternatives on either side of this optimum. In such a case voter preferences are said to be single peaked. Under single peaked preferences the median voter decides, in the sense that the most preferred alternative of the median voter is the Condorcet winner – i.e. is capable of beating all other alternatives in a pairwise contest. This result, called the Median Voter Theorem, is illustrated in Figure 6.1. In this figure there are five voters with single peaked preferences V_1 to V_5. It is easy to see that V_3, the most preferred position of the median voter, will in pairwise contest beat, say, V_4, since voters 1, 2 and 3 will support V_3 but only voters 4 and 5 will support V_5.

The notion of single peaked preferences has a certain intuitive appeal when issues have a single dimension: thus in a referendum to decide, say, expenditure on the National Health Service, it is plausible that an individual voter will have a most preferred position, and that the further a given level of expenditure is away from this position, the more unhappy he will be. Although the notion of

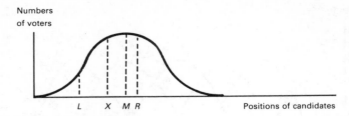

FIGURE 6.2   Median voter outcomes under two-party competition

single peakedness can be extended to multi-dimensional issues (cf. Plott, 1967; Mueller, 1989, ch. 5) the results are far more complex and intuitively less appealing and will not be discussed here. An interesting discussion, however, is found in Ng (1979, ch. 5).

However, if there are a large number of voters, each of whom distils the complexity of issues confronting the country into a personal ideological position (extreme left, soft left, centrist, right-ist, extreme right, etc.), then the median voter theorem can be used to predict outcomes in a two-party democracy (cf. Hotelling, 1929; Downs, 1958). Suppose that voters are distributed across the spectrum of ideological positions, from 'Left' to 'Right' as shown in Figure 6.2, and that each voter votes for the party closest to his ideological position. If the initial party positions are given by L and R then R wins; R obtains the support of voters to the right of R as well as the support of voters between X and R where X is the mid-point of the segment LR; L obtains support from voters to the left of L as well as from those between L and X. However, L can increase its vote – as can R – by moving closer to the centre. Then inter-party competition will ensure that the two parties will occupy an ideological position corresponding to that of the median voter.

6.4   INTEREST GROUPS, COLLECTIVE ACTION AND RENT SEEKING

Voting is one way that people can reveal their preferences; another, more direct way is to form, with other like-minded persons, a special interest group and then to lobby government for particular courses of action favourable to that group. The trouble is that it does not follow from the fact that a group of people have a common interest that they will form an interest group and bear the cost of collective action. For, as Olson (1965) pointed out, collective action is bedevilled by the familiar 'free-rider' problem of public economics: a rational self-interested person would not join (and participate in the costs of) an interest group since he cannot be excluded from any benefits that might accrue from the activities of the group. Thus many groups that would gain from collective action will not in fact, for this reason, be organised.

However, at the same time, there are several instances, in the real world, of collective action. Olson (1965) argued that such cases usually satisfied one or the other of two conditions. First, the number of persons that would need to act collectively should be sufficiently small, so that if one person decided not to participate the group would be ineffective and no benefits would accrue. Second, the group should have access to 'selective incentives' by which it could reward or punish individuals who either have or have not borne the costs of collective action. Trade union 'closed shop' arrangements by which only union members can get jobs is an example of 'selective incentives'. Selective incentives are less often available to potential entrants and to low-income groups than to established and well-off groups. Thus it is the employed rather than the unemployed that are organised, and it is the professional groups – doctors, lawyers, teachers – that are better organised than the relatively underskilled occupations. Consequently Olson (1982) observed that, in the main, collective action would be anti-egalitarian and pro-establishment.

One of the reasons that collective action would be retrogressive is that it would often lead to 'rent seeking'. Tullock (1967) was the first to analyse rent seeking though the term itself was introduced by Krueger (1974). It is a well-known proposition in economics that monopoly price will be higher (and output lower) than under competitive conditions. This in turn leads to the monopoly earning a rent – equivalent to the loss in consumers' surplus from not producing the competitive output at the competitive price – the size of which is shown by the area of the triangle L in Figure 6.3. If the establishment of the monopoly were an otherwise costless affair then this would be the social cost of monopoly.

However, in order to seek such rents interest groups would be prepared to invest resources in order to secure a monopoly position. Hence the true cost of a monopoly is not just the loss in

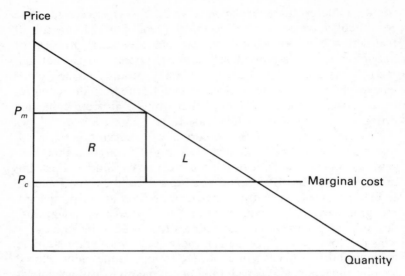

FIGURE 6.3 **The social costs of monopoly with rent seeking**

consumers' surplus but also the total resources invested in rent-seeking activities. It is usual to think of such activities in terms of businesses lobbying governments for some regulation in their favour – for example an airline (or cartel of airlines) lobbying for monopoly rights over a particular route. However, rent seeking need not always take this form and a trade union lobbying the management of a company for 'single union' recognition is an instance of rent seeking purely within the market structure.

More generally one can categorise (cf. Buchanan, 1980) three types of social costs associated with rent seeking: (i) expenditure undertaken in an attempt to secure a monopoly; (ii) the efforts of government officials to react to such expenditure; and (iii) third-party distortions caused by the rent-seeking activity. Thus, for example, in a country with exchange controls, commodities may only be imported with an import licence. Businesses may then lobby government to be granted monopoly rights to import certain commodities. This in turn may lead to government officials wishing to be involved with areas where lobbying is particularly intense. The prospect of earning relatively high rewards either from monopoly rents (as a businessman) or from the largesse of businessmen (as a bureaucrat or politician) may in turn dictate the choice of career for school-leavers and university graduates.

The above analysis, however, begs the question: what is wrong with seeking rent? The answer is nothing, if rent seeking is the consequence of a productive activity, for example patenting a cure for AIDS. However, many rent-seeking activities produce profit but no output. Such activities have been described in the literature (cf. Bhagwati, 1982) as 'directly unproductive profit-seeking' (DUP) activities. Much of the analysis of DUP activities has come from the international trade literature (cf. Colander, 1984), probably because many of the restrictions that governments place on economic activities – thereby creating the potential for generating rents – are directed at foreigners. Tariffs, quotas, import licencing, etc., are all instances where foreign trade restrictions both cause, and are caused by, lobbying activities.

The consequence of contemporary interest in rent seeking and DUP activities is that a great deal of government activity is regarded by conservative economists and politicians as being the result of rent-seeking activities; the fact that conventional economic analysis assumed that the only costs associated with such activities were deadweight costs, led to a gross underestimate of the social costs of rent seeking. The work of Tullock (1967), Buchanan *et al.* (1980) and others has tried to show that in fact the social costs could be much higher.

6.5 THE GROWTH OF PUBLIC EXPENDITURE

The preceding sections examined the demand side of the public choice equation by looking in some detail at the behaviour of voters. This section, and the next, turn to the supply side and examine the behaviour of governments. In this section we observe that in most countries of the OECD there has been a tendency over the past thirty years for public expenditure to grow, both in real terms and as a proportion of GDP. We then enquire into the possible causes of the growth of government. In the next section we ask whether, given this secular growth in public expenditure, there might be cyclical variations in expenditure, such that such variations might be described as being politically motivated.

The most striking fact about public expenditure in the United Kingdom since 1960 is its growth. In 1960 the real value of general government expenditure in the UK was, at 1980 GDP prices, £50 million; by 1985 it had more than doubled to reach £113 million. Over this period general government expenditure grew, in real terms, at an average annual rate of 3.3 per cent; the corresponding growth in real GDP was 2.3 per cent. As a consequence general government expenditure rose, as a percentage of GDP, from 35 per cent in 1960 to a peak of 48 per cent in 1975. After the cuts imposed as a consequence of the financial crisis of 1976, it fell to 46 per cent in 1977. Thereafter it again rose, reaching a peak of 46 per cent over the years 1981–3, since when it has fallen. This experience of the UK has largely been mirrored in other countries of the OECD (cf. Saunders and Klau, 1985, for a detailed analysis).

Klein (1976) in reviewing explanations for the growth of public expenditures distinguishes between three such explanatory modes. The first mode, which was the most general, explained trends in public expenditure by changes in the societal system and placed emphasis on the structural determinants – social, economic and demographic – of public expenditure. The second mode narrowed the focus by concentrating on the political system and emphasised factors like inter-party competition and party ideology. The third mode, which was the most specific, sought an explanation in the context of the organisational setting within which public expenditure decisions were made.

The argument that there are broad societal factors tending to continually raise the level of public expenditure has of course a great deal of plausibility. Thus, in the context of expenditure on social services, Glennerster (1979) argued that since the late 1950s the UK has seen a growing political demand for social services. The relations between social structure, the economic system and public expenditure are of fundamental importance in understanding this trend. Self (1980) noted that though the decline of kinship and neighbourhood groups as a supportive socio-economic system is of very long standing in the Western world, since 1945 high employment levels and high activity levels combined with increased personal mobility and spending power have reduced the claims of community and family life to minimal levels. According to this view, therefore, a large part of public expenditure has been absorbed in coping with the effects of social and economic change. In some cases the effort has been to prevent declines in welfare, in others it has been to provide alternative social structures.

The idea that the increased wealth and income of industrialised societies would lead to an increased demand for the public provision of goods and services can of course be traced to Adolf Wagner, who posited in 1890 that increased state expenditure was due to (a) 'increased friction causing greater demand for public services', (b) 'highly income elastic demand for collective and quasi-collective services', and (c) 'the fundamental inefficiency of private enterprise' that required the state to provide superior quality goods and services as the state grew richer. Thus according to this law (a) would explain the growth of administrative services and (b) and (c) would explain the growth of expenditures on health, education, social services, etc.

Within the framework of societal explanations of the growth of public expenditure is the Peacock and Wiseman (1961) 'displacement hypothesis'. According to this hypothesis, there is an upper limit to the amount of taxation the electorate is prepared to tolerate, and this 'tolerable level of taxation' effectively acts as a constraint on the growth of public expenditure. However, large-scale societal disturbances raise public expenditures and also the acceptable levels of taxation. After the crisis, the increased levels of expenditure are maintained, and as a result there is a permanent displacement of private by public expenditures. On the basis of expenditure trends in the 1950s, Peacock and Wiseman 'predicted' in 1961 that over the next twenty years, although public expenditures would grow, they would not increase substantially as a proportion of national income.

Political explanations for the growth of public expenditure (cf. Brittan, 1975) essentially argue that if the benefits of public expenditures are more visible to voters than the associated costs through taxation, then inter-party competition for votes will succeed in raising the level of public expenditure. Thus the direction of the inter-party competition effect depends crucially on the assumption regarding the relative visibility of the costs and benefits of public expenditure. There is some evidence that in the UK there is widespread ignorance about the impact of direct taxation (Brown and Dawson, 1969), though there also appears to be a great deal of ignorance on the part of social security claimants about the level of their entitlements (Micklewright, 1985).

However, the effects of cut-backs in public services may be quite visible, and have in the UK, in the recent past, been the source of public disquiet.

The basic model of inter-party competition can be extended in two directions. First, as Breton (1966) argues, there may be competition not only between parties for votes but also between voters for scarce public resources. Second, the model of inter-party competition needs to be qualified by taking account of the role of 'political ideology'. Thus while competition may explain the general rise in expenditures, ideology may determine both the rate of increase as well as the composition of expenditures (cf. Borooah and van der Ploeg, 1983).

One of the key assumptions of the British socio-economic scene, held by politicians, administrators and electorates, is the desirability of the welfare state. This assumption, even if it does not lead to the expectation of annual growth in the public provision of goods and services, certainly leads to the expectation that governments will not significantly reduce the level of such provisions. The political support model would therefore suggest that there is a lower limit to the level of public expenditure which is politically feasible, and that within the culture of the welfare state this limit may be reached before cuts of any significance are achieved. At the same time, constraints of prudent economic management suggest that there is an upper limit to the level of public expenditure that is feasible without making the burden of taxation intolerable. This would suggest that there are very narrow limits within which party ideology can make an impact on public expenditures. Indeed the evidence for the UK is that competition between parties is more in terms of good economic management than in terms of attaining public expenditure levels; for such management, public expenditure is of course seen as an important instrument.

The explanations for the growth of public expenditure that have the narrowest focus are those which concentrate on the behaviour of the protagonists in the public expenditure planning process. Perhaps the best description of this process is provided by Jenkins (1985), who writes that it

> is the nearest that modern Whitehall gets to war. The campaign season is brief, from July to October. The protagonists are always the same, the Treasury and the spending departments.

But the outcome is never predictable. At the end of each year the participants agree there must be a better way of settling the issue. Yet the following summer the season opens with the procedure unreformed.

The basis for the dispute is the Treasury's public expenditure survey committee (PESC), which is an interdepartmental group composed of departmental finance officers and Treasury officials and chaired by a Treasury deputy secretary. The purpose of PESC was to create an annual review procedure, encompassing the whole of the public sector, for a number of years ahead, which broke down expenditure by function and by economic category and which therefore enabled the spending of different departments to be coordinated and also enabled public expenditure to be integrated into overall economic policy. However, notwithstanding the merits of its conception, 'the PESC round', in practice, has, proved to be, under both Labour and Conservative governments, the focus of confrontation between Treasury parsimony and the expenditure ambitions of the spending ministers.

The organisational explanation for the growth of public expenditure in the UK is that the system for planning and controlling such expenditure is 'out of control', in that whatever the level of expenditure planned and approved by ministers, PESC is unable to ensure that the out-turn of expenditure does not exceed the planned level. To understand why public expenditure plans were, almost always, exceeded in their out-turn, one has to distinguish between the pre-1976 system of planning in terms of the volume of expenditure, and the current practice, which began in 1976, of 'cash limits'. Before 1976, public expenditure was planned for in real terms over the planning horizon of 4–5 years, the main aim being to plan the provision of given levels of public goods and services against a background of forecasts about the future availability of resources.

If real public expenditure and GDP were projected to grow at the same rate, differential productivity growth between the public and private sectors of the economy would ensure that the money value of public expenditure would increase as a proportion of GDP. This so-called 'relative price effect' occurs because, while productivity gains offset to some extent the rising cost of labour in the private sector, it is conventionally assumed that there is no productivity growth associated with the public provision of goods and services. There is of course nothing inevitable about the 'relative price effect', which relies for its operation on the assumption that in spite of differential productivity growth, wage growth in the public and private sectors is the same. Thus the effect can be frustrated by governments deciding to hold wage growth in the public sector below private sector levels. However, most governments in the UK had decided that the political costs of trying to achieve this were too great to justify the attempt.

By 1975 it was acknowledged by the Treasury that the monetary cost of the public expenditure was out of control. The solution proposed was to change to a system of 'cash limits', and such a system was introduced in 1976. A 'cash limit' is defined as an administrative limit on the amount of cash that the government proposes to spend on certain services, or blocks of services. The only programmes excluded from 'cash limits' were demand-determined ones – mainly social security payments – and, as a proportion of total public sector expenditure, such exclusions amounted to about 38 per cent. Of equal importance as 'cash limits' was the setting-up of a monitoring system to enable the Treasury to identify areas of overspending before it was too late to take corrective action. After 1976, therefore, there was a change of emphasis from the planning of expenditure to the control of public expenditure.

The system of cash limits has survived the thirteen years since its inception in 1976. Although since 1979 public expenditure plans have been consistently exceeded, the breach has been the result of items not subject to cash limits, and, by and large, cash limits on the various expenditure blocks have held up. However, the prognosis for the future is generally regarded as poor. This is for three reasons. First, cash limits have been used to influence public sector pay settlements by including in their announcement a budgeted pay figure. However, in each year the actual pay settlement has exceeded the budgeted figure, thus damaging the credibility of cash limits. Moreover, the reduction in the volume of public services required to stay within the cash limits, as a consequence of this breach, has so far not proved unacceptable. There is no guarantee that this will continue to hold in future, particularly if the gap between the pre-specified inflation rate and the actual inflation rate becomes too great.

Second, the success of cash limits has been at the expense of capital expenditure, and since 1976 the condition of the public sector capital stock has undeniably deteriorated. Any attempt, however, to reverse this neglect will place an additional strain on the system. Finally, the weakness of cash limits is that any flexibility in their implementation is liable to be interpreted as a licence to overspend; the credibility of cash limits therefore depends on their rigid enforcement. This is particularly important when it is remembered that there do not appear to be any sanctions that can be imposed on those who breach their cash limits.

6.6 THE POLITICAL BUSINESS CYCLE

The last section discussed reasons for the upward trend in public expenditure in the UK over the past thirty years. We now turn, in this section, to movements around this trend. The key proposition about political business cycles is that economic activity tends to revolve around election dates, with governments seeking favourable economic outcomes just prior to an election and postponing unfavourable outcomes to after. Interest in the political business cycle was due to Nordhaus (1975) who focused on the short-run trade-off between inflation and unemployment. The context of this emphasis was to debate in the 1960s and early 1970s about how vertical the price-expectations augmented Phillips curve was, and by how much the short-run Phillips curve could be shifted.

The basic behavioural assumption in the Nordhaus model was that the electorate was only concerned about the level of unemployment and the rate of inflation, and its support (or lack of support) for the government depended only on the outcome of these two variables. This meant that events in the economy relating to, for example, real incomes, balance of payments, social security benefits, etc., were ignored, and also that divisions within the electorate along, say, class lines were irrelevant in determining the government's support level. The government, for its part, was then assumed to follow policies that, given the preferences of the electorate, would guarantee its re-election. Under these assumptions, Nordhaus showed that the optimal outcome would be a political business cycle of the following form.

Immediately after an election the government follows policies to

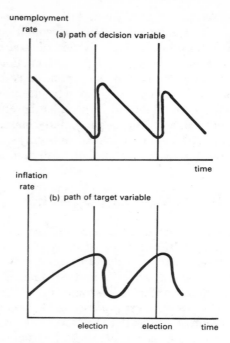

FIGURE 6.4　The optimal political business cycle

raise the level of unemployment which in turn lowers the rate of inflation and depresses inflationary expectations. The rationale for such a policy is that it is an 'investment' in the future which shifts the short-run Phillips curve closer to the origin in the latter years of the government's life. Closer to the next election policies are followed which reduce the level of unemployment at the expense of an increase in the actual inflation rate; however, since the Phillips curve has been shifted inwards the inflation rate associated with the reduced unemployment level is not as great as it would have been if the post election 'investment' had not been undertaken. Thus on election eve the government secures a low level of unemployment in conjunction with a 'moderate' rate of inflation and after securing re-election repeats the cycle which is illustrated in Figure 6.4.

Apart from the restrictiveness of the behavioural assumptions relating to the electorate – whereby it, as a homogeneous entity, cares only about unemployment and inflation – the existence of Nordhaus's business cycle depends on the further assumption that voters are backward-looking and never contemplate the consequences of government policy; as a consequence they never anticipate that hard times follow good times, and this leads to the cycle being perpetuated.

If, more reasonably, it was assumed that the electorate not only knew its likes and dislikes but also understood and took account of politically motivated economic policy, then this could prevent the appearance of the political business cycle à la Nordhaus. By penalising the government for its cyclical policies, the electorate could ensure through strategic voting that the economy was always characterised by low levels of unemployment and relatively high rates of inflation.

Nordhaus (1975), in a survey of nine countries, conceded that, over 1947–72, there was no evidence for his political business cycle in Australia, Canada, Japan and the United Kingdom, very modest evidence for France and Sweden and reasonable evidence for only Germany, New Zealand and the USA. Macrae (1977) cast further doubt on the empirical relevance of Nordhaus's model, by showing that for the USA evidence for the political business cycle was confined to the Kennedy and Johnson years and that there was no evidence for such a cycle during the Eisenhower and Nixon administrations.

The empirical irrelevance of the Nordhaus (1975) model is not surprising since there are strong reasons that might prevent governments from behaving as predicted. The derivation of optimal political-economic strategies is, in most practical situations, complicated and cannot expect a government to be able to 'optimise on the economy'. This difficulty is of course compounded if the government does not possess the required information or is faced with conflicting views on the behaviour of the economy and the electorate. Consequently, the formulation of *ex-ante* economic policy is, for most governments, a questionable proposition. Instead, a government is more likely to carry on with the established policies until a crisis arises, when it might modify or abandon existing policies in response to the crisis. This *ex-post* formulation of economic policy may be found in the 'feedback' approach to the theory of economic policy (cf. Tustin, 1954; Phillips, 1954), though the approaches there are typically normative, whereas the purpose of political economics is to provide a positive explanation of economic behaviour.

Reacting to these criticisms Frey and Schneider (1978) put forward a satisficing model of government behaviour which ran as follows. The primary objective of a government was to promote its ideology. However, in order to pursue this objective a government had to remain in office, and a political crisis would exist for the government if re-election was judged unlikely. Consequently, in the absence of a political crisis a government would implement its ideology and in the presence of a political crisis a government would follow 'popular' policies. The criteria to judge whether a given situation represented a political crisis would of course be flexible since low popularity is less serious just after an election than just prior to an election.

In the light of these comments, they suggested that a government would adjust its policy instruments (taxes, subsidies, public spending, etc.) according to a three-tier political economic reaction function. The first component would only be active when there was a popularity deficit and usually involved reflationary measures such as cutting taxes or implementing public works. The implicit assumption underlying such a strategy was that the popularity deficit was caused by too-high unemployment or a too-low growth in disposable income rather than a balance of payment crisis or too much inflation, since the latter two factors would require deflationary measures. In other words such a simple vote-satisficing strategy typically failed to take account of the cause of the popularity crisis.

The second component of the political-economic reaction function would be active when there was scope for discretionary policy, i.e. when there was a popularity surplus. A Conservative administration might cut public spending and taxes, whereas a Labour government might take the opportunity to increase taxes to finance an expansion of the public sector. The third component of the political-economic policy rule would be active regardless of the government's popularity, since it captured purely economic factors. For example, the unemployment benefit component of public spending might rise when the unemployment level rose.

6.7 CONCLUDING REMARKS

This chapter has tried to convey the flavour of the area of economics known as Public Choice by focusing on a limited number of topics within it, and attempting to address them within the general framework of the demand for, and the supply of, government. Given the limitations of space, the topics have not been discussed in the full richness of detail. The interested reader is directed to Buchanan and Tullock (1962), Borooah and van der Ploeg (1983) and Mueller (1989) for a more complete discussion of these issues. Constraints of space have also meant that several topics of importance were left out. Among these was the behaviour of bureaucracies, the seminal work here being that of Niskanen (1971). Notwithstanding these defects it is hoped that the chapter will provide a useful introduction to the subject.

7 Issues in Multi-Level Government

DAVID KING

7.1 INTRODUCTION

Much of the discussion in public sector economics assumes implicitly that the public sector in any country consists of a single government body. In practice, however, virtually every country has several levels or tiers of government. For there is usually one or more tiers of local authorities – and perhaps a tier of state authorities – in addition to the central government. This chapter looks at the main issues which arise with multi-level government.

These issues fall into two broad areas as follows. First there is the issue of the assignment of functions, that is the question of which functions might most appropriately be handled by the central government and which by the states and local authorities – hereafter called subcentral authorities. Intimately bound up with this issue, there is the question of how large the subcentral authorities should be. Second, there is the issue of finance. This raises several questions. To what extent should the subcentral authorities have independent tax-raising powers and to what extent should they rely on transfers – or grants – from the central government? Given that all subcentral authorities seem to have some tax-raising power, there is the question of which tax or taxes are most suitable for them. And given that some grants are paid in every country except, perhaps, Yugoslavia, there arises the final question of how grant payments should be allocated between the various authorities and what effect grant payments have on the recipients' spending levels. These issues are considered in the following sections. (For a fuller discussion of these issues, see especially Foster *et al.* 1980; King, 1984; Oates, 1972.)

7.2 THE ASSIGNMENT OF FUNCTIONS

In his celebrated textbook, Musgrave (1959) pointed to three areas of public sector activity: resource allocation, income distribution, and stabilisation. He gave only a brief treatment of fiscal federalism but concluded that 'the heart of fiscal federalism thus lies in the proposition that the policies of the Allocation Branch should be permitted to differ between states, depending on the preferences of their citizens. The objectives of the Distribution and the Stabilization Branches, however, require primary responsibility at the central level.'

Broadly speaking, this conclusion has stood the test of time, but it is useful to consider why this result is still felt to be a fair conclusion and the extent to which it might be qualified. The following sections look at the assignment of various types of function, starting with the provision of public goods, though many of the issues raised there arise also with other functions.

Public good provision

Much of the general public sector economics literature supposes that the principal resource allocation concern of governments is to provide public goods: that is, products which have benefits that are non-rival – in the sense that they can be consumed simultaneously by different people – and which are non-excludable – in the sense that once the product is provided for one person then it will not be possible to exclude from consumption other people whether or not they pay anything to the producer. Typical examples include defence, and law and order: once an army is established to keep out a foreign would-be invader, or a police force to apprehend criminals, then all citizens can benefit simultaneously, so the benefits are non-rival; and they accrue to citizens irrespective of whether or not they pay any money to the supplier of the army or the police force, so the benefits are non-excludable. It is the non-excludable feature that chiefly explains the interest of the public sector in public goods, for if people who do not pay can still benefit, then everyone has an incentive to be a free-rider and leave others to compensate producers, and the result is that without government intervention levels of provision could be well below the Pareto-efficient levels.

It is sometimes held that public goods can be divided into two groups: national public goods and local public goods. Their assignment is said to depend on how large an area the benefits of the public good affect. Thus defence is an activity where the benefits seem to be nation-wide, so this would be a national public good, while a flood-prevention scheme or a park might benefit only a small part of a country, that is just one locality, so they would be local public goods. Now if all public goods could be divided into two such groups, then it is easy to see that there would be a good case for having the central government provide the national public goods and for having subcentral authorities provide the local public goods. To see this, consider each type of good.

If defence activities benefit a whole country, then the activities of any subcentral authority in this field would chiefly benefit non-residents, and so would be external to the authority's own citizens. Consequently, there could be much under-provision as subcentral authorities might choose to ignore these external benefits when deciding on their production levels. If provision were handled at the central level, then the problem would disappear since the central government would take into account the benefits to all citizens.

On the other hand, if flood protection benefits only a small local area, then it would benefit only a minority of the central government's own voters, so the central government might choose to levy no taxes for this service and so spend no money on flood protection. This problem might seem less acute with parks, since the central government might find a wide demand for parks which means it could indeed raise taxes to provide them. But here there is the issue of local variety and choice. People in different areas might differ in their views about how much money they wanted to spend on parks and on what sort of parks they wanted. As Oates (1972, pp. 11–12) has explained, economic efficiency is attained by providing the mix of output that best reflects the preferences of the individuals who make up society; so if all individuals are compelled to consume the same level of output of a local public good or service when variations in consumption among different subsets of the population are possible, then the result is an inefficient allocation of resources, unless, of course, subcentral provision carries with it disadvantages outweighing this gain.

One problem with this approach to deciding the functions of

subcentral authorities is that there are few if any public goods whose benefits necessarily accrue to all the citizens in a nation. With defence, for example, it is possible that the EC countries could give further powers to the European parliament without sacrificing control over their armed forces, so it is possible that Europe will for a time resemble a nation where defence is a subcentral responsibility and where most of the benefits of any one member's armed forces accrue chiefly to that country's citizens. So it is not axiomatic that defence has to be a central government responsibility.

Another problem with this approach is that even where a public good may seem to have very local benefits, as with a park, the advantage of giving control over the level and type of provision to local citizens may not be decisive in deciding that subcentral provision is most efficient. One possible disadvantage of such a policy is that local services such as parks provide some external benefits to visitors which local citizens would ignore. Another possible disadvantage is that subcentral authorities might be too small to enable economies of scale in production to be fully exploited; a possible solution to this problem would be to require small authorities to purchase services off large private producers, but with some services, at least, there must be a question over how far the type and level of provision could be tailored to meet local preferences if production was on a scale sufficient for more than one authority.

In fact, the relevant economies of scale include not only those concerned in the actual production of public goods but also those involved with subcentral authority organisation. The issue of organisation costs has been discussed by Breton and Scott (1978) who point out that organisation includes administration by individual authorities and negotiations between authorities. Breton and Scott also note that the signalling of voter preferences is another cost associated with public provision, but it is not clear whether this cost would fall or rise if a subcentral activity were transferred to the centre.

The upshot is that each public good must be looked at on its merits. There will usually be advantages and disadvantages of provision by small authorities. The main disadvantages of provision by small authorities concern their tendency to ignore external benefits and their modest scale of production. The main advantage comes from increased local control: the importance of this will be stronger the more preferences vary between areas. Another possible advantage is that subcentral authorities may be more likely to indulge in experiments and innovation, partly at least because they will not be under pressure to maintain a uniform service across the country.

Consequently, it seems that instead of trying simply to divide public goods into national and public ones, some attempt should be made to find the optimum (population) size of authority for the production of each. (See Oates, 1972, and King, 1984, for further analyses of optimum size.) The optimal size for each function will be where any gains from increased size – such as a greater ability to exploit economies of scale and the tendency for external effects to become internalised as authorities include more people – just balance the losses from increased size – that is, the tendency for larger areas to be less able to respond to varying preferences. Where economies of scale and external effects are very important, as is likely with defence, then central provision – or even provision by international groups bound by treaties – may appear to be best. Where economies of scale and externalities are modest, as with parks, the possibility is much stronger that local provision will be preferred.

It must be stressed that there is rather more to the implications of local control than has been considered so far. In a celebrated paper, Tiebout (1956) pointed out that subcentral provision does not only mean that provision can vary from area to area in accordance with the wishes of local majorities. The fact is that members of local minorities who do not like the choices made in their areas can migrate – or 'vote with their feet' – to other areas. If migration were costless, and if there were a very wide range of localities to choose from, then everyone could end up with provision very close to their preferences.

While the concept of 'voting with one's feet' seems to strengthen the general advantages of subcentral provision, Tiebout went on to argue that it could even result in public goods being provided in Pareto-efficient quantities. This would be a great additional merit of subcentral authorities, and there is an extensive literature discussing the extremely unrealistic assumptions needed for this particular outcome to emerge. (See Wildasin, 1986, for a survey of this literature; and see Zodrow and Mieszkowski, 1986, and

Mieszkowski and Zodrow, 1989, for recent contributions.)

It is clear that deciding which size of authorities should provide public goods is likely to be a tricky issue. In fact, though, such goods account for relatively few items produced by most subcentral authorities. Police – or law and order – seems to be the most important example. Roads might just be taken in the same category, but price-exclusion could become feasible in time if vehicles were all fitted with devices that identified them to roadside equipment so that each vehicle's journeys could be recorded on computers and appropriate bills sent to its owners.

Services provided to handle externalities

Some subcentral services were probably incorporated into the public sector on externality grounds. These services include refuse collection and disposal, and fire services. For if refuse services were handled by the market, then there would be external health and nuisance costs associated with the uncollected rubbish of those who refused to pay. And if fire services were handled by the market, then there would be externality problems associated with fires in properties whose owners could not or would not pay to have them extinguished; this problem would be especially acute with terraced houses and flats.

As far as the assignment of services provided to handle externalities is concerned, very similar points arise to the points considered in the last section. Provision by small authorities enables services to be tailored to local wishes – for instance, meeting local preferences about how frequently refuse collections should be made – but it also carries the risks that the authorities would be too small to enjoy economies of scale and that they would ignore benefits to people in other areas. As before, there will be an optimum authority size for each service.

Services where marginal costs are zero

Other common local services include the provision of items such as museums, libraries and art galleries. Why are these provided by the public sector at all? Perhaps part of the answer is that these facilities are generally not crowded, so that the marginal cost of admitting an extra person is zero. In turn the efficient price is zero, and this can be achieved only if costs are met through taxes. If public provision is decided on, then the usual factors affecting the optimal size of authority need to be weighed up. It may appear, for instance, that collections of national importance need to be handled centrally because their benefits are widely spread, whereas collections of only local interest may be appropriate for subcentral authorities.

Merit goods and redistribution

In practice, the most important local authority function in many countries is the provision of education. Like other social services, this is what Musgrave and Musgrave (1976, pp. 65–6) have called a merit good. It is an item which governments provide because they feel too little would otherwise be provided, perhaps because people were too poor or because they were ignorant of the benefits. Again similar arguments to those already considered arise over the appropriate size of area. But here a further issue arises. The point is that there is often a large redistributive element in the provision of merit goods, and as noted earlier, subcentral intervention in redistribution is felt to be problematic.

Why is this? At first sight it seems arguable that subcentral authorities would be quite suitable for redistribution. Pauly (1973) has argued that people care more about the poor in their own neighbourhood than they care about the distant poor, so there seems a good case for allowing redistribution polices to vary from area to area in response to varying preferences about the appropriate degree of redistribution. And against this point it is doubtful if there are many economies of scale in redistribution to act as an argument for central control. Admittedly the case for subcentral responsibility could be weakened by a consideration of externalities, for it is true that help to the poor in one area may bring benefits to people elsewhere who are concerned about the plight of the poor in general.

However, the main objection to subcentral redistribution is that the authorities which pursued the most progressive policies would very likely find themselves in an untenable position, with poor people coming in from other areas to enjoy the high benefits and rich people being driven out by the high taxes. It has been said (Foster *et al*. 1980, p. 51) that the migrant poor in sixteenth-century England caused a problem for the more generous areas. More recent evidence from the United States suggests that the poor there are also mobile to some extent, and this has discouraged the adoption of decentralised measures to help the poor (Brown and Oates, 1987).

It is important, though, to keep this matter in perspective. The poor are not likely to migrate if differences in benefits are modest, so there could be a case for having redistribution done primarily by the central government with modest topping-up done by subcentral authorities. Returning to the related matter of merit goods such as education, there could be a case for prescribing that the central government should substantially control the amount of redistribution entailed with the provision of these items, while still allowing local authorities considerable discretion in the type of services they provide.

It has been suggested that this prescription has some relation to education provision in the United State (Bell, 1988); for there local authorities typically provide education services while only producing a modest amount of the funds needed from their own taxes. It is argued that taxes are redistributive so that migration problems make it harder for local authorities to establish their own tax policies than it is for higher tier authorities. In practice, the local authorities rely greatly on state grants rather than central government grants, and migration between states may tie the states' hands to some extent, but probably not as much as migration between local authorities would tie theirs. Curiously, perhaps, the opposite course to the one prescribed in the last paragraph seems to apply to education in the United Kingdom, for here the central government has fairly tight control over the type of education provided by means of regulations including a national curriculum, yet the amount spent on education is at the discretion of individual local authorities.

Stabilisation

Just as the subcentral role in redistribution may be modest, so too their role in stabilisation is likely to be very small. Of course preferences about macroeconomic policy may vary from area to area – for instance, views about the need for deflationary policies to combat inflation may be quite different between areas with high unemployment and areas with low unemployment. So the possibility of allowing at least some subcentral intervention deserves consideration. The trouble is that on consideration it is hard to see how subcentral authorities could play much of a role.

One problem is that it is hard to find suitable instruments for subcentral authorities to use. For instance, monetary policy is always a central government tool, though in the future it might not seem so in western Europe if political integration proceeds faster than monetary union. Certainly the prospect of numerous subcentral authorities each able to finance its expenditure by borrowing from its own 'central' bank would alarm anyone concerned about inflation. Other tools that seem denied to subcentral authorities are exchange rate adjustments and tariffs or quotas, since countries invariably have a single currency and no internal trade barriers.

There is, though, a possibility of some form of subcentral fiscal policy. Subcentral authorities might seek to run surpluses in good times and use up the accumulated balances (or borrow) in bad times to help promote some form of counter-cyclical tendencies in their own areas. Indeed, Gramlich (1987) has contended that local counter-cyclical policies have an advantage over central ones, as deflationary events, such as rises in energy prices, can have more effect on some areas than others. But the problem here is that even if subcentral authorities did run deficits and surpluses, they might have little effect on their own economies. This is because subcentral economies are typically very open with high marginal propensities to import. So a cut in taxes in a bad year might simply lead to a flood of imports as consumers spent more and thus have negligible effect on home production.

Perhaps a more fruitful, though more modest, area for macroeconomic intervention by subcentral authorities would be in regional policy. Many countries devote some resources to attempts to get new industrial development located in depressed areas. There is clearly a case for the funds for this activity to be provided centrally as needs are greatest in the poorest areas, but there is also a case for having at least some of the funds given to subcentral authorities to spend. They may know how best to attract industry to their areas, and they may approach the problem with more urgency than the central government. Moreover, as Bennett

(1990) has argued, most subcentral authorities can play an important role in development by using a wide range of measures such as advice bureaus for prospective investors, environmental and infrastructure improvements, training programmes, and suitable sites for new industrial buildings.

Legislation

There is one further area of subcentral action, and it has received scant attention. This is the possibility of subcentral authorities acting as legislators. In principle they could take decisions on matters as diverse as whether shops could open on Sundays, on noise or smoke abatement, on penalties for criminal behaviour, on speed limits on main roads and on rules for casinos and public houses. It has been suggested (King, 1991) that in many respects laws resemble public goods. For instance a law to the effect that only smokeless fuels could be burned would produce non-rival and non-excludable effects.

On this basis, there is an efficiency argument for subcentral discretion in legislation to enable varying preferences to be met and to encourage experiments to be carried out. And against this proposal the issue of economies of scale may be virtually irrelevant. However, the issue of external effects on people in other authorities may be important, at least on some issues. For instance, on the question of penalties for criminal offences, exceptionally severe penalties in one area could affect citizens elsewhere in several ways. For its criminals might be encouraged to move to other areas and citizens, elsewhere who disapproved of severe penalties on principle, would be worried.

This seems to be an area where there will be growing debate. For in the EEC at least the issue of which legislation should be taken at EEC level and which at individual country level is one which has so far been given little theoretical consideration.

7.3 THE FINANCE OF SUBCENTRAL GOVERNMENT

Much of the literature of fiscal federalism is devoted to the question of how subcentral authorities might best be financed. The sheer extent of the literature suggests that this issue is a complex one with no perfect solutions. This is unfortunate: for subcentral authorities often provide costly services, so they do have large revenue requirements. Broadly speaking these requirements can be met from four sources; loans, charges, taxes and grants.

Loans

The key issue with loan finance is whether there should be any controls over its use. Certainly there are controls in many countries, usually to the effect that loans may not be used to finance current spending. But it is not immediately apparent that controls are needed, especially if Ricardo's equivalence theorem is recalled.

This theorem was put forward by David Ricardo in obscure appendices to the *Encyclopaedia Britannica*. Although there is some debate about exactly what he meant, the general belief is that he suggested that the implications of tax finance and loan finance would be identical if people were fully rational. Suppose that a central or subcentral government decides to spend £10 million in the current year and that interest rates are 10 per cent. If the government raises taxes for £10 million, then people will have £10 million less to allocate to private consumption and saving than they would otherwise have allocated to those activities. If the government borrows, say by issuing bonds that never mature, then it will need to raise taxes of £1 million each year indefinitely to finance its interest commitments. Knowing this, citizens should save £10 million in what might be termed 'special' funds so that the interest they receive each year from these funds meets their annual tax obligations. And as a result of establishing these special funds, citizens have to cut back on the private consumption and other saving that they would have done by £10 million. So the effects of the two types of finance seem to be the same.

If the two types of finance do have identical effects, then there seems to be no point in special controls over subcentral borrowing. However, Ricardo himself felt that the two types would have different effects. He doubted whether people would react to government borrowing by saving additional funds sufficient to meet even their own future tax commitments, yet for equivalence to work their extra savings would have to be sufficient to meet the tax burdens of future generations also. So economists have traditionally been sceptical about the equivalence of tax and loan finance. Indeed, many introductory macroeconomics texts simply ignore the possibility that government borrowing would cause people to save more in view of the future tax burdens that will be needed to pay the interest. Interestingly, a recent paper in the United States has argued that consumers there do behave in a way that makes Ricardian equivalence a reasonable approximation (Evans, 1988). However, the issue has yet to be settled, even there.

If the traditional sceptical view is correct, then it suggests an important reason why there might need to be restrictions on the use of loans by subcentral authorities. For it suggests that the macroeconomic consequences of loan-financed subcentral expenditure could be much greater than the macroeconomic consequences of tax-financed subcentral expenditure. The point is that, on this traditional view, when loan-financed government expenditure takes place then total demand rises as a result of the expenditure, and there is little or no offsetting fall in total demand from the effects of the loan finance as this will induce little or no extra saving. In contrast, when tax-financed government expenditure takes place, although total demand is pushed up by that expenditure, it could be pushed back down almost to its original level by an almost equal fall in private consumption induced by the tax rises. In so far as the central government is concerned with stabilisation, then it will be principally concerned about loan-financed subcentral expenditure and may wish to regulate this with controls.

But suppose Ricardian equivalence were true. Would there then need to be any controls over subcentral borrowing? The answer is that there would be a case for limiting loan finance to capital projects alone, for fear that if loan finance were used for current spending then the level of current subcentral spending could be raised to the point where it was excessive – that is, where its marginal benefits fell short of its marginal costs.

The point is that many people migrate from area to area. So people who migrate know that if their own subcentral authority finances some current spending from loans, then they will enjoy all the benefits of that spending but will not have to pay much in the way of costs; consequently they may vote for spending whose benefits equal the expected costs to them even though the benefits fall far short of the true costs. There may be a check on this tendency through capitalisation, that is through induced falls in house prices; because immigrants to any one area which has to impose high taxes to meet the interest on loans used to finance past current spending will not buy property in that fiscally unattractive area unless the value of property there is relatively low. But this check will not deter tenants from voting for high spending. And it will not operate if voters in all areas opt for extravagant subcentral spending; for then no areas would be relatively unattractive so there would be no reason why property values should fall.

Charges

The possibility of having subcentral authorities make more use of charges for their services is frequently raised. (For general studies of charging, see Bird, 1976; Foster *et al.*, 1980; King, 1984; and Seldon, 1977.) Numerous issues arise but they will be not be explored here because they concern the principles of charging *per se* and do not have any specific relevance to the problems caused by multi-level government. However, a few general comments may be made.

First, the desirability of using charges needs to be weighed up for each service separately, or, more precisely, for each part of a service. For instance, it may be felt appropriate to charge for school dinners but not for school lessons, to charge for handling industrial refuse but not domestic refuse, and to charge for city-centre parking but not for rural parking.

Second, in the consideration of each service or part of a service, both efficiency and equity factors need to be considered. Equity arguments generally favour charges. For it seems equitable for road costs to fall chiefly on the heaviest road users, for refuse costs to fall chiefly on those with the most rubbish, and for museum costs to fall chiefly on those who most frequently visit them. Of course the introduction of charges could have undesirable distributional effects on the poor, especially for expensive services such as education where there is a major redistributional impact with tax-financed zero-price services; but these effects could in principle be neutralised with the use of vouchers or extra cash benefits to the groups concerned. On the other hand, efficiency arguments often support zero-price tax-financed services, at least for those services usually provided by subcentral authorities; for, as shown earlier, these services are often ones where public goods characteristics, or externalities, or zero marginal cost situations suggest that any serious attempt at conventional markets would result in market failure.

Perhaps it is the strength of the efficiency arguments that has resulted in little effective increase in charge finance in most countries in recent years. The one really significant service were charging might just be introduced is school education. It would be quite possible for subcentral authority schools to charge for their services and for parents to meet all or some of the fees with the help of vouchers which they could be given by the central government. One implication of such an arrangement is that voucher levels would probably be the same in all areas (except, perhaps, for supplements in areas where labour costs were high); so if subcentral authorities set their fees at voucher levels, then there would be very great uniformity in expenditures per pupil between areas and so great uniformity in the amount of redistribution taking place in each area as a result of state education.

It is fair to say, though, that advocates of education vouchers are usually concerned to promote parental choice. So there would be some support by them for allowing parents to use vouchers at independent schools also; and if the charges in independent schools exceeded the voucher levels, then parents would meet the extra costs themselves. In this situation, expenditures per pupil could vary substantially within authorities as well as between them. Suffice it to say here that no country has yet adopted a general education voucher scheme, but if such a scheme were introduced, then it would greatly reduce the need that subcentral authorities have for tax or grant revenues.

Taxes versus grants

Assuming that loan finance is confined to capital projects, then all subcentral authority current spending that cannot be met from charges has to be financed by means of taxes or grants. At first it might seem a matter of indifference as to which source is used, but this is not so. Two reasons why there may be significant differences will be noted here. (For a fuller discussion of the arguments for and against decentralised taxes, see Groenwegen, 1990.)

The first reason relates to the issue of how far each subcentral authority can vary its total income, and hence its total expenditure, in order to meet rises or falls in the demand for its services by its local voters. Given that the prime advantage of having subcentral authorities at all is to enable them to cater for varying preferences, it clearly seems reasonable to argue that they should be able to vary their total expenditures as well as the allocation of their expenditures. In this context, a key point to grasp is that if subcentral authorities can levy high-yielding taxes at rates they themselves determine, then they will have substantial control over their total income; but if they rely largely on fixed lump-sum grants from the central government, then they will have little control.

It must be stressed that the mere presence of some subcentral taxes may not in itself guarantee much freedom for subcentral authorities to determine their own budgets. For instance, the states in Austria and Germany have substantial tax revenues, but these come from taxes whose revenues they share in constitutionally decreed proportions with their central governments, and individual states have no say over how large their tax revenues are. And subcentral authorities in many countries find that even if they can set their own tax rates there may be upper limits on the amounts of tax revenue they can raise, as for instance occurs in the United Kingdom with 'capping' arrangements.

Conversely, the presence of a high degree of grants does not necessarily make it hard for subcentral authorities to vary their total revenues because there may be a scheme of 'effort-related' grants. Under such a scheme, the grant paid to any area depends on how much it raises in taxes, that is on how much tax effort it makes. In a simple scheme, the grant paid to an area could be made proportional to its tax income. Thus an authority might find that if it raised £10 million in taxes then it would receive £40 million in grants, while if it raised £20 million in taxes it would receive £80 million in grants. So, even though its taxes always account for a small proportion of its total income, a doubling of its tax income still leads to a doubling of its total income.

However, effort-related grants like these are rare, not least because such schemes effectively 'subsidise' increases in subcentral spending and hence are likely to encourage excessive or super-optimal spending. In the example just considered, the citizens in the authority concerned might vote to pay an extra £10 million in subcentral taxes knowing that this would secure them an extra £40 million in grants and so enable their authority to provide extra services which cost £50 million in all; and they might vote for these extra services even though they valued the extra benefits to themselves at, say, only £11 million. The citizens could well approve of this situation since they are themselves paying only £10 million in extra taxes for services whose benefits they value at £11 million. But in a world of scarce resources it is unsatisfactory that a total of £50 million is spent on services which yield benefits worth just £11 million.

The second reason why there are significant differences between taxes and grants concerns the point that when grants are paid by the central government then it will be concerned with how they are spent. After all, it has had to take the unpopular decision to raise taxes to finance the grants, and it is answerable to its voters for how those grants are spent. So it may well feel entitled to lay down numerous regulations concerning subcentral authority services, thereby reducing the freedom of subcentral authorities to respond to local wishes.

The choice of subcentral taxes

The discussion in the last section points to the conclusion that if subcentral authorities are to satisfy their main *raison d'être* and respond to local wishes, then they will find it best to rely substantially on the yield of taxes levied by themselves. But which taxes are most suitable for subcentral authorities?

A useful starting-point is to suppose for a moment that each subcentral authority concentrates on supplying local public goods from which all its citizens derive equal benefits; and suppose, too, that the cost per head of providing these services varies in strict proportion to the level at which they are provided. Thus area X may provide services which cost £200 per head while area Y may provide better services which cost £300 per head. In these circumstances there is much to be said for subcentral poll taxes, for then the amount of subcentral tax paid by each citizen will be £200 in X and £300 in Y. So the tax paid by each citizen will equal the cost of providing that citizen with services. This means that citizens will be encouraged to locate efficiently. For instance, citizens currently in X who want better services and who are prepared to pay their share of the costs will go to Y.

In contrast, if the areas levied an income tax, then the tax rates might be 4 per cent in X and 6 per cent in Y. As a result, poor people would be encouraged to move from X to Y, where services actually cost £100 a person more, even though they would not be willing to pay £100 more and would not value the improvement at £100 more. Poor people would be tempted to make the move because, on their low incomes, the extra cost of the higher tax rate could be under £100; indeed the extra cost could even be zero if their incomes were below the tax threshold. Conversely, rich people might move from Y to X where services cost £100 per person less, even though they might be willing to pay over £100 more to live in Y, because with their high incomes the extra tax cost of living in Y could be well over £100 above the cost of living in X.

Essentially, there is the redistribution problem once again. So some writers (such as Musgrave, 1983) have argued that subcentral authorities should keep off highly progressive taxes. But should they levy poll taxes? The analysis suggests that they should only if all people in each area actually derive equal benefits so that the cost per person is the same for all. In fact, an empirical study in the United Kingdom has suggested that rich people tend to make more use of local services than the poor – for instance their children are more likely to stay on at school after the compulsory school-leaving age and they are likely to have more cars and use roads more (Bramley *et al.*, 1989). And a theoretical general equilibrium model in the United States has argued that in practice the efficiency losses from a progressive income tax are unlikely to be large enough to warrant concern (Goodspeed, 1989).

Some might argue that there would be a case for a progressive tax even if it did give an inducement for the rich to live in areas with low services and vice versa. This argument arises if subcentral services are normal goods, and there is evidence in the United States, at least, that income is an important argument in the demand function for local public spending (Schokkaert, 1987). The point is that if local services are 'normal' then a poll tax is likely to lead to rich people generally congregating in areas characterised by high taxes and high services while poor people congregate in areas characterised by low taxes and low services. A value judgement might be formed that it was undesirable for better public services to be generally provided for rich people, even though they were prepared to pay more. In practice, a progressive tax might simply do enough to counteract the tendency for the rich to want to live in high tax areas, and vice versa, and so ensure there was no systematic tendency for rich people to live in areas with the best services.

It is clear that the issue of whereabouts the ideal tax would come on the spectrum that has a very regressive poll tax at one end and a very progressive income tax at the other is one which could be extensively debated. In practice many subcentral authorities raise property taxes, and so there is naturally much interest in trying to establish what the incidence of property taxes is. This is a very complex issue which can only be touched on briefly here. It was traditionally argued that a property tax was regressive. This 'old' view looked separately at domestic and non-domestic property taxes and argued that the former, at least, were regressive. The argument stemmed from a belief that taxes on domestic property fell chiefly on the occupants of such property. This is obvious enough in the case of owner-occupiers, and was taken to apply to tenants because the long-run elasticity of supply of housing is presumably very high. The argument was that as the tax fell on occupants, then it would be regressive, because poor people typically devote a higher proportion of income to housing than rich people do. As for the tax on non-domestic property, this too should fall on occupiers since the supply of such property is highly elastic in the long run; occupiers will pass the tax on in a mix of lower wages, higher prices and lower profits, but whether the incidence here is regressive or progressive is hard to say.

However, this 'old' view was challenged in the 1970s (see Mieszkowski, 1972; Aaron, 1975). The 'new' view then put forward assumed that the aggregate supply of capital goods in a country is highly inelastic. If so, then a tax on non-domestic property which in any way reduces the earnings of its owners will encourage capitalists to switch into other untaxed assets such as plant and machinery. This could lead to lower prices for consumers which largely offset the higher cost of housing resulting from the domestic property tax, so the overall incidence of the tax on them may be negligible. In contrast, capitalists will get lower returns from non-domestic buildings, as a result of the tax, and also from the other assets whose supply has risen. So a property tax may chiefly hit capitalists and thus be progressive.

This result is most plausible if property taxes are levied uniformly throughout a country. What happens if tax rates vary from authority to authority? Here it is best to look at the rate set in any area as a combination of the nation's average rate and the local difference from the average. The effect of the national average may be progressive for the reasons just outlined, but the incidence of all deviations could fall on local citizens and be regressive. Consider an area with a relatively high property tax. The incidence of its high domestic property tax will not be noticeably offset for its citizens by lower prices on other items, as any tendency for its high non-domestic tax to drive capitalists into other assets will not specially benefit its citizens any more than it benefits citizens in other areas through lower prices. The results of this 'new' view were initially derived from fairly simple models. Later work has tried to embody more elaborate general equilibrium models; these models have offered a fair measure of support to the 'new' view (see Lin, 1986; Zodrow and Mieszkowski, 1986).

The discussion so far has suggested that the choice between a poll tax, a property tax and an income tax, or perhaps the choice of a mixture of these, could be much affected by studies on their incidence and views of the desirable incidence for subcentral taxes. But property taxes have been widely used as subcentral taxes without any special regard to their incidence. This is no doubt partly the result of some special advantages as a local tax (OECD, 1983). These advantages include: the fact that with a property tax it is always clear which authority is entitled to the tax on any taxed subject – which is not so for income taxes or poll taxes in relation to people with two homes; the fact that the administration costs of a property tax are generally found to be much lower than with an income tax (where complex tax returns may be needed) or with a poll tax (where it is necessary to monitor all moves by all tax-payers); the fact that the yield of a property tax can be predicted very accurately in advance – which is not so for an income tax (or with a poll tax if there is widespread evasion); and the fact that some tax will be levied on businesses, which is reasonable to the extent that businesses derive some benefits from subcentral services such as roads and the police – whereas businesses pay no poll tax or personal income tax. Businesses could be made to pay a subcentral corporation tax on profits, but there is always a problem of deciding how to allocate the profits of a multi-area firm between the areas in which it operates.

However, while property taxes have some advantages over a poll tax and an income tax, it must be conceded that the poll tax has the advantage that all voters are made to contribute something towards the local exchequer so that no voters regard subcentral services as 'free' (see King, 1990, for an appraisal of the property tax in England); and an income tax has the virtue that, not being regressive, it can yield high sums and help ensure that subcentral authorities can have a fair degree of financial autonomy.

This discussion of subcentral taxes can be concluded with three further points which arise if it is desired that such taxes should help authorities provide services at the levels which their citizens are prepared to pay for.

First, there is no point having a subcentral tax whose base is highly mobile between areas. For instance, an area which sets a high rate of corporation tax in order to try and finance high service levels may simply drive capital away (McLure, 1986). Similarly, an area which set a high rate of any sales tax would tend to find that many people switched their purchases to other areas.

Second, another group of unsuitable taxes are those where much of the incidence is exported to non-residents, for these mean that spending rises are effectively 'subsidised' by non-residents (see Gordon, 1983, for an analysis). This point argues against subcentral corporation taxes; for at least some of the incidence of any one area's corporation tax will be exported to non-resident owners, workers and customers. This point also argues against sales taxes, at least some of whose incidence will be exported on to non-resident customers and producers.

Third, there is no point having taxes whose burdens are imperceptible to local citizens. This point also argues against sales taxes and corporation taxes where the true burden on those who pay is very hard for them to gauge.

The need for grants

Virtually all subcentral authorities rely to some extent on grants from higher-tier governments. Why are grants so common? There are perhaps three main reasons for grants.

First, there are grants to correct for externalities. Some subcentral services will yield benefits to non-residents, as noted earlier. Roads are a common example. In deciding on how much of these services to provide, authorities will typically ignore these external benefits, and thus under-provision is a probable outcome. In principle this problem could be overcome by a system of grants that met a percentage of the costs of the service in question. In practice, the problem could prove hard to solve this way. For one thing, there would have to be a separate system of grants for each service which generated externalities. For another, it would be very hard to work out the correct percentages of costs to meet by grants for each area – the correct percentages would typically be different for each service for each area. So there is still good reason to suppose that where externalities are large, then subcentral authorities are inappropriate providers.

Second, there is the problem of finding suitable subcentral taxes. It might be possible to arrange for subcentral authorities to be financially independent by allowing them to raise an income tax along with a property tax and/or a poll tax. Generally, however, subcentral authorities are given an array of taxes which, if levied at rates deemed 'reasonable' by the central government, raise less than the central government wishes the authorities to spend. So the government shares some of its own tax revenue with the subcentral authorities by paying out revenue-sharing grants.

Third, there may be inequalities between different areas which the government feels must be ironed out by means of equalisation grants. These grants raise several issues which must now be addressed. (See Bramley, 1990, for a recent discussion of this topic.)

The case for equalisation grants

The basic rationale for equalisation grants stems from a realisation that if they were not introduced, then subcentral tax rates might vary widely even between two areas providing services at comparable levels. Consider a particular example: suppose that all subcentral authorities provide schools and levy an income tax. For a given level of education, income tax rates will have to be highest in those areas where income per head is low, or where the number of schoolchildren in relation to total population is high, or where the labour costs of teachers are high. The problem can be expressed more generally by saying that tax rates will have to be highest in those areas where taxable resources per head are low, or where needs per head are high (where needs are related to the numbers of units of local authority output required to provide particular levels of services), or where unit costs (that is the costs of providing units of output) are high.

Now there are two reasons why it might be decided to address this situation by means of equalisation grants. First, there is an equity argument: without grants, equals in different areas may pay different amounts in local taxes and yet receive the same levels of services in return. Second, there is an efficiency argument. This arises because the inequalities in tax rates for similar service levels could lead to migration from unfavourable areas to favourable ones. Such migration will in itself use up resources; moreover, it could lead to people locating themselves in areas where their contributions to output were less than before if the lower wages they received were more than offset by an improved local fiscal package. It must be conceded, though, that there is also an efficiency argument against equalising differences in unit costs. For if people move from areas where services are costly to areas where services are cheap, then the total cost of providing people with a particular level of services will fall.

It is sometimes argued that there is no need to have equalisation grants at all on the grounds that capitalisation adjustments in home prices will prevent migration actually taking place and will also preserve equity. Thus if one area is disadvantaged in some way and people seek to leave, then home prices there will fall while home prices in relatively attractive areas will rise. These home price changes could act in a way that leaves the total cost of living in each area the same – once home costs and local service costs are taken into account – and so eliminate migration and restore equity.

There are, however, two reasons for not placing too much reliance on this capitalisation process and so for opting to have a system of equalisation. First, it is really land prices that will alter. In the long run, at least in rural areas, land for homes may have its price set at levels determined in the market for agricultural land. Thus the supply of land for homes may be perfectly elastic in rural areas at the level of agricultural land prices. If so, then land price differentials may not emerge as a result of local fiscal differences so that migration and inequity will occur. Second, even if the supply of residential land were perfectly inelastic, as might occur in built-up areas, so that appropriate price differentials could occur, there would still be an equity case for equalisation grants. For without such grants owners of homes would face continual windfall gains and losses whenever the taxable resources or the needs or the unit costs in their areas altered, and these gains and losses would be allocated in a capricious way.

Types of grant scheme

In general, schemes of equalisation grants usually seek also to pursue the revenue-sharing objective noted earlier whereby the central government shares some of its tax revenues with local authorities because they have inadequate tax power. So the usual type of grant scheme is one which pays grants to all areas, but gives most to those with low resources, high needs and, perhaps, high costs.

There are many types of equalisation grant cum revenue-sharing grant schemes in operation in different countries, and there are other schemes which exist only in the theoretical literature. Inevitably, the degree of equalisation actually achieved varies from scheme to scheme. However, it is perhaps fair to say that the more effective schemes all have one feature in common. This is that they all specify some particular standard rate of tax for each local tax and work out the tax revenue that each local authority would get with those rates (R^*), and they each specify some particular level for each local service and work out the total expenditure that would be incurred in each area if it provided services at these levels (E^*), and then they give each to each area which actually raises the revenue R^* a grant equal to $E^* - R^*$. Consequently, if each area set taxes at the standard rates, then each would have a total income of E^* and each could provide services at the standard levels.

Now while the most effective schemes may have in common the feature that areas with a revenue of R^* receive a grant of $E^* - R^*$, they differ in their treatment of areas which choose not to have a revenue of R^*. One simple possibility is actually to pay $E^* - R^*$ to each area irrespective of its tax effort – that is, to have lump-sum grants. Such a scheme has the virtue that all changes in local spending fall on local taxes, so there is no implicit 'subsidy' or 'tax' on spending increases caused by the grant scheme. However, lump-sum grants result in inequity between areas with common tax efforts unless they happen to make the standard effort.

To see this, consider two areas A and B. In area A, R^* is $0.25E^*$. If it sets the tax rates specified for R^*, then it will be given a grant of $0.75E^*$ (that is $E^* - R^*$) and will be able to spend at E^*; and if it doubles its tax rates so that its tax revenue is $0.5E^*$, then its grant will still be $0.75E^*$, so that its spending will rise to $1.25E^*$ and services will be 25 per cent above the standard levels. In contrast, in area B, R^* is $0.75E^*$. If it sets the tax rates specified for R^*, then it will be given a grant of $0.25E^*$ (that is $E^* - R^*$), so it too will be able to spend at E^*; but if it doubles its tax rates so that its tax revenue is $1.5E^*$, then its grant will still be $0.25E^*$, so that its spending will rise to $1.75E^*$ and services will be 75 per cent above the standard levels. So there is no equity between people in areas with common tax rates where those tax rates are different from those specified for R^*.

This problem can be solved by making the grant paid to each area depend on its tax effort. In effect, in addition to specifying a level of spending for areas which set the tax rates needed for R^*, the scheme specifies the level of spending that can be met for any possible level of tax effort, where tax effort can be defined as actual tax receipts divided by R^*, so that an area with a revenue of R^* would be regarded as making a tax effort of 1 while an area with a revenue of $2R^*$ would be regarded as making a tax effort of 2, and so on. Now areas making an effort of 1 would still be given enough grant to finance a spending level of E^*, but the government would have to specify the spending level for each other tax effort. For a tax effort of 2, the government might specify that the grant scheme should facilitate spending levels of, say, $1.6E^*$.

To see how this works, return to A and B. Suppose A and B each started with a revenue of R^* so that each made an effort of 1. Then the tax revenue would be $0.25E^*$ in A and $0.75E^*$ in B; and each would be given the grant needed to take total income up to the level needed for E^*. Then suppose both areas raised their efforts to 2, so that A received a tax revenue of $0.5E^*$ and B one of

$1.5E^*$. This time A would find its grant rising from $0.75E^*$ to $1.1E^*$ so that its total spending was $1.6E^*$. In contrast, area B would find its grant falling from $0.25E^*$ to $0.1E^*$ so that its total spending was also $1.6E^*$.

Of course a key problem with grants of this effort-related type is that they do implicitly subsidise a tax increase in local spending. In A's case, spending rises are subsidised, while in B's case they are taxed. This problem clearly provides one argument for lump-sum grants. A further advantage of lump-sum grants is that they are simple to administer. For with these schemes, the grant to each area can be announced in advance and the total grants paid out can be easily calculated in advance. With effort-related grants, the grant to each area depends on the tax rates it sets. The question arises as to whether the government sets the formula for the grant scheme before or after the areas set their tax rates. If the government acts first, then it will not know exactly how much it will have to pay out until the last tax rate has been set. If the government acts last, then the authorities will not know when they set their tax rates exactly how much grant they will receive.

The effects of grants

Having considered why grants may be paid, there remains the question about what effect they will have on recipient authorities' spending. This issue has been extensively discussed in recent years in the context of the 'flypaper effect'.

To see the meaning of this effect, it is simplest to consider a system of lump-sum grants. Suppose the authority in an area receives a lump-sum grant of £1 million. This money is available to its citizens whose votes will decide how it is spent. They may vote for subcentral taxes to be cut. They could, for instance, vote for a £0.6 million cut in taxes so that their private spending would rise by £0.6 million while their subcentral authority's spending would rise by only £0.4 million.

In principle, it seems that the voters should opt for a similar allocation between subcentral and private spending increases if they instead acquired an extra £1 million through cuts in central taxes. In that case the citizens would be expected to vote for rises in subcentral taxes to the tune of £0.4 million, so that once again private spending would rise by £0.6 million while their subcentral authority's spending would rise by £0.4 million.

However, in a review of the empirical evidence for the United States, Gramlich (1977) found that when the money available to citizens rose through central tax cuts, then only 5–10 per cent of their extra money was devoted to subcentral authority spending, whereas when the money available to them rose through a rise in grants to their authority, then 40–100 per cent was devoted to that subcentral authority's spending. The term 'flypaper effect' was coined for this phenomenon because the money given to the citizens by the central government tended to stick in whichever sector, private or public, it arrived.

Numerous models were developed to explain this (see King, 1984, for a survey). These suggested various factors which might cause this paradoxical result. For instance, voters might be under an illusion where they interpreted a rise in grants as a fall in the unit cost of subcentral services, and this could encourage them to react to a rise in grants by voting for a big rise in subcentral authority spending. Or maybe voters often want subcentral authority spending to rise but do not vote for this because they think subcentral taxes (such as a property tax) are regressive and fear the effects of rises in their rates on the poor. If the central government cuts its taxes, this may not help the poor much, so voters may opt for only small rises in subcentral taxes and spending; but if grants are increased, then voters may be happy for much of the grant revenue to be allocated to subcentral authority spending.

Curiously, no sooner were these models developed than grants in the United States tended to be cut. The 'flypaper effect' evidence suggested that subcentral spending would fall sharply, but it did not; instead, it has been argued that subcentral taxes rose to make up the loss (see Gramlich, 1987). Of course it may be that this is simply a result of the fact that it is notoriously harder to cut public spending than to increase it – partly because it is easier to hire officials than fire them – in which case the predicted sharp fall may occur, but only slowly. Equally, it is fairly clear that more research is needed to understand fully the effects of grants.

One weakness of much of the discussion of grants has been to say little about the role of the central government. If the central government raises its payments of grants, then it must generally raise its taxes at the same time to finance the grants, so the citizens in many areas may not find themselves any better off at all – indeed the citizens in some areas could be worse off. So, to say the least, it is not very satisfactory to look at the effects of grants in any model which does not also look closely at how they are financed.

It is therefore appropriate to end by mentioning work by Logan (1986) and Grossman (1989) which does attempt to bring the central government in more fully. This work builds on the proposition that if grants delude voters into thinking that the costs of subcentral services are lower than they really are – because their subcentral tax payments cover only part of the cost of these services – then grants should also delude voters into thinking that central services are more costly than they really are – because their central tax payments cover more than the cost of central services. So while a rise in grants might raise the amount of subcentral spending that people want, it should also reduce the amount of central spending that they want. Thus a central government which does raise its grant payments may be wise to cut its other spending if it wants to retain popular support. A corollary would seem to be that if a central government wished to raise its own spending, then it might receive support for this provided that it simultaneously cut its grant payments.

8 Public Finance in Developing Countries

RICHARD M. BIRD

The goals or objectives of public finance in developing countries are those of economic policy as a whole: economic growth, internal and external stability, and the attainment of an appropriate distribution of income and wealth. Taxation and expenditure are by no means the only or the most important means of achieving such national objectives. Nevertheless, since the budget is one of the most pervasive instruments of government policy in any economy, the effects of budgetary policy on such general public policy objectives as growth, stability and distribution must be taken explicitly into account in formulating tax and expenditure policy.

8.1 ECONOMIC GROWTH

A major policy concern in every developing country is to increase the level of per capita output. A useful, if oversimple, way to think of economic growth is in terms of an aggregate production function:

$$Y = f(K, L, T, R, S)$$

where Y is the level of capacity output, K the stock of available capital services, L the available labour force, T the stock of applied technical knowledge, R the available natural resources, and S stands for the various social and cultural characteristics that affect the ability to produce (Bruton, 1965). R, S, and T affect the level of output chiefly through their effects on K and L. The level of available resources (R), for example, depends largely on the

183

state of technology, and technical improvements are implemented largely through new investment in physical or human capital or through organisational changes. *S* refers to everything else: the organisation of markets, the extent and effectiveness of the price system in allocating resources, the level of institutional development, and so on. In the first instance, then, growth can be thought of as the outcome of increases in the quantity of *K* and *L*, where *K* and *L* represent a heterogeneous collection of physical capital and workers with different skill levels, respectively. In addition, of course, the level of output at any point in time depends on the level and composition of demand.

Simple as it is, this way of approaching the problem of growth serves to set up the problem of public finance in a developing country in a useful way. The level and rate of economic growth depends on (i) the initial conditions in the country in question (e.g. *T*, *R*, and *S*); (ii) the behaviour of the key 'active' parameters in the growth process (*K*, *L*); (iii) the level and composition of demand; and finally (iv) on exogenous shocks and on the response of the economic system to such shocks. Budgetary policy may, in principle, affect many of these factors in various favourable and unfavourable ways.

In addition to the role of fiscal (and monetary) policy in influencing the level and composition of demand, the 'supply-side' aspects of public finance policy have attracted considerable interest in recent years. Public spending policy may, for example, influence *R* by encouraging systematic exploration of natural resources and by ensuring such resources are developed optimally in terms of linkages with the rest of the economy. Similarly, public spending may increase a country's 'absorptive capacity' – its ability to make good use of additional capital by developing such cooperating factors as trained manpower and physical infrastructure (Wolfson, 1979). Tax policies, of course, may also affect incentives to save, work and invest (Gandhi *et al.*, 1987).

Perhaps the simplest way to view the effects of public finance on growth is to consider the relationship between investment and growth in the equation:

$$\dot{y} = i/k = vi \qquad (8.2)$$

where $\dot{y}$ is the rate of growth in output, i is the rate of investment (net I as a percent of national income Y), k is the incremental capital–output ratio or ICOR (the number of units of I needed to raise Y by one unit a year), and v is the inverse of k (that is, the 'productivity' of net investment in terms of increased output). This simple formulation shows clearly that growth can be increased in two quite different ways; by increasing investment or by lowering the ICOR, that is, increasing the efficiency with which investment is used (Gillis *et al.*, 1987).

The latter may be achieved by altering the structural composition of I (e.g. through changes in public investment patterns or by tax changes to induce changes in private investment), by developing appropriate physical infrastructure and other cooperating factors, or by using prices and markets more efficiently (e.g. by reducing the 'excess burden' or 'deadweight loss' of the tax system and government regulations and controls or by lowering the cost of capital through monetary and fiscal policy). ICOR is thus clearly as much a policy variable, affected by both sides of the public budget, as is the level of investment. Nonetheless, the primary concern of 'supply-oriented' public finance policy in most countries has clearly been to increase the level of net investment in order to increase the rate of growth.[1]

Increased investment must of course be balanced by increased saving if the fullest and best level of resource utilisation is to be attained without undue internal and external instability in the form of price inflation and balance of payments deficits. If the aim of public policy is to attain a given level of investment without macroeconomic imbalance, the appropriate budgetary stance is

$$G - T = S_p - I_p + (M - X) \qquad (8.3)$$

where G is *total* government spending (including investment), T is current government revenues, S_p and I_p are, respectively, private saving and private investment, and $M - X$ (imports less exports) is the deficit (or surplus) on the current account of the balance of payments. As this formulation suggests, public finance is not only important in setting the levels of G and T but also in affecting both the balance of payments (M, X) and the surplus (or deficit) of private sector savings (S_p, I_p).

Equation (8.3) may be revised slightly to show the task, and dilemma, of tax policy as follows:

$$T = G + (I_p - S_p) + (X-M) \qquad (8.4)$$

One aim of policy in a growth-oriented country will generally be, for instance, to increase private investment. Reduced taxes on investment may produce this happy result. At the same time, however, increased private investment will require *increased* taxes to avoid inflation, unless fortuitously offset by either increased private saving or increased foreign saving (net imports).

The most obvious 'growth' objective for tax policy is thus to provide the resources needed for public sector capital formation and other necessary development-related expenditures in a non-inflationary manner. At the same time, however, many developing countries wish to encourage private investment in new physical capital (at least in certain lines of activity) through tax 'incentives'. The aim of increasing private investment may also shape the design of business income taxes in general. Higher taxes may, for instance, be imposed on retained profits than on distributed profits in order to encourage distribution, the development of capital markets, and the flow of savings to the highest-return investment opportunities. Or, more likely in most developing countries, the opposite policy, of favouring retained earnings, may be followed to encourage corporate reinvestment.

There is almost no limit to the tax gadgetry which may be used to stimulate economic growth and, in particular, investment. Nonetheless, such policies are of uncertain effectiveness in achieving their alleged goal, in part because we know so little about the relationship between the financial factors that are influenced by tax policy and the real factors underlying growth performance. This uncertainty, combined with the inequitable and administratively complicated character of most tax incentives, suggests that many countries have overestimated the net benefits that can be achieved through incentive policy (Gandhi *et al.*, 1987).

Taxes (and expenditures) also affect the supply of labour and social risk-taking, of course, so it seems logical to ensure that at the least these effects do not contravene the basic policy goal of growth in a developing country. This does not mean, however, that taxes should be designed specifically to make people work as hard and take as many risks as possible or that taxes are necessarily the best, or even good, instruments for this purpose. Indeed, the best approach in the circumstances of most developing countries is probably more to avoid doing too much harm through budgetary policy than to try to stimulate and direct growth through ingenious fiscal devices. The cost of attempting to direct market forces through public finance measures may be not only an unsustainable growth pattern but also a severely distorted and ineffective budgetary system. Creating a tax-free sector of economic activity within a country, for example, in effect establishes an on-shore 'tax haven' with accompanying pressures and strains on the limited administrative capacity available. The potential rewards seem too little in most cases to run such risks. Most developing countries would thus seem well advised to avoid fine-tuned tax incentive policy.

8.2 INCOME DISTRIBUTION

A somewhat similar conclusion may be drawn with respect to the role of taxation and expenditure in achieving other public policy goals: namely, it is better not to try to do too much. Objectives such as stabilisation and distribution are even more likely than growth to give rise to political conflict among different social groups, for example. The extent to which these goals are attained, and the methods by which they are attained, are thus inevitably as much political problems as economic problems. Moreover, policies intended to achieve one goal may reduce the likelihood of achieving another. Tax concessions to investment, for instance, may raise the rate of growth in certain situations but often only at the cost of increasing the inequality with which wealth and income are distributed. On the other hand, sometimes measures aimed at one objective may simultaneously move a society toward another. Heavy taxes on land, for example, may induce more efficient utilisation of existing assets and raise the level of output, while at the same time reducing inequality (Bird, 1974). The relevance and importance of such arguments can usually be determined only by a close examination of the situation in each particular country.

The connection between the distribution of income and the rate of economic growth has sometimes been considered to be a simple, straightforward matter. As noted above, economic growth may be viewed as primarily a function of the rate of investment, which must be matched by savings. Since it is supposedly well known that the rich save more than the poor, the characteristically unequal distribution of income in poor countries should at least have the virtue of permitting a higher rate of economic growth than would otherwise be possible.[2]

The implications of this view for tax policy in particular seem clear – and have been much heralded by recent advocates of the so-called 'supply-side' approach to taxation. High taxes on the rich should be avoided, since private saving is the well-spring of economic growth. In particular, light taxation of industrial profits and capital gains would appear to be an essential part of a growth-oriented tax system. In this view, redistributive taxation is a luxury which poor countries can ill afford. Tax policies which appear to be redistributive in character may at times need to be legislated for political reasons. To foster growth, however, such policies ought either to be largely vitiated by incentives or else not really enforced. Since the interests of the well-to-do in maintaining their position are thus buttressed by the economic argument that it is really better in the long run for the poor that the rich are rich, it is not surprising that in fact few developing countries have very progressive tax systems (DeWulf, 1975).

Even in the 'classical' case, however, where growth is limited by inadequate savings and where the rich are savers, the saving 'instinct' may prove to need considerable stimulation in the form of low taxes on the rich, and such policies may build up problems for the future.[3] Other countries, in which growth may also be characterised as 'savings-limited', but where the rich spend rather than save, may find redistributive tax policy a more efficient way of producing growth than tax concessions. Moreover, if the key constraint holding back growth is inadequate foreign exchange, as has been argued to be true for some countries at some times (McKinnon, 1964), increasing savings as such is not a very useful growth policy anyway. In these circumstances, if the rich are spenders (especially on imported goods), the needed changes in the pattern of final demand may again point toward redistributive tax policy (Bird, 1970).

Some of these relationship can be usefully illustrated in a simple 'three-gap' growth model, as follows (Ize, 1989). The first element in such a model is the growth equation already given:

$$\dot{y} = vi \tag{8.2a}$$

In addition, the resource balance requirement set out in equation (8.3) above can be reformulated as

$$i = S_h + S_f \tag{8.5}$$

where S_h is domestic savings (both public ($S_g = T - G$) and private (S_p), and S_f is foreign savings ($M - X$), which in turn depends on the current account balance (CA), itself a function of investment (i) and the real exchange rate (e).

$$S_f = CA(e, i) \tag{8.6}$$

In the real world, some of the key variables in this model are generally constrained in various ways. S_h, for instance, is constrained on the one hand by minimal consumption requirements which limit private saving (S_p) and on the other by fiscal rigidities limiting government saving (S_g), such as the difficulty of raising taxes (T) or reducing expenditures (G). S_f, on the other hand, is constrained by the limited supply of international capital inflows to any particular country, while the real exchange rate, e, is constrained by social and institutional factors which limit real wage changes and hence domestic relative prices. Moreover, i may be constrained by private reluctance to invest in the uncertain and risky economic and political environment characterising many developing countries.

Since this model has three equations and five unknowns, it has as many solutions as there are combinations of these constrained variables, taken two at a time. For example, if both domestic and foreign saving are constrained, then

$$g_0 = v[\overline{S}_h + \overline{S}_f] \tag{8.7}$$

This is the case of savings-constrained growth, which was implicitly assumed in the earlier discussion of the 'classical' model. If S_f and the real exchange rate are constrained, then

$$g_0 = vCA^{-1}(\overline{S}_f, \overline{e}) \tag{8.8}$$

where CA^{-1} is the inverse of the current account. This is the case of foreign-savings constrained growth (McKinnon, 1964). Finally, if i and any other variable are constrained, then

$$g_i = \bar{v}\bar{i} \tag{8.9}$$

This is the case of investment-constrained growth.

Which model dominates depends on which constraint is binding. For example, in the savings gap model, it is assumed the private sector will readily invest all available resources, and the balance of payments will permit the import of all needed capital goods. In the exchange gap model, on the other hand, even if savings increases it cannot be used for investment because there is inadequate foreign exchange to permit such imports. This formulation is obviously very limited, with no monetary sector, no way for real interest rates to affect either ICOR or the propensity to save, and so on. Nonetheless, it does serve to show clearly that the traditional 'classical' role of budgetary policy in growth set out above is only one of a number of possibilities and, in particular, that even a strictly growth-oriented policy does not necessarily mandate neglect of distributive policy.

The connection between income distribution and economic growth in any country is thus a factual matter. Surprisingly little is known about the relevant facts, but on the whole there seems to be little case in most countries for pursuing actively inegalitarian policies in the name of economic growth. Indeed, while the role of redistributive progressive taxation is undoubtedly limited, there is good reason to be concerned about the extent to which government budgetary policies adversely and unnecessarily affect the poor in many developing countries (Bird and Horton, 1989).

8.3 STABILISATION

The characteristic of the tax system most relevant to the objective of price level and balance of payments stability is its 'elasticity' with respect to changes in the level of income, that is, the extent to which tax yields rise when money national income rises. The more elastic the tax system, the less the need to rely on (often inflationary) deficit financing to maintain and expand the level of public sector activity in a growing economy.

Whether an elastic tax system is desirable or not is less clear, however. As noted above, in some cases it may be argued that properly structured taxes and expenditures may help loosen both the immediate and the long-term import constraint on growth, for example, by fostering export-oriented growth. Moreover, additional taxes will in any case generally be needed to transfer resources to the public sector (or through the public sector to private investment). Most analysis along these lines implicitly assumes, however, both that government expenditure is 'useful' and that the structure of government expenditure is determined independently of the structure of the tax system. Those who question either of these assumptions may be less enamoured of the results of a highly elastic tax system.

Governments are obviously constrained in what they can do when revenues do not accrue automatically as a result of economic growth and inflation but must instead be obtained painfully and openly. Making the cost of expanded government activity more visible may constitute an important means of making governments more responsive to the real needs and desires of citizens, as the 'public choice' literature suggests (Mueller, 1989). But the result may also be to restrain unduly the growth of the public sector, particularly when taxes are less elastic than current expenditure and are collected with a lag, as is frequently true in developing countries suffering from inflation (Tanzi, 1977). The desirable level of tax elasticity in a particular country thus depends not only on economic considerations but also on basic questions of political philosophy and practice. Nonetheless, it is usually essential for taxes to be at least as responsive as expenditures to changes in real income and price levels if recourse to inflationary deficit finance is to be minimised.

8.4 ADMINISTRATIVE FEASIBILITY

As Musgrave (1969) pointed out, the taxes collected by developing countries largely reflect the administrative feasibility of grasping particular 'tax handles' such as trade or natural resources. A safe general statement about most developing countries is that the administrative aspect of budgetary policy is overwhelmingly important. Similarly, tax reform proposals should not, for example, depend upon such inevitably tenuous matters as assumed tax incidence (DeWulf, 1975) or an assumed relationship between such unknown magnitudes as the elasticity of factor substitution and the elasticity of labour supply (Gandhi *et al.*, 1987). When the success of a tax policy is sensitive to variations in such largely unknown facts, the policy is not a good bet. A strategy of not putting all one's water in one probably leaky bucket seems advisable in most countries.

In particular, as mentioned earlier with respect to tax incentives, policies which depend for their success on administrative 'fine-tuning' are almost inevitably doomed to failure in the circumstances of most developing countries, or at least to such perversion in the process of implementation as to produce quite different results than those intended. The best tax policies are thus those that offer little latitude for usually undertrained, underpaid, and under-motivated officials further down the line to mess them up (Bird, 1989a). On the other hand, there are clearly many distortions and much fragmentation in the economies of most developing countries. The tax system, like all other policy instruments, will inevitably be used to some extent to deal with these problems. In view of the administrative constraint, however, any necessary interventionist component of budgetary policy should be as general in nature as possible and should not depend on the discretionary decisions of officials.

Moreover, since the problems requiring correction may well have arisen in the first place as a result of other government policies (overvalued exchange rate, inappropriate credit policy, etc.) the indicated direction for budgetary policy may not always be intuitively obvious. Examples are the common (and usually correct) advice to levy compensating domestic excise taxes on goods taxed by high luxury import taxes (Gillis and McLure, 1971) or, more controversially, to tax capital goods in order to increase utilisation and reduce the rate of unnecessary investment in excess capacity (Due, 1988). Such corrective policies may indeed be useful in particular cases. On the whole, however, as emphasised earlier, it would seem best for developing countries to be cautious and careful in such fiscal intervention, in order to avoid creating still more unforeseen distortions in the economy leading to still more interventionism and still greater strain on administrative capacity.

In general, budgetary policies must therefore be designed so that they will work with a poor administration. Reform proposals that simply presume, implicitly or explicitly, that administration will be improved are dangerously naive. Such proposals have too often been seized upon as a sort of panacea to enable governments to solve this or that problem *without* tackling the hard task of introducing the sort of technically competent, honest and dedicated administration that such proposals usually assume already exists, or can readily be brought into being. Those proposing tax reforms must therefore understand thoroughly the existing administration and assess realistically the possibility of rapid improvement. Unfortunately, all too many reform proposals in developing countries would complicate, not simplify, the work of an already overloaded administration and hence are generally likely to fail. Even competent honest and dedicated tax officials in most countries – and it is amazing how many of them there are, even in the most corrupt countries – can seldom do their jobs properly, for lack of adequate political support on the one hand and the minimal resources needed on the other.

The solution to this problem is simply to try to design a tax reform that 'works', that is, produces better results than the present system with an administration of the calibre of that which now exists, and is likely to continue to persist in most developing countries (Bird, 1989a). Complex proposals such as Kaldor's (1965) interlocking income, expenditure and wealth taxes or his tax on the presumptive income of agricultural land should as a rule be shunned. Such schemes have not worked, and they will not work, in the conditions of most developing countries. Too often tax designers have let themselves be led astray by the futile search for the perfect fiscal instrument, not realising that the perfect is often the enemy of the good, in the sense of a roughly acceptable tax system – that is, one that can be administered roughly and still produce acceptable results.

In the income tax field, for example, the key to success is invariably a good withholding system supplemented by some sort of legally based presumptive assessment method on the hard-to-tax groups (Bird, 1983). Both of these approaches work best if rates are not too high or steeply progressive. In the sales tax field, for some countries the best that can be done is a physically controlled excise system of varying dimensions – most revenues come from alcohol, tobacco, and fuel in any case – though some use of the value-added principle is both feasible and desirable within limits in many countries, largely to reduce cascading (Cnossen, 1977). Small, open countries with little domestic production and relatively low tariffs on most items may achieve much the same results by levying a uniform tariff on imports, while exercising due care to avoid fostering inefficient industrial development (Bird, 1989b). As for wealth taxes, simple flat-rate taxes on urban and rural property are likely the best that can be achieved in all but the most advanced developing countries (Bird, 1974).

The 'brave new world' of tax reform sketched in the previous paragraph may not sound either very brave or very new but it is the world in which most developing countries live. Since those who would change the world must first understand it, starting from this realistic basis would appear to offer a better prospect of attaining a genuinely fair, generally efficient, tax system than the finest academic dream of perfection.

8.5 CONCLUSION

The task of the public finance analyst in a developing market economy is more complicated than in either an industrialised market economy or a traditional centrally planned economy. In addition to all the tasks customarily assigned to taxes in industrial countries, the tax system in developing countries must generally take on some of the plan-implementation functions of taxes in centrally planned countries. When this more complex task is imposed on the inevitably less developed administrative machinery and lesser knowledge of critical empirical parameters in the developing countries, it should occasion no surprise that actual performance so often falls far sort of what might be considered ideal in an unconstrained world.

Moreover, how people feel about taxes at least to some extent reflects how they feel about expenditure. Governments which enjoy widespread popular support and which most people think are doing a good job are more able to depend on a certain degree of public acceptance of the need for taxation than are governments in countries in which the popular belief is that nothing good comes from the capital city. When people are antagonistic to government, when they feel that it is wasting their money and not acting in their best interest, taxes are clearly likely to be even more unpopular than usual.

This argument should not be misunderstood. It does not, for instance, rest on the view that a good tax system is one in which there is a high degree of 'voluntary compliance'. Voluntary compliance in this sense is a myth. Even if every individual citizen fully supports all government actions and willingly accepts a resulting high tax level in principle, it will still be in his or her individual interest to reduce his share of the total tax burden, and he or she must be expected to take every reasonable measure to do so. Any effective direct tax system rests primarily upon taking money away from people before it gets into their hands and scaring them into paying the balance, and not on their goodwill. The boundaries of what is considered 'reasonable' in terms of tax evasion in any society are very elastic, however, and how far they are stretched will depend at least in part upon how the government is perceived by its citizens.

A telling demonstration of this point may be found in the well-known study by Peacock and Wiseman (1967) of the growth of public expenditure in the United Kingdom. A central argument in this study is that the pattern of expenditure growth reflects changes in what they call the 'tolerable' level of taxation. At any one time, the argument goes, there is an accepted level of taxation in any country which governs, within limits, the level of sustainable government expenditure. Only when this tolerable level of taxes is increased – as commonly happens in wartime, for example – can there be a corresponding increase in expenditure. After the war (or other emergency) passes, although the immediate need for expenditures is clearly lessened, people are now accustomed to a higher level of taxation, and politicians and officials seldom have difficulty in finding sufficient good things on which to spend to prevent taxes from falling back to their pre-war level. The level of expenditure will thus, as a result of the 'displacement' of taxes that occurred during the war, remain permanently higher than it would otherwise have been.

Studies for a number of other countries have shown a similar linkage between tax and expenditure levels, to a greater or lesser degree. Countries in which the role of the public sector in development is taken seriously have amply demonstrated their ability to

raise taxation, and hence expenditure, to what were once considered wartime levels (World Bank, 1988). Consider, for example,
the case of Nicaragua, in which a 'state-minded' government
raised the level of taxation from 10 per cent to 40 per cent of (a
declining) GNP is only six years, or India, where taxes have
increased from 7 per cent to 17 per cent of GNP in the course of
the last twenty years.

Budgetary *increase*, whether in India, Nicaragua or anywhere
else, however, is not necessarily budgetary *reform*, in the sense of
a change in the structure of the budget that improves both its
distributive and allocative effects. On the contrary, the evidence is
overwhelming that in almost every developing country in which
taxes have increased significantly, the bulk of the increased revenues has come not from the direct taxes on income, expenditure
and wealth customarily stressed by tax reformers, but rather
from a variety of indirect taxes on consumption (Tanzi, 1987a) –
taxes which have equally conventionally been condemned as
regressive and (in the forms they have generally taken in developing countries) inefficient. In Nicaragua and India, for
example, virtually the entire increase in tax revenues is attribut-
able to such indirect taxes. This preponderance of indirect taxation offers yet more evidence of the administrative constraint on
budgetary policy stressed above.

The initial call for increased taxes by many analysts in the early
postwar period (e.g. Lewis, 1966) rested on the belief that, as
assumed in the sample models sketched earlier, such increased
taxation was needed to generate the increase in savings needed to
finance the investment that was in turn needed to produce the
desired rate of economic growth. Calculations like those in equation (8.4) of the so-called 'required' rate of taxation were at one
time almost mandatory in developing countries and are still by no
means uncommon. Nevertheless, even the first link in this chain of
reasoning is highly questionable – a fact first pointed out in a
prescient article by Stanley Please (1967). As Please noted, as a
rule the observed increases in tax revenues in developing countries
have been matched, or more than matched, by increases in current
expenditures, with the result that there has been no corresponding
increase in public sector saving. Empirical studies of this so-called
'Please effect', like those of the displacement effect mentioned
earlier, are by no means conclusive. Nevertheless, there is enough

evidence in enough countries to cast substantial doubt on the validity of the traditional chain of reasoning that development requires additional saving, and that increased taxation is the best way to secure the needed additional saving.

Indeed, quite apart from the 'two-gap' (foreign exchange constraint) and 'three gap' (investment constraint) variants of this model sketched above, this argument has been called into question on two distinct grounds – the 'supply-side' concern with the disincentive effect of taxes on private saving (a concern dating back at least to Bauer and Yamey, 1957), and the Please concern that increased taxes will be eaten up by increased expenditure (often in the form of a higher public sector wage bill) and hence yield no increase in public savings. Of course if *both* of these bad things happened, as some suggest has occurred at times in some countries (e.g. Jamaica in the 1970s), the result of increasing taxes might be a net *decline* in savings, and hence perhaps a fall in the rate of economic growth. The Kaldor–Lewis vision of a world in which increased taxes fuel increased development is thus completely reversed in the Bauer–Please world, in which the opposite occurs.

Such an outcome is bad enough. But matters will clearly be much worse if the expenditure financed by the increased taxes is itself so structured as to do little good in developmental terms. The evidence in some countries that the structure of much government expenditure is at best misguided and at worst almost a complete waste from the point of view of development, is stronger than the evidence underlying the attack on taxation as a means of generating public saving. Almost every developing country could use substantial expenditure reform to accompany, support, and perhaps even to some extent replace tax 'reform', in so far as the latter means, as it often does, tax increases.

Political scientists sometimes define the two principal functions of government as delivering services and managing conflict. Traditionally, economists have considered only the first of these objectives. Those who study public expenditure cannot similarly close their eyes to reality, however. Even the best-intentioned government can live up to its good intentions only if it is in power, and it can stay in power only if it can muster sufficient support. Some may support it because they agree with its intentions; others because they dislike its opponents even more. The evidence in all countries, however, is that some critically needed support comes from those groups to whom, so to speak, government delivers the goods, often in terms of public expenditures favouring their interests – whether it be food subsidies to urban workers, irrigation projects in a particular region, new military equipment, or the subsidisation of inefficient but employment-generating public enterprises. Moreover, just as in the case of tax policy, expenditure policy does not implement itself: it is implemented by a public bureaucracy which expects, and generally receives, its own substantial share of the public sector pie.

There is, it must be emphasised, nothing evil about this process. In the real world, unlike Utopia, things get done by rewarding those whose support and cooperation is needed to ensure that they get done. The result of this natural process, however, is that it is excessively naive to expect that an extra dollar of tax revenue will necessarily provide an extra dollar of either public saving or benefit to whatever group or groups are the supposed target of public sector policy at any particular time. Either a substantial fraction of the dollar will go to other, perhaps also worthy (but undoubtedly powerful), groups, or well over a dollar in taxes will be needed to deliver the promised dollar's worth of services to the target group. Increased taxes leading to increased spending on education – or whatever – may indeed provide more education in the end, although even this is far from certain in many countries: what is not subject to question, however, is that the result will certainly be to provide more, and better-paid, jobs for teachers and those who staff the educational bureaucracy. Subsequent pleas for still more taxes to finance still more education may understandably be received with scepticism by those once burned.

The point is simply that at the present time it is probably more important in most developing countries to spend wisely than it is to tax more (Bird, 1984). Just as the need to invest huge sums in new sources of energy may be reduced by much cheaper measures to curtail energy-inefficient activities, so the need for new taxes can be reduced by measures to curtail inefficient expenditure activities. Citizens in most countries seem to think that there are many such activities. They are right, even if they are seldom able to articulate clearly exactly where they think the money is wanted, and even if they always seem to be convinced that any expenditures directly benefiting them are fully justified.

The existing structure of expenditure (like that of taxation) is, in a sense, the necessary result of the economic and political structure of a country. Drastic changes in expenditure (or tax) patterns cannot be expected in the absence of similarly drastic changes in these underlying factors or exogenous events which alter the relevant costs at the margin of spending (or taxing) in one way or another (Hettich and Winer, 1988). It may therefore seem to be hopelessly quixotic to call for a serious attempt to reform public expenditures in developing countries in such a way as to get more developmental impact for each tax dollar.

Such a conclusion is too pessimistic, however. Reforms in budgetary processes, in expenditure analysis, management, control and appraisal systems are neither glamorous nor easy to accomplish. But experience in a number of countries shows that some things can be done along those lines and that such changes can have some beneficial influence, at least at the margin (Premchand, 1983). Such changes may, over time, lead to less need for more taxes to accomplish desired policy ends. If the result is to induce a little more faith that something useful will result, as well as greater accountability to citizens over how the money is spent then there is likely to be less resistance to increases when they are necessary.

9 The Distribution and Redistribution of Income

PETER J. LAMBERT

9.1 INTRODUCTION

The 1970s and 1980s brought renewed interest, both theoretic and empirical, in matters of income distribution and redistribution. How may we evaluate trends in income distribution through time, and differences between countries? Is the income tax 'a good thing'? What constitutes an improvement in an income tax?

Questions like these are of popular concern, and in the last twenty years economists have developed a structure within which answers can be given. Yet the bulk of what has become known, though now familiar to social policy analysts and researchers in welfare economics and public finance, passes by the student audience almost entirely. A growing body of distributional analysis, beginning with the celebrated Atkinson theorem of 1970, has set the framework and language for questions of distribution and redistribution. This material is not inherently inaccessible. Because the focus is on measurement, it only takes a little mathematics and a little economics to appreciate what has been achieved.

In this chapter we describe the methodology that has been established for the comparison of alternative income distributions in terms of well-being. The distributions in question can be from a given country at two different times; from two different countries and times; from one country and at one time, but before and after application of an income tax; or after application of two alternative income taxes. A single set of techniques covers all possibilities. The field of potential applications is rich and politically relevant.

Atkinson's 1970 theorem provided the first means to make such distributional comparisons, linking Lorenz curve configuration with social welfare. The impact of Atkinson's theorem was such that the structure, and agenda, for subsequent research effort was largely determined. As things now stand, two basic analytical constructions, one being the aforementioned Lorenz curve, and the other a variant of it called the generalised Lorenz curve, introduced by Shorrocks in 1983, comprise the economist's toolbag. The Atkinson and Shorrocks theorems have become standard among researchers, but they have not yet percolated into the student textbooks. We aim to remedy this shortcoming here, with a minimum of analytical fanfare.[1]

9.2 PRELIMINARIES

Before embarking on a description of how to evaluate differences in income distribution, there are three prior questions to be settled. First, what is it that we wish to measure as income? Should it be the flow of money to each family, or to each adult, leaving out children, or to each household, however many adults, or to each individual, attributing a share of parental income to children? This is the question of the *income unit*. Second, there is the problem of the *time unit*. Should we measure the flow of income per week, or per year – or indeed, per lifetime? Then there is the problem of the *income concept*. We may focus only on earnings and self-employment income; or broaden the scope to include unearned income, or transfer payments; or seek also to allow for imputed items such as the value a household can be reckoned to derive from the ownership of its own home and from the existence of public-sector activities like education and defence. Much real-world debate on income distribution and tax and benefit policy is about these essential preliminaries themselves – about what should be the appropriate income unit, time period and definition of income. But we bypass these matters here, simply assuming, in order to progress, that they can be resolved.

Summary income distribution tabulations, in which numbers of incomes and their values are classified by income ranges, are published by government statisticians in most countries. In contrast to this highly aggregated level of presentation, of what is known as *grouped data*, it has become feasible in recent years and in the many developed countries to store income distribution *micro data* on mainframe computers, and to make subsets of this data available to the researcher for use on personal computers. Increasingly, distributional issues will be addressed by confronting micro data with powerful computers and sophisticated software. This development we bypass too, since our purpose is to describe methodology at a theoretical and conceptual level.

The dimensions of income distribution that spring most readily to mind are total and spread. How big is the cake and how is it divided? Abstracting from the issue of population size, we may ask, what is average income and how unequally are incomes distributed around this average? This is a descriptive or statistical question, but it is inextricably linked with prescriptive or normative ones. How good or bad is this or that distribution of income? Is the presence of inequality a bad thing? Is one distribution of income in some sense better than another?

9.3   THE LORENZ CURVE

We may measure the inequality in an income distribution in terms of the shares of total income accruing to various groups of income recipients. For example: how much of the cake do the poorest 20 per cent get? How much do the richest 10 per cent get?[2] We may go on to look at the situation after tax of these same income units, to see how taxation affects inequality. A graph known as the Lorenz curve summarises all of the quantile share information contained in an income distribution.

We first order the income units by magnitude of income, starting with the lowest; and then plot, against cumulative proportion of the population so ordered (running from 0 to 1 along the horizontal axis), the cumulative proportion of total income received by these income units. The resultant curve will look something like that in Figure 9.1. So long as inequality is present, every 'top quantile' group receives more than its (population) share of total income, and every quantile group that begins with the lowest income receives less than its share. The curve thus lies below the 45°-line.

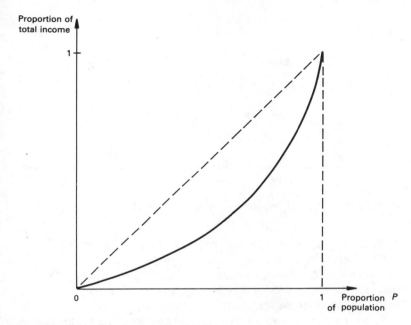

FIGURE 9.1 Typical Lorenz curve

The inequality in two different income distributions can be compared visually by looking at plots of both Lorenz curves on the same graph. The dotted lines in Figure 9.1 delimit the boundaries for such curves. If all incomes were equal, the Lorenz curve would run along the 45°-line: the bottom quantile would be any quantile, and the share in total income equal to the share in the population. We call the 45°-line the *line of perfect equality*. If, at the other extreme, one person held all income, the rest having next-to-nothing, the Lorenz curve would run along the horizontal axis, and then vertically, as also shown.

Figure 9.2, (i) and (ii), shows two hypothetical Lorenz curve configurations. The distributions *A* and *B* might be for different countries, or for the same country at two different times – or, for that matter, for the same country and time period, but for two different populations and/or income concepts. (*A* could be teachers and *B* semi-skilled workers; *A* could be for earned income and *B* include unearned income; etc.) In case (i), we would describe distribution *B* as being 'more unequal' than distribution

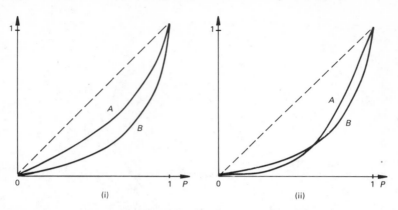

FIGURE 9.2   Two hypothetical Lorenz curve configurations

A. In case (ii), we would say that A has 'more inequality at the bottom, and less at the top' than does B.[3]

Figure 9.2(i) illustrates a situation of Lorenz dominance. We say that A Lorenz dominates B. The bottom $100p$ per cent of income recipients in distribution A have a greater share in total income than do the corresponding group in distribution B, and this is true for every p between 0 and 1. Intuitively, one may feel approval for the way the cake is distributed in A relative to the way this is done in B, and hold perfect equality in mind as the 'ideal' way to divide a cake. But Lorenz curves say nothing about the sizes of the respective cakes, and so cannot tell us which distribution of income is superior in terms of well-being. Non-income characteristics are also suppressed by Lorenz curves. Because of differences in people's needs, equal purchasing power of all income units is unlikely to be secured along the 45°-line. If populations A and B differ, different unequal distributions may represent the appropriate 'ideals' in the respective cases.[4]

When comparing real-world income distributions, it is often found that Lorenz curves across. For example, Kakwani (1984) found Lorenz crossings in more than 30 per cent of 2556 possible pairwise comparisons of income distribution between 72 countries. The most prevalent case he found was of a single Lorenz crossing.

When we wish to distinguish the Lorenz curves associated with two income distributions A and B, in what follows, we shall write them $L_A(p)$ and $L_B(p)$, where p is rank by income (running from

$p=0$ to $p=1$), or simply as L_A and L_B. Distribution A *Lorenz dominates* distribution B if:

$$L_A(p) \geq L_B(p) \text{ for all } p \in [0, 1], \text{ and } L_A \neq L_B$$

The Lorenz curves of two distributions A and B are identical if and only if one distribution is a scaled-up version of the other. In the case that A and B are income distributions before and after application of an income tax, we shall denote the relevant (pre-tax and post-tax) Lorenz curves as L_X and L_{X-T}.

9.4 COMPARING INCOME DISTRIBUTIONS IN TERMS OF WELL-BEING

The Lorenz curve shows how the cake is divided, but it does not reveal the size of the cake or the number of mouths. What, then, can be deduced, in terms of well-being, about the respective distributions when two Lorenz curves do not intersect? Are we entitled to say that the dominating distribution is better in some precise sense? What can be said about well-being when Lorenz curves cross?

Other information is needed in addition to Lorenz curve configuration to enable a convincing story about relative well-being to be told. As we shall see in what follows, the additional information of mean incomes, and sometimes also variances of income, can be used to extract considerable normative significance from the information contained in a given pair of Lorenz curves.

The much-celebrated theorem of Atkinson (1970) was the first to give terms under which a Lorenz curve inequality comparison has normative significance. Before we can state it, we need an assumption. It is that the social welfare in an income distribution will be measured as average utility according to a strictly concave utility-of-income function:

Assumption 1

Social welfare in an income distribution $\{x_1, x_2, \ldots, x_N\}$ will be measured as:

$$W = [1/N] \sum U(x_i)$$

where $U'(x) > 0$ and $U''(x) < 0$ for all $x \geqslant 0$.

This is a large assumption, and it is not enough simply to introduce it so baldly. But let us first state Atkinson's theorem, and then proceed to a discussion. It will be convenient in all that follows to write as W_1 the class of social welfare functions described in Assumption 1, and write $W \in W_1$ for one such social welfare function. (The '1' is because other classes are coming later.)

Theorem 1 (Atkinson)

Let A and B be two income distributions with equal means, $\mu_A = \mu_B$. Then:

$$L_A(p) \geqslant L_B(p) \text{ for all } p \in [0, 1] \Leftrightarrow W_A \geqslant W_B$$
$$\text{for all } W \in W_1$$

This result provides a clearcut recommendation for the Lorenz-dominating income distribution, if we take social welfare to be average utility. The most equal division of any cake of a given size is welfare superior according to the view that social welfare be equated with average utility, and this is so for every strictly concave utility-of-income function $U(x)$.

There are a number of quite distinct rationales for evaluating the welfare in an income distribution as average utility-of-income, and concavity of $U(x)$ has a different interpretation in each case.

One approach to specifying the social welfare in an income distribution is to define it over the personal utilities of the participants. A social welfare function constructed according to this criterion is called individualistic. The general aim is to allow the income recipients to be the best judges of their own well-being when making social judgements.

A very simple story is as follows. Suppose that each individual in society has the same tastes – in that, given an income of x, each individual would choose to spend it in the same way as all others, and would derive the same pleasure from consuming the goods so purchased. Let this 'pleasure' be measurable on a numerical scale, and call it $U(x)$. Now aggregate it across all individuals to measure welfare. In this context, strict concavity of $U(x)$ means diminishing marginal utility of income, a familiar economists' proposition. The poor man can make better use of an extra £1 than the rich man, on everybody's common pleasure scale. Since it is total (or average) pleasure which matters, greater equality in income distribution is favoured.

The assumption of identical tastes for all individuals is, of course, too unrealistic to provide a convincing interpretation of Atkinson's theorem. For international comparisons of income distribution, there is the added problem that people do not, in general, have the same consumption opportunities in different countries. At best, this simple approach to specifying individualistic social welfare lends normative support to Atkinson's result of a hypothetical kind: the Lorenz-dominating income distribution would generate more pleasure if populated by the same kind of (identical) individuals, able to buy the same kind of goods, as in the dominated distribution.

In contrast to this very simple depiction, sophisticated arguments from social choice theory can be brought to bear, which also support the construction of an individualistic social welfare function as in Assumption 1. According to this rationale, concavity of $U(x)$ is, simply, a restriction ensuring inequality aversion.[5]

A different approach entirely is to seek a criterion for ranking income distributions that is, unlike the individualistic one, free from the effects of people's self-interest. Which of two alternative distributions of income A and B would you prefer, if, hypothetically, each pertained to the same society, and you were going to be dropped into that society by parachute to assume the role of the first person you came across? As Harsanyi (1953) has argued, when first propounding this 'veil of ignorance' thought-experiment, such an approach to choice of income distribution 'would show the required impersonality to the highest degree' (p. 434).

Under the rules of this game, the relative frequency with which any given income level occurs in an income distribution is the probability of assuming an income of that magnitude. Inequality of income gets represented as risk: you may find yourself occupying either extreme of the distribution, or a central position, and must

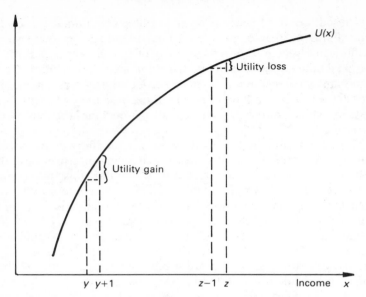

FIGURE 9.3   Social decision-maker's imposed utility of income function: transfer from z to y

weigh up the prospect for each distribution under consideration. Under certain assumptions,[6] you will, if risk-averse, seek to maximise the expected value of a concave utility function $U(x)$ defined over possible outcomes x.

Another approach to social choice, which is formally equivalent to the veil-of-ignorance construct, is through the social decision-maker. If a socially concerned and personally disinterested individual were to make a choice between income distributions, how would he proceed? Suppose that he imposes on each distribution his own (social decision-maker's) utility-of-income function $U(x)$. This will not necessarily be the same function as that of some other social decision-maker. But if each such observer uses a strictly concave utility, they will all favour the Lorenz-dominating distribution in any choice where mean incomes are equal and Lorenz curves do not intersect. Strict concavity of an imposed decision-maker's utility function connotes *transfer approval*. See Figure 9.3: if and only if $U(x)$ is everywhere strictly concave, will the deemed loss in utility from taking £1 from any particular income recipient he more-than-compensated by the gain from giving it to somebody else further down the distribution.

What does the Atkinson theorem have to say about cases where there is Lorenz dominance between two income distributions, but mean incomes differ? We may illustrate this possibility with two real-world examples.[7]

Case I In 1970, national income (GDP) per capita in the Philippines was about twice that in India (both expressed in US dollar terms), but India had a higher Lorenz curve.

Case II The UK Lorenz curve for 1967 lay inside the Tunisian one for 1970. In 1970 terms, UK real GDP per capita in 1967 was $4\frac{1}{2}$ times Tunisian real GDP per capita in 1970.

Since Lorenz curves are unaffected by scaling incomes up or down, we may scale down by one-half the incomes in the Philippine distribution, and scale up by four-and-one-half times the Tunisian incomes, to create new comparisons for which mean incomes are now equal and the Lorenz comparisons are unchanged. Having done this, we can apply Atkinson's theorem:

Case I The distribution of Indian incomes is welfare superior to the distribution of ($\frac{1}{2}$ of Philippine incomes). This does *not* amount to a recommendation for the Indian over the Philippine distribution, but it does bring some normative insight to statistical fact; and,

Case II The distribution of UK income is welfare-superior to the distribution of ($4\frac{1}{2}$ times Tunisian incomes). Now obviously the distribution of $4\frac{1}{2}$ times Tunisian incomes is preferred to the distribution of (1 times) Tunisian incomes! (This is true for any increasing utility-of-income function, and not just the strictly concave ones in Assumption 1.) The recommendation for UK 1967 over Tunisia 1970 is clear.

In Case I, the size of the cake and the way it is divided are in conflict. The Philippine cake is bigger – twice as big – but the Indian one is more equally divided. We cannot readily see which cake is preferable. But in Case II, the bigger (UK) cake also has the more equal slices. Atkinson extended his theorem to cover cases like this:

Corollary 1 (Atkinson)

Let A and B be two income distributions. If $\mu_A > \mu_B$ and $L_A(p) \geqslant L_B(p)$ for all $p \in [0, 1]$, then $W_A \geqslant W_B$ for all $W \in W_1$.

A major generalisation of Atkinson's theorem was provided by Shorrocks (1983).[8] To describe this, we must first define the generalised Lorenz curve for an income distribution A, as:

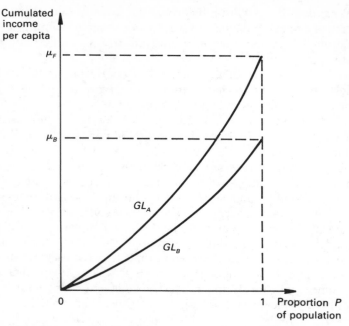

FIGURE 9.4   **Generalised Lorenz curves (showing dominance)**

$$GL_A(p) = \mu_A \cdot L_A(p)$$

Computing generalised Lorenz values amounts to cumulating income per capita upwards, from $p = 0$ to $p = 1$. Shorrocks showed that generalised Lorenz dominance is precisely the criterion that is necessary and sufficient for welfare approval in general:

Theorem 2 (Shorrocks)

Let A and B be two income distributions. Then $W_A \geqslant W_B$ for all $W \in W_1 \Leftrightarrow GL_A(p) \geqslant GL_B(p)$ for all $p \in [0, 1]$.

Given two income distributions, we simply compute (mean income) x (ordinary Lorenz curve values), equivalently cumulated income per capita, and plot new curves, to see whether we have a configuration for which a robust welfare distinction is available. See Figure 9.4.

This resolves some, but not all, income distribution comparisons for which Lorenz curves cross; and some comparisons where there is Lorenz dominance, but it is the smaller cake which is the more equally divided. Kakwani (1984) has studied the success rate of generalised Lorenz dominance in resolving cases where the Atkinson theorem and corollary fail. For example, for the India–Philippines example we cited earlier, where:

$$\mu_{Philippines} \simeq 2\mu_{India} \text{ but } L_{Philippines}(p) < L_{India}(p) \text{ for all}$$
$$p \in (0, 1)$$

Kakwani found that:

$$GL_{Philippines}(p) > GL_{India}(p) \text{ for all } p \in [0, 1]$$

so that the Philippine distribution, with the higher mean, can be recommended despite having more inequality. Below we summarise Kakwani's findings for 248 pairwise comparisons between the 1970 distributions of real GDP in US dollar terms of 23 countries:

Comparisons between A and B for which:	Number of cases:
1 $\mu_A \geqslant \mu_B$ and $L_A \geqslant L_B$	116
2 $\mu_A > \mu_B$, $L_A \leqslant L_B$ but $GL_A \geqslant GL_B$	46
3 L_A and L_B cross but GL_A and GL_B do not	46
4 GL_A and GL_B cross	40

The Shorrocks theorem resolves all cases of types 2 and 3; the Atkinson theorem and corollary deal only with cases of type 1. As an example of the sort of international comparison which can now be established, consider the following chain, derived from Kakwani's classification, where the numbered arrow $\rightarrow$ connotes in each case a welfare improvement of the relevant type:

$$\text{Malawi} \xrightarrow{3} \text{India} \xrightarrow{1} \text{Pakistan} \xrightarrow{2} \text{Korea} \xrightarrow{2} \text{Costa}$$
$$\text{Rica} \xrightarrow{2} \text{Chile} \xrightarrow{3} \text{Canada} \xrightarrow{1} \text{USA}$$

It is clear from the number of 2's and 3's in this chain that the Shorrocks result has delivered a significant increase in analytical power.

However, many of the most interesting pairwise comparisons in Kakwani's sample turn out to involve generalised Lorenz curve crossings. For example, no pair of countries among the following:

{Australia, Canada, West Germany, New Zealand, USA}

except for Canada $\overset{1}{\rightarrow}$ USA, can be unambiguously ranked in welfare terms, because of generalised Lorenz curve intersections.

The Atkinson and Shorrocks results do not help in cases of type 4, but we can go further by imposing an additional restriction on the utility functions defining the class W_1 of social welfare functions. By narrowing this class, without losing its appeal, we can increase the number of pairwise comparisons of income distribution for which an unambiguous and convincing welfare recommendation can be had.

Strict concavity of $U(x)$ is necessary and sufficient to ensure that every transfer from rich to poor increases welfare. We saw this in Figure 9.3. 'Whereas a mild egalitarian will certainly appreciate a small transfer from a rich person to a poorer one,' says Kolm (1976) of this condition, '. . . he may go one step further and value more such a transfer between persons with a given income difference if these incomes are lower than if they are higher. Thus, he would prefer to transfer £1 from a person who earns £500 a month to one who earns only £100, than to transfer £1 from a £900 earner to a person who already earns £500' (p. 87). Our additional restriction is to confine attention to those social welfare functions in W_1 which satisfy Kolm's principle. This is, in fact, equivalent to requiring a positive 3rd derivative of the utility-of-income function[9]:

Definition 1

Denote by W_2 the class of social welfare functions:

$$W = [1/N] \sum U(x_i)$$

for which, in addition to $U'(x) > 0$ and $U''(x) < 0$, also $U'''(x) > 0$ for all $x \geqslant 0$.

Although multiple crossings of ordinary Lorenz curves are theoretically possible, they are, according to Shorrocks and Foster (1987), 'in practice . . . less common than single intersections'

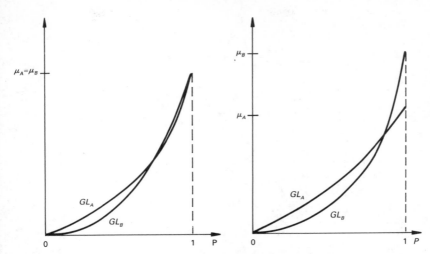

FIGURE 9.5 **Single intersection of generalised Lorenz curves: (i) equal means, (ii) unequal means**

(p. 491). Kakwani (1984) finds that generalised Lorenz curves 'are likely to cross less often than . . . [ordinary] Lorenz curves' (p. 205). If this is so, then the most prevalent scenario, and the one we shall consider next, is that of a single generalised Lorenz curve crossing, as depicted in Figure 9.5, (i) and (ii).

There are two cases to consider: equal means and unequal means. In both cases, as drawn, GL_A is dominant in the neighbourhood of $p = 0$. Mean incomes are determined at the other end of the scale, namely at $p = 1$:

$$\mu_A = GL_A(1) \text{ and } \mu_B = GL_B(1)$$

Hence we have $\mu_A < \mu_B$ in case (ii). The social welfare results for these two generalised Lorenz configurations, (i) and (ii), are as follows, where we have denoted by σ_A^2 the variance of income in distribution A, and similarly for B:

Theorem 3 (Dardanoni and Lambert)

Suppose that the generalised Lorenz curve for distribution A crosses that for B once, from above.

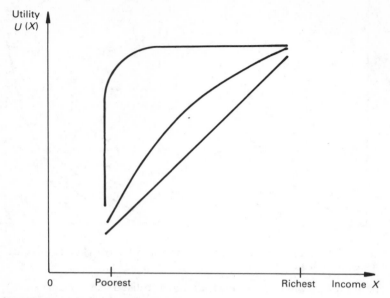

FIGURE 9.6   Degrees of concavity

(i) If $\mu_A = \mu_B$, then $W_A \geqslant W_B$ for all $W \in W_2 \Leftrightarrow \sigma_A^2 \leqslant \sigma_B^2$.

(ii) If $\mu_A < \mu_B$, and $\sigma_A^2 < \sigma_B^2 - (\mu_B - \mu_A)(2z - \mu_A - \mu_B)$, where z is the highest income in either distribution, then $W_A \geqslant W_B$ for all but the least inequality-averse social welfare functions $W \in W_2$

Some remarks are in order. First, note that due to its dominance in the neighbourhood of $p = 0$ in both cases, A is the income distribution in which the poorest are better-off (remember, generalised Lorenz curves cumulate incomes from the lowest upwards). This is why the recommendations are (of inequality-averse utilities) for A, and not for B.

In the equal mean case, all that is needed for unanimous welfare approval by W_2 is a lower variance in addition to the poorest being better-off. In the unequal mean case, we need a lower variance still, and the recommendation excludes the least inequality-averse of the social welfare functions in W_2. Why is this?

Inequality aversion can be thought of as *concavity* of the utility-of-income function $U(x)$. Look at Figure 9.6. This shows two extremes of concavity. At one extreme, the utility function has become so arched that it forms virtually a right-angle. The only income transfer which is valued by this utility is a transfer to the poorest income unit, no matter from whom. In any choice among income distributions, concern focuses entirely on the poorest income unit(s): that cake is preferred whose smallest slice is larger, regardless of all other considerations. At the other extreme, we have the case where $U(x)$ has lost its concavity entirely, and is linear in income. Now rich-to-poor income transfers involve zero gain in utility. For this limiting attitude to inequality, a bigger cake is always preferred, regardless of how it is sliced.

Precisely in the unequal-mean case in Figure 9.5(ii), the preference of the most inequality-averse utilities is opposed to that of the least inequality-averse utilities in W_2. The one is determined by dominance of generalised Lorenz curves in the neighbourhood of $p = 0$ (this tells in which cake the smallest slice is larger); and the other, at $p = 1$ (this tells which cake is bigger). So, for part (ii) of Theorem 3, we have necessarily to restrict the spectrum of attitudes to inequality, excluding the least inequality-averse utilities, to secure a unanimous preference recommendation for A. In fact, the more the variance of A falls below that of B, the smaller the set of utilities that need to be excluded from W_2, and the correspondingly stronger is the welfare recommendation for A.[10]

Cases where generalised Lorenz curves cross more than once are probably uncommon in practice. But in an interesting construction, Davies and Hoy (1987) have shown how to deal with such cases. Simply, we compare variances for appropriate subpopulations, defined by the points of intersection of the generalised Lorenz curves, and piece together the normative implications rather like the pieces of a jigsaw puzzle. The key observation is that, if intersections take place at $p=p_{i-7}$ and $p=p_i$, then cumulated income per capita is the same under A as under B for both the poorest $100p_{i-7}$ per cent and the poorest $100p_i$ per cent of income units: it is therefore the same for the sub-population in between. So for such a population (for whom the generalised Lorenz curves are just the relevant portions of GL_A and GL_B 'writ large') the comparison is an equal-mean one.

Theorem 4 (Davies and Hoy)

(a) If GL_A crosses GL_B an even number of times, first from above, and if under A variance is less for each sub-population but the last, than it is under B, then A is preferred to B for all $W \in W_2$;

(b) If GL_A crosses GL_B an odd number of times, first from above, and if under A variance is less for each sub-population but the last, the strength of the recommendation for A, by all but the least inequality-averse social welfare functions in W_2, depends on the mean–variance relationship in the last sub-population.

Thus far, we have ignored non-income information about income units, if available, in measuring social welfare simply as average utility-of-income. Non-income information may be hard to come by. For example, when making international comparisons, the raw material may consist solely of incomes and their frequencies. On the other hand, we may have additional information, but deliberately seek welfare prescriptions that are free from it, regarding utility-of-income as the appropriate ethical construct for the purposes at hand. But if non-income information is judged relevant, and can be taken into account, then new questions can be addressed. For example, can we find conditions under which transferring income from single-person income units to families with children, or to those with special needs such as old age or infirmity, is welfare-improving?

One way forward in such cases is to use the available non-income information to 'equivalise' incomes. An equivalence scale is a device to convert the incomes of different income unit types to a common base measuring income-unit purchasing power. Each income-unit's income is divided by the conversion coefficient relevant to its circumstances. For example, the differing needs and expenses of pensioner households can be recognised by attributing them a higher coefficient than younger but otherwise comparable households. The 'equivalised' incomes of the component sub-distributions by income-unit type are then pooled, to form an overall distribution of equivalent income. There are conceptual and practical problems with equivalence scales,[11] but, setting these aside, we may perfectly well regard all of the results that have gone before as applying to distributions of equivalent income.

But there is another way forward, which enables analysis to be carried out in money income terms, while still retaining the essential elements of the average utility-of-income approach. This is particularly convenient for income taxes, because they are denominated in money income terms. The approach is due to Atkinson and Bourguignon (1987). It gives rise to an important new dominance criterion, that of sequential generalised Lorenz dominance. We describe here what is involved.

First, the available non-income information is used to subdivide the population into groups $i = 1, 2, \ldots, n$ with different levels of need. The idea is that, for each given x, some income units possessing an income of x are more deserving of additional resources than others, by virtue of their composition, age, handicap or whatever. For example, Atkinson and Bourguignon cite as an example, with $n = 5$, the following classification:

$i = 1$: families with three or more children
$i = 2$: families with two children
$i = 3$: families with one child
$i = 4$: couples
$i = 5$: single persons

of income units which, we might agree, rank from the neediest $(i = 1)$ downwards.

These differences in need are recognised by the social decision-maker. He attributes a different utility-of-income function $U^i(x)$ to income units in each group. Each $U^i(x)$ is increasing and concave: the decision-maker is inequality-averse when focusing on income distribution within any group. As between groups, his attitude to the hierarchy of needs is reflected in systematic differences between the utility-of-income functions $U^i(x)$, $1 \leq i \leq n$:

Assumption 2

For each $i = 1, 2, \ldots, n-1$, $dU^i/dx - dU^{i+1}/dx$ is positive and decreasing in x.

This says two things. First, the social marginal valuation of income dU^i/dx at each income level falls as i rises. This means that among all the income units possessing any particular level of income, the social evaluator regards those income units in the group $i = 1$ as the 'most needy' – in that they are the most deserving of any additional unit of resource – and he ranks the categories in descending order in this respect. Second, the marginal utility differential reflecting the acknowledged difference in need decreases with income. This means that less social concern is shown for differences in needs at higher income levels than at lower ones.

The social welfare function evaluates average utility-of-income across the whole population. It therefore takes the form:

$$W_A = \sum p_i W_{Ai}$$

where p_i is the proportion of income units belonging to group i (assumed positive), A_i is the distribution of needs group i incomes, and W_{Ai} is average utility-of-income within needs group i as measured by $U^i(x)$; hence $W_{Ai} \in W_1$. Let us denote by W_3 the class of social welfare functions having this form.

Theorem 5 (Atkinson and Bourguignon)

$W_A \geqslant W_B$ for all $W \in W_3$ if and only if there is generalised Lorenz dominance under A for the sub-populations consisting of the j most needy groups, for each $j = 1, \ldots, n$.

This is Atkinson and Bourguignon's sequential generalised Lorenz dominance criterion. The procedure to follow is, take first the most deserving group, then add the next-most deserving group, and so on, until all groups are included, checking at each stage for generalised Lorenz dominance of A over B. If this obtains, A can be recommended.

Sequential generalised Lorenz dominance demands conventional generalised Lorenz dominance, of GL_A over GL_B, and a lot more. In particular, a necessary condition on mean incomes is as follows:

$$\sum_{i=1}^{j} p_i [\mu_A^i - \mu_B^i] \geqslant 0 \text{ for each } j$$

(just evaluate all curves at $p = 1$). Clearly, this condition does not preclude changes in distribution being recommended which involve the transfer of income from the less needy to the more needy, but transfers in the other direction cannot be supported.

With this recent development, we conclude our description of the methodology that is currently available for making welfare comparisons between income distributions. Next we turn to the effects on income distribution of income taxation, and of changes in income taxation. Is a welfare recommendation available for the typical income tax, and what kind of income tax reforms will be welfare-improving?

9.5   REDISTRIBUTION

We begin by considering the properties of a progressive income tax. An income tax is progressive if the higher is an income unit's income, the greater the fraction of its income that gets taken in tax. It is intuitively believable that, in this case, income shares in the smaller post-tax cake will be more equally distributed than in the larger pre-tax cake. The formal result, that post-tax incomes are distributed more equally than pre-tax incomes:

$$L_{x-T}(p) \geq L_x(p) \text{ for all } p \in [0, 1]$$

when the tax is progressive, was first demonstrated by Fellman (1976) and Jakobsson (1976), and independently by Kakwani (1977). See Figure 9.7.

Theorem 6 (Fellman/Jakobsson/Kakwani)

Let $t(x)$ be the income tax liability of an income unit with income x. Suppose that $x-t(x)$ and $t(x)/x$ are both increasing with income x. Then for every pre-tax income distribution, $L_{x-T}(p) \geq L_x(p)$ for all $p \in [0, 1]$.[12]

Let us put aside for the moment discussion of real-world income taxes, to consider the implications of this result. A progressive tax is inequality-reducing; but in what sense is this 'a good thing'? Positive taxation *per se*, progressive or not, can only reduce social welfare – since it reduces people's incomes, over which social welfare is defined. Clearly we must look to the other side of the coin, which is the way benefits from government activity are conferred on income units,[13] to find a welfare rationale for income

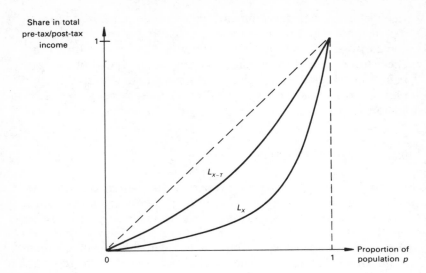

FIGURE 9.7　**The inequality-reducing effect of a progressive income tax**

taxation. But progression in the income tax schedule is 'a good thing' compared with another obvious way to raise the same revenue from the same pre-tax income distribution:

Theorem 7

For every social welfare function in W_1, progressive income taxation reduces social welfare by less than would equal-yield proportional taxation applied to the same pre-tax income distribution.

The reasoning is that (i) the Lorenz curve for post-tax income under a proportional tax coincides with the Lorenz curve for pre-tax income; hence (ii) there is a Lorenz dominance relationship between the actual post-tax distribution and this hypothetical one; (iii) the equal-yield requirement ensures cakes of the same size are being compared; and (iv) Atkinson's theorem applies to this comparison:

$$L_{X-T}(p) \geqslant L_X(p) \equiv L_{X[1-t]}(p) \text{ for all } p \in [0, 1] \Rightarrow W_{X-T}$$
$$\geqslant W_{X[1-t]} \text{ for all } W \in W_1.$$

where t is the average rate of the tax.

We speak of a progressive income tax as being 'redistributive'. What is meant by this? Transferring income from rich to poor is an act of redistribution, in anyone's language – but how can we talk of an income tax, which only takes away from people without necessarily returning the proceeds to others, as redistributive? The answer is that we are implicitly making a comparison, not between the progressive tax and no tax at all, but rather between the inequality-reducing tax and the distributionally neutral tax with the same yield.[14] Relative to this hypothetical alternative, the progressive tax does indeed redistribute, from high to low incomes, and the Lorenz curve is shifted inwards as a result.

Now we must turn to the matter of real-world income taxes. Do they satisfy the preconditions of the Fellman/Jakobsson/Kakwani theorem? Certainly, you and I will each experience an increase in average tax rate when our incomes increase (provided we are both taxpayers). But income tax is typically levied differently on different people, according to circumstance (for example, single and married people may be taxed differently, and special allowances given for old age, mortgage, number of children, and so on). If you and I are in different circumstances, there may not be an increase in average tax rate as between your (lower) pre-tax income and my (higher) one. Indeed, I may no longer be better-off than you after tax (if I was before).

In the real world, the income tax liability of an income unit depends not only upon that unit's income, but also crucially upon its composition. Thus it cannot be said that, *as between different income unit types*, the average tax rate on gross income increases with income level. Progression is only a meaningful feature for such an income tax *as restricted to income units all of the same type*. When the typical income tax is so restricted, tax liability is indeed a function of income x alone, and satisfies the postulates of the Fellman/Jakobsson/Kakwani theorem.

Thus the Fellman/Jakobsson/Kakwani theorem has to be confined to a population of income units treated homogeneously for tax purposes, to be valid. The same is true of Theorem 7, which followed it, and will also be the case when we discuss tax reforms in a moment. In particular, this analysis stops well short of explaining why (or indeed, whether) a typical income tax, separately progressive on each of the different income unit types, is welfare-superior to a single, flat-rate equal yield tax. Interfering in dis-

distribution may, or may not, be capable of justification in these (social welfare) terms. Since differences in tax treatment arise largely from perceived differences in need, the real challenge here is, rather, to justify separately progressive income taxes using the Atkinson and Bourguignon framework of analysis, i.e. for the class W_3 rather than for W_1.[15]

9.6   INCOME TAX REFORM

A wider question is, given our income taxes, can the periodic reforms to which they are subjected be justified in social welfare terms?

Tax reforms designed to benefit some but at a cost to others occur whenever government seeks to pursue a redistributive policy: for example one of poverty alleviation; or of redress of perceived disincentives for entrepreneurs; or of easing the tax burden for middle-income groups.

Let us confine our attention to an income unit type enjoying homogeneous tax treatment, so that tax liability is a function of income alone. If the old and new income tax schedules cross, they do so at break-even levels of income separating gainers from losers. In the simplest case, of a single crossing, reform involves redistribution from one end to the other of the post-tax income distribution. In the case of a double crossing of tax schedules, the reform involves either redistribution from the middle to both ends of the post-tax income distribution, or vice-versa. See Figure 9.8, (i) and (ii).

These are politically relevant cases to consider. If protection of the poorest in tax reform is a perennial political imperative, redressing disincentives for the entrepreneurs, at the top end of the income distribution, became so in the political climate of the 1980s. If middle-income recipients are the losers from this dual process, as in Figure 9.8 (ii), can the reform be supported in social welfare terms?

Simplification of a highly graduated marginal rate structure can work to the benefit of both ends of the income distribution, as Minarik (1982) has pointed out in respect of a proposal to replace the US individual income tax by a flat rate tax with increased low income relief: 'with tax cuts for the top and bottom, it is the middle

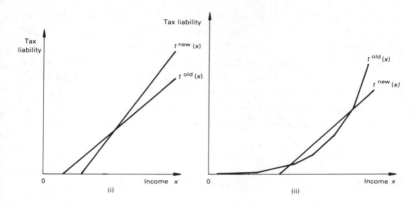

FIGURE 9.8 **Single and double crossing income tax reforms: old and new schedules**

that is left holding the bag' (p. 238). A change in the balance of taxation between different component taxes can, too (e.g. from the personal income tax in the UK to the National Insurance Contribution on earned income). The argument here could be one of 'earmarking' taxes to their ultimate purposes or, a less worthy suggestion, that some forms of tax are less conspicuous than others, and the change of balance might feel like a tax-cut to voters.

Reform can as well work in the opposite direction. Suppose that income taxes are to be cut for middle-income recipients, perhaps in fulfilment of a political commitment. Tax-cuts for middle-income units can be very expensive (since these incomes are very numerous), and if undertaken may subsequently have to be re-couped by adjustment to other forms of tax. It is quite conceivable that middle-income units will pay *only a part* of the subsequently regained revenue (for example, this would be so if consumption taxes were to be put up). In that case, middle-income units still gain ultimately, though not by as much as first thought, and at the expense of the two ends of the income distribution.

To determine whether such income tax forms can be recommended, we may apply the generalised Lorenz curve methodology. For a single-crossing reform which benefits the bottom end of the income distribution at the expense of the top, and for a double-crossing reform which benefits both ends at the expense of the middle, the effect of the reform on the generalised Lorenz curve for post-tax income is very easy to determine. In all but one case, that of a yield-reducing double crossing reform, to which we will return, there is at most one crossing of old and new generalised Lorenz curves. Furthermore the new generalised Lorenz curve begins (in the neighbourhood of $p = 0$) above the old one. The welfare results which follow from this happy situation are these:

Theorem 8 (Dardanoni and Lambert)

If a single crossing reform which cuts the tax liabilities of low incomes is:

(a1) yield-neutral or yield-reducing, it is favoured by all $W \in W_1$;
(a2) yield-increasing, it is favoured by all but the least inequality-averse social welfare functions in W_2 provided that it sufficiently reduces the variance of post-tax income.

If a double crossing tax reform which cuts the liabilities of low and high incomes is:

(b1) yield-neutral, it is favoured by all $W \in W_2$ provided that it reduces the variance of post-tax income;
(b2) yield-increasing, it is favoured by all but the least inequality-averse social welfare functions in W_2 provided that it sufficiently reduces the variance of post-tax income.

The single-crossing result in (a1) is the easiest to understand. In the yield-neutral case, the reform amounts to a series of rich-to-poor income transfers. In the yield-reducing case, there are in addition other net additions to low incomes. All inequality-averse social welfare functions favour rich-to-poor income transfers, and of course all favour net additions to incomes too; hence the results. In case (a2), of a yield increase, there is a net loss of post-tax income, from upper-income units. No social welfare function approves such income reductions *per se*. The increased tax 'take' can be made palatable, however – but not to the least inequality-averse, who will never approve of any reduction in total (or mean) disposable income. The way to secure welfare approval is to couple the increased 'take' from the richest with additional transfers from them to the poorest – and at the same time to reduce sufficiently[16] the variance in post-tax income.

In the yield-neutral double-crossing case (b1), we can gain some understanding of the result as follows. Transfers to the less well-off are approved by every inequality-averse social welfare function; transfers to the better-off, by none. The criterion expressing the balance required for the approval of the restricted class of social welfare functions is variance-reduction.

A double-crossing tax increase can be recommended if the variance in post-tax income is sufficiently reduced. This is (b2). The conditions for welfare approval of a double-crossing reform benefiting both ends of the distribution and involving a yield decrease, not dealt with in these theorems, are in fact less stringent. The effect may be to cause a double crossing of generalised Lorenz curves, but the reform can be seen as providing net additions to upper and lower incomes in addition to transfers from the middle. A mean-variance condition is again decisive.

What do these results imply for the particular reforms discussed earlier? First, yield-neutral tax simplification, or change of balance, which benefits the richest and poorest income units of any given type is welfare-improving if variance-reducing. Second, any move to reduce income tax for middle-income recipients and recover the lost revenue from increased consumption taxes, levied across a wider income spectrum, would be disapproved if the end result was increased variance in people's disposable incomes.[17] Lastly, such an income tax cut for middle incomes only partly recovered from broader-based taxation would be disapproved by all but the least inequality-averse of social welfare functions if variance were not sufficiently controlled.

Finally, let us not overlook the fact that many of the politically most sensitive tax reforms involve redistribution between income unit types treated differently by the tax. Can a reform which transfers post-tax income from single people to married people with children, or to old people, say, be recommended in social welfare terms? To address this sort of question, the Atkinson and Bourguignon differences-in-need approach is required. The next steps will be taken by those able to push the analytics along in this direction.[18]

9.7 CONCLUSION

In this chapter we have described a methodology for making robust social welfare comparisons between income distributions. By applying this methodology to income taxes, we have been able to throw welfare light upon certain politically relevant types of income tax reform. We have also identified some open questions for income taxes and income tax reforms.

There is another, related literature upon which we have not touched, however. This concerns the summary measurement of income inequality and of redistributive effect for income taxes. If an unambiguous social welfare recommendation is not available as between two income distributions or tax schedules, we can always reduce each alternative to a numerical index (of inequality or redistributive effect), appeal to this literature, and make a recommendation. That is another story.[19]

Finally, we must point to a major problem which has gone unrecognised in this chapter. It is that the introduction of an income tax, or tax reform, alters the terms on which people can trade their leisure for income, and so may affect the pre-tax distribution of income (which, in these pages, we have held constant to evaluate the effect of the tax or reform). The possibilities for deeper analysis in this respect are considerable.[20]

10 Asymmetry of Information in Public Finance

ROSELLA LEVAGGI[*]

10.1 INTRODUCTION

A large and interesting class of problems in economics involves delegated choices in which one individual or organisation has the responsibility for taking decisions in the interest of one or more others. A usual claim in economics is that an optimum exists because each agent realises that he could not do better for himself than by accepting the prevailing settings and maximising his objective function using those constraints.

Under certain carefully specified conditions the 'invisible hand' will create the necessary conditions for the economic system to be efficient, and the amount of information required for the economic system to work efficiently will be very low – no one needs to know or care about the intentions, constraints or information pertaining to anybody else – and it will ensure that the information is truthful – no one else will have the incentive to pretend that his preferences are different from what they are.

However, this ideal world is hard to find in real life. In the real world some individuals may transact their business in such a way as to create an incentive to misrepresent important aspects of their own characteristics or their actions and in those cases a form of incentive has to be introduced in order to ensure that the more informed party reveals this information truthfully. The essence of the incentive problem which I shall examine here is a kind of master–servant contract, the type of relationship that may exist between a patient and his physician, a firm and its employee, an insurance company and its clients or a central planning board and its satellite agencies. In all these examples one of the two parties is better informed than the other: the patient may not feel well but is unable to translate this feeling into a disease; the firm is not able to know the effort of its employees; and the insurance company is not completely informed about all the personal characteristics of its clients. A wide range of economic problems fits this framework and may cause market failures. Private or government agencies can take steps to protect their interests if markets do not work and can formulate incentive schemes to circumvent these problems.

Designing a good system of incentives is a problem that has been recognised for a long time. In principle such a system ought to encourage the parties to truthfully reveal their private information. In this chapter I will first briefly present the asymmetry of information problem and the different situations that can arise in this context, and I will then explain by using some public finance problems how it is possible to create a system by which the most informed party does not cheat. The last part of this chapter will then explain a particular and new application of the asymmetry of information framework to the relationship between central and local government.

10.2   ASYMMETRY OF INFORMATION

The common feature which links together all the asymmetry of information models is the presence of a master–servant[1] relationship in which the roles of the two parties have to be clearly specified. The master has a specific objective he wants to achieve using the effort of a servant and has the power to devise the rules of the game. An objective function to be maximised is the usual representation of the master's problem. The master, however, has to choose between a bounded set of optimising rules, i.e. he cannot choose any rule he likes. There are two basic reasons why the set of rules is bounded:

(a) he does not have all the information that would give him a completely free hand;

(b) the servant is not a slave – that is, his cooperation must be obtained voluntarily. This constraint is usually defined as the participation constraint.

TABLE 10.1   Asymmetry of information or master–servant problems

Definition	Moral hazard; or
Private or hidden information; or adverse selection; or screening	unseen action; or Principal and agent
Key distinction	
Agent is *passive*	Agent is *active*
Examples	
Public goods	Share cropping
Central–local government	Employees producing output
Firm choosing employees	

In economic terms this means that the servant has his own objective function whose arguments can differ from the master's objective function. The servant is also allowed to have some freedom of action. Essentially he may choose whether or not to take up the deal on the terms offered by the master: in most models this element is represented by a minimum reservation utility level that must be granted to the servant in any event. This participation constraint limits the set of enforceable rules that the master may choose to lay down and in some extreme cases is itself the cause for the presence of 'market failures'.

Starting from the seminal paper by Ross (1973), numerous models have been developed to deal with the problem of incomplete information but a definite taxonomy of the different problems has not yet been developed. Almost every author uses his own terminology to define similar problems. In order to make the exposition easier I have recorded in Table 10.1 a classification of the asymmetry of information models based on the definitions of Cowell (1986), Rasmusen (1989) and Rees (1985 a and b).[2] As we can note from the table, the key distinction is represented by the role played by the agent: if he has just to report information on personal characteristics he will be 'passive', while if he has to perform an action he will be labelled 'active'.

The two main classes will now be examined in turn by using real-world public finance examples. Let us then start with the unseen action models.

Unseen action – principal and agent theory

Unseen action (or principal and agent) models reflect situations in which some action taken by the servant cannot be directly observed: what can be observed is the outcome, which is determined in part by the unseen action and in part by random events independent of the action taken by the servant. The master is facing a true moral hazard problem. The failure to induce the 'optimal' effort level by the servant derives solely from his limited ability to monitor the servant's effort.

This theory is intended to apply to any situations with the following structure: one individual called the agent, A, must choose some effort from a given set of efforts, (x). The particular outcome Y which results from his choice depends also on which element α from a given state of the world will prevail at the relevant time, so that uncertainty is intrinsic to the situation. The outcome Y generates utility to a second individual, the principal, denoted by P.

A contract is to be defined such that P makes a payment to A in exchange for his effort. A's utility depends both on this payment and on the value of the action x. It is usually assumed that P has a Von Neumann–Morgenstern utility function depending on the net value of the output, i.e. the output he receives minus the reward he has to offer to the agent. In formal terms we can write his utility as:

$$E[U(Y - S)]$$

with $U' > 0$ and $U'' \leqslant 0$,[3] so that risk-loving behaviour is ruled out. In general, in order to simplify the matter, risk-neutrality is assumed, i.e. $U'' = 0$. The agent is generally postulated to have a Von Neumann-Morgenstern utility function depending both on the reward received and his effort. In general, the agent's utility function can then be written as:

$$U(S, x) = S - f(x)$$

It is important to stress the particular assumption that characterises the utility function for the agent: additivity as well as separability in effort and reward is assumed throughout the analysis. The agent, like the principal, can be either risk-averse or risk-neutral.

Output is produced according to the following production function:

$$Y = g(\alpha, x)$$

P is assumed to know the technology used by A to produce the output in which he is interested but he does not know the realisation of α and hence he cannot observe x.

The lack of observability of x and α means that P has to design a contract such that the agent does not cheat and, in order to provide his participation, will receive a minimum utility in any state of the world. The optimal solution will usually imply that the effort value chosen by the agent is not optimal since he either receives a reward higher than his effort or the most productive combination is never reached. Rasmusen (1989) distinguishes between *moral hazard with hidden information* and *moral hazard with hidden action* according to when the realisation of the random variable occurs. In the first case the servant knows the state of the nature before he signs the contract; in the second type of contract the servant and the master share the same information when they sign the contract, but the servant is able to observe the state of the nature before choosing his effort. I will now illustrate the problem and the solution offered by the literature by using an example that, according to Rasmusen classification, would belong to the 'moral hazard with hidden information' class.

Public enterprise

Public enterprise provides a good example for a simple application of the unseen action – principal and agent models.[4] Let us suppose that the government owns a plant producing an output Y from labour x according to the production function:

$$Y = \alpha x$$

where α is the state of the world, a random variable which, to simplify matters, can take only two possible values, namely α_1 with probability p and α_2 with probability $(1 - p)$. It is also assumed that α_2 is a more favourable state of the world, i.e.:

$$\alpha_2 > \alpha_1 > 1$$

The government hires an agent to produce output and its problem is to fix the output level and the reward it has to give the agent. In this context I will assume the two parties agree to share the output according to γY; where γ is the share of output to be granted to the agent; then $0 \leqslant \gamma \leqslant 1$.

Finally I will assume that the agent has a specific utility function of the form:

$$v = \gamma Y - x^2$$

At the time at which the contract is set up, both parties share the same beliefs about α but the agent will know its realisation before he chooses his effort.

The government knows the technology and wishes to choose two output levels, Y_1 and Y_2 (depending on the realisation of the state of the world) and γ to maximise his expected return.

Let us first assume that the government could observe α or infer it from other firms on the market. In this case the problem could be written as:

$$\text{MAX } (1 - \gamma) \left[p Y_1 + (1 - p) Y_2 \right] \tag{10.1}$$

$$\text{subject to } \gamma Y_i - x^2 \geqslant 0^5 \tag{10.2}$$

The constraint in the problem assures that the agent will receive at least a non-negative utility from his effort and represent the participation constraint.

In this case it is possible to show that it is optimal for the principal to fix $Y_i = \gamma \alpha_i^2$ and $\gamma = \frac{1}{2}$.[6] The optimal solution can be illustrated by using Figure 10.1 in which both the objective function and the constraint are straight lines because they are both linear in Y.

The problem for the principal here is quite simple: he has to maximise his utility, represented by the downward-sloping indifference curves (W), increasing in a north-easterly direction, subject to giving to the agent a minimum utility represented by the shaded area which encloses the set of points for which the two

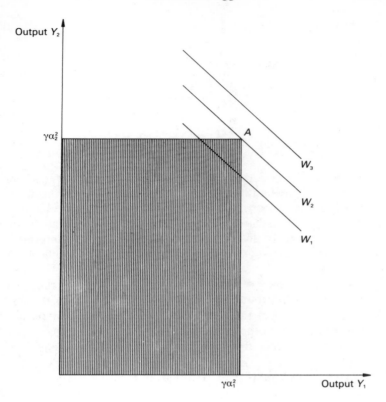

FIGURE 10.1 Perfect information

constraints are satisfied. The optimal solution will then be represented by point A.

Let us now see how the optimal solution changes in the presence of asymmetry of information. I will now assume that the government, although it does know the technology, cannot observe α_i.[7]

In this case a new constraint, the so-called 'incentive compatible constraint', has to be added to the problem and its role is to ensure that the agent will always have the incentive not to cheat, i.e. to reveal truthfully the state of the world which has occurred. The new problem can be written as follows:[8]

$$\text{MAX } (1 - \gamma) \, [pY_1 + (1 - p) \, Y_2] \tag{10.1a}$$

$$\text{subject to } \gamma Y_i - x^2 \geqslant 0 \tag{10.2a}$$

$$\left.\begin{array}{l} \text{subject to } \left[\gamma Y_2 - \left(\dfrac{Y_2}{\alpha_2} \right)^2 \right] \geqslant \left[\gamma Y_1 - \left(\dfrac{Y_1}{\alpha_2} \right)^2 \right] \\[3ex] \text{subject to } \left[\gamma Y_1 - \left(\dfrac{Y_1}{\alpha_1} \right)^2 \right] \geqslant \left[\gamma Y_2 - \left(\dfrac{Y_2}{\alpha_1} \right)^2 \right] \end{array}\right\} \tag{10.3}$$

The first of the equations in (10.3) assures that the agent will be better off by revealing that state α_2 has occurred when this is the case, while the second equation assures that the same happens when state α_1 is realised. Since α_1 is a worse state than α_2 the second constraint is always satisfied: the agent has no interest in reporting α_2 and having to deliver Y_2 if the worse state of the world has occurred!

Assuming for ease of exposition that $p/(1 - p) > 1$ then it is possible to show[9] that the optimal solution is $Y_1 = \alpha_1^2 \gamma$ and $Y_2 = \gamma(\alpha_2^2 - \alpha_1^2)$, i.e. the output target for the most favourable case is lower than in the previous case.

The maximum payoff for the principal in this case is equal to:

$$(1 - \gamma) \, [p\alpha_1^2\gamma + (1 - p)\gamma(\alpha_2^2 - \alpha_1^2)]$$

while in the previous case it was equal to:

$$(1 - \gamma) \, [p\alpha_1^2\gamma + (1 - p)\gamma(\alpha_2^2)]$$

then the principal is worse off.

The optimal solution to this problem can be presented by using Figure 10.2 in which both the objective function and the constraints are straight lines since they are linear functions of Y_1 and Y_2.[10]

The incentive compatible constraints are represented in Figure 10.2 by the downward lines BB' and CC'. The introduction of those constraints reduces the feasible set from $Y_2\alpha_2^2 \, A \, Y_1\alpha_1^2$ to the area $BB'DC$. The point A is now no longer feasible and the new optimal solution will then be represented by point D.

The previous example has shown that it is possible to devise

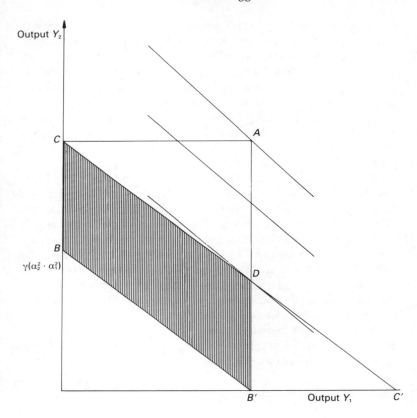

FIGURE 10.2   Hidden information case

systems in which the markets still work efficiently even without
having all the relevant information. I will now turn to examine the
second big category of asymmetry of information models, i.e.
cases in which the 'agent' has private information.

Private or hidden information

Private information models reflect situations in which the servant
knows something that could be kept hidden from the master.

These models are designed for situations in which the relationship between the two parties involves the transmission of some messages. The agent has usually the ability to misrepresent the information he has to pass on to the principal, to his own advantage. According to the role played by the agent, Rasmusen (1989) distinguishes between *adverse selection models*[11] in which the servant possesses some characteristics that he keeps hidden from the principal to his own advantage, and *signalling and screening models* in which the agent has to report his private information to the master.

Even when this private knowledge is announced, it is always possible for the servant to give a misrepresentation to his own advantage as long as he is relatively sure that the master will not be able to discover his cheating. The private information usually depends on the realisation of some random event; however, the servant is usually assumed to observe the realisation of this event either before he sets up the contract with the master or before the contract is enforced. Examples in this class include allocation mechanisms, nonlinear pricing in monopoly markets, auction-design and public goods production.

The problem of incentive compatibility in models dealing with public goods arises precisely because the characteristics of each agent are not known by the planner *a priori*.

An optimal grants-in-aid allocation rule

Another important problem in public finance that can be modelled as a private information model is the allocation formula for grants-in-aid from central government to local governments. Local governments are better informed than central government about their preferences for public goods and this parameter is essential to central government to design an optimal system of grants. The optimal grant formula will be examined in a *dynamic* framework that focuses around the political life-cycle of local authorities.[12]

Central government's objective is to minimise the size of the grant to be given to local authorities subject to a set of carefully specified constraints.[13] The literature on fiscal federalism[14] points out the reasons why central government might be interested in giving grants to local authorities. The explanations usually provided relate to:

—grants designed to encourage sub-central authorities to take account of external effects of their services (*spillover grants*)
—grants designed to correct fiscal imbalances between the various tiers of government (*revenue sharing grants*)
—horizontal equalisation grants.

In my model all those considerations are picked up by the target level of expenditure that central government wants each local authority to reach and that I label Ψ^*. Making local authorities spend at least Ψ^* is the main economic constraint that central government faces in the process of minimising the amount of grant.

Local authorities' behaviour is described by a Cobb Douglas social welfare utility function defined over two goods: y, a composite private commodity, and X which represents local public services. β is a parameter summarising the characteristics of each local authority with respect to its preferences for expenditure. β lies in the closed interval $[\beta_1 \ \beta_2]$ with $\beta_1 > 0$ and $\beta_2 < 1$.

Local authorities maximise their utility function over their political life-cycle, i.e. during the period they are in power,[15] which for most British local authorities is equal to four years.[16] I will also assume that the community welfare is independent of time, i.e. there is no discount rate on utility in different periods of the life-cycle. The utility function for authority i can be written in a very general form as:

$$\sum_{t=1}^{4} [(1 - \beta) \ln y_t^i + \beta \ln X_t^i]$$

which has to be maximised subject to the budget constraint.

In the absence of any grants from central government the budget constraint for each period t could be written as:

$$X_t^i + y_t^i = M_t^i$$

If, for ease of exposition, we assume that (a) resources can be freely transferred through time, and (b) there is no rate of discount on money available at different periods of time, then the budget constraint for the life-cycle of each local authority can be written as:

$$\sum_{t=1}^{4} [X_t^i + y_t^i] = \sum_{t=1}^{4} M_t^i$$

where M_t^i represents the amount of local income available.

In order to simplify the analysis I will assume that M, as well as Ψ^* is constant through time. The problem faced by each local authority can be formalised as follows:

$$\text{MAX} \sum_{t=1}^{4} [(1 - \beta) \ln y_t^i + \beta \ln X_t^i]$$

$$\text{subject to } \sum_{t=1}^{4} [X_t^i + y_t^i] = 4M$$

By using a standard Lagrangean approach it is possible to derive the following set of demand equations:

$$X_{NG, t}^i = \beta M^i$$

$$y_t^i = (1 - \beta)M^i$$

where X_{NG}^i represents the level of expenditure chosen by each local authority in absence of any grant from central government.

I will also assume that $X_{NG, t}^H = \beta_2 M < \Psi^*$ such that even a local authority with the highest possible preference for expenditure would not be able to reach the target level with its own resources. This assumption has been introduced in order to rule out the possiblity of having negative grants. I will start by describing the optimal grant formula in a world with no uncertainty in order to compare the optimal contract with the one that will arise in an asymmetry of information world. The environment in which central government has to operate in the first case[17] can be described as follows:

(i) Central government can observe the amount of local income available in each region, M, and set the amount of local public services to be provided, Ψ^*.

(ii) Before the start of the period central government observes the true preferences over local public services which will be in turn be used to determine the size of the grant for each authority.

(iii) Open-ended matching grants and lump-sum grants are the two instruments available to central government to reach its objective.

(iv) Preferences parameters are peculiar to any authority considered – i.e. it is impossible to infer authority i's preferences by observing the relevant parameter for authority j[18] – and are fixed throughout the lifetime of the authority such that local authorities must be consistent in their cheating.

Given assumption (iv) the model can be designed to cope with the optimal allocation rule for just one authority and it will then be replicated for the entire population by changing the relevant parameters characterising each local authority.[19] In terms of the exposition that follows these assumptions allow us to drop all subscripts i for local authorities.

From assumption (iii) central government can reach its goal by using open-ended matching grants and lump-sum grants. A matching grant is equivalent to a reduction in the price paid for expenditure, while a lump-sum grant is equivalent to an increase in the income available. From consumer theory we know that, provided the substitution effect is not zero, a matching grant, by having both an income and a substitution effect, boosts expenditure to a higher level than does a pure lump-sum grant. It is then optimal for central government to use this instrument in order to achieve its goal. The formal proof of this proposition is given in appendix 2, but a diagram might be sufficient to describe the problem and its solution.

Consider Figure 10.3 in which a local public good, X, is measured on the horizontal axis and a private composite commodity, y, is measured on the vertical one. The diagram is drawn for a generic period t. Since I have assumed for ease of exposition that M is constant through time, the same diagram can be replicated for all the other periods of the life-cycle.

The local authority's budget constraint is represented by the line MM. The before grant optimal allocation is represented by A, the point at which the budget constraint is tangential with the Indifference Curve (IC) I_0. Now suppose central government offers the locality a matching grant in the form of a percent contribution to the unit price. The local authority's budget constraint pivots to $M M_1$. The locality moves to A_1 on indifference curve I_1. Provided price elasticity of demand is positive, demand for local public goods will increase, in this case from X_0 to X_1; the resource cost will amount of Mc, of which $y_1 c$ is financed by central government. If the amount $y_1 c$ had been given as a lump-sum grant the local

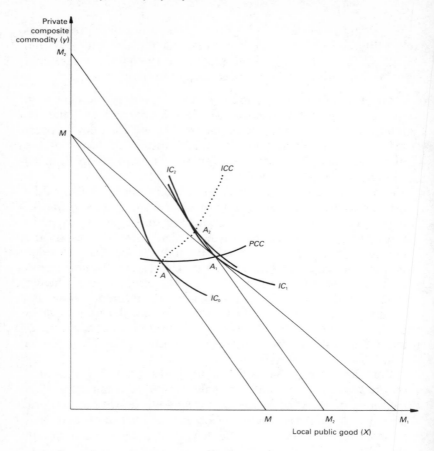

FIGURE 10.3   Income consumption curve problem

authority would have a budget line M_2M_2 and would be able to achieve a more desired position A_2, but its demand for local services would have been less than at A_1 because the matching grant is effectively a price reduction which, as I have explained before, has a substitution as well as an income effect, and this is reflected by the fact that the price consumption curve (PCC) lies to the right of the income consumption curve (ICC) after the initial position.

The ICC problem

Let us now assume that central government does not know the preferences for services provided locally. An asymmetry of information between central and local government arises. Local authorities are better off by cheating. Local authorities know that central government wants them to achieve a provision Ψ^* of local public goods: by reporting a lower β than the true one, they receive a grant which is greater than the amount they would be entitled to had they reported their true preferences. In terms of the environment I described in the previous section, assumption (ii) is replaced by:

(iia) Central government knows that the true β for any local authority lies in the closed interval $[\beta_1, \beta_2]$. Since no other information is available the distribution of β, $f(\beta)$ is assumed to be uniform.[20] Before the start of the period each local authority has to report to central government its preferences over local public services which will in turn be used to determine the size of the grant. The preference parameter declared by local authorities will be labelled β_d to distinguish it from β, the true one.

Ceteris paribus, the grant that each local authority receives depends negatively on β_d, i.e. the more it prefers expenditure, the less grant it needs in order to reach Ψ^*. It is clear that it will have an incentive to report a β_d as low as possible such that it will be entitled to receive a greater grant. The cheating clearly depends both on the possibility of the cheating being observed and on the consequences that it might bring about.

From assumption (iv), it follows that the optimal solution can be restricted to a context characterised by central government and one local authority.[21] Central government can observe local income in each period and it knows Ψ^*, but it has to rely on local government with regard to preferences for local public services. The only information available is that the true preference parameter lies in the closed interval $[\beta_1, \beta_2]$. Before the start of the period central government asks local authorities to report their preferences β_d, and on the basis of the parameter reported it sets the grant for period one. From period one onwards it can infer β_x by observing the expenditure for local public services that each

TABLE 10.2   Two-party game

Period one
(a) Central government asks local authorities their β.
(b) On the basis of the reported β it sets up the matching grant.
(c) Local authorities set up their expenditure.

Period two onwards
Central government infers β from (c) in period t-1 and sets up the new matching grant accordingly.

---

local authority has actually chosen. Since I have assumed that local authorities have Cobb Douglas utility functions, β_x can be obtained by inverting the demand equation, namely:

$$X_t = \beta_x \frac{M}{g_t}, \qquad \beta_x = \frac{X_t g_t}{M}$$

The basic game played by the two parties is presented in Table 10.2.

In the next sections I will show graphically the gain a representative local authority might have in cheating in the first three years of its life-cycle. The analytical proofs are presented in Levaggi (1991).

The local authority after reporting β_d has to be consistent with its cheating and cannot spend more than Ψ^* on local public goods,[22] at least in the first three periods of its life-cycle. However, this surplus can be used both for private consumption and for savings. This procedure can be considered a form of 'creative accounting' behaviour and again links this model to the political-cycle literature.

The gain our representative local authority achieves by cheating can be illustrated using a set of diagrams which compares the indirect utility derived from cheating with that obtained by truthfully revealing its preferences. If it reports its true preference the local authority would be entitled to spend Ψ^* and y^* as illustrated in Figure 10.4.

I will now examine what happens if the local authority cheats. By cheating on the β it reports, our local authority will spend Ψ^* on local public goods, but since it is entitled to a higher grant it will

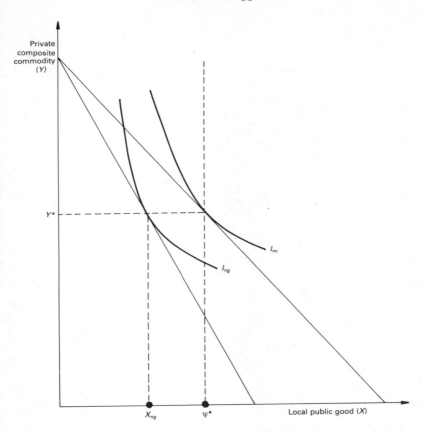

FIGURE 10.4   No cheating case

actually be able to spend more on private goods and to save resources for the last period.

In the first three periods, the local authority cheats on its true preferences and receives a higher amount of grant than it should be entitled to. This situation is illustrated in Figure 10.5.

The local authority receives a grant according to the $PCC\beta_1$ price consumption curve up to point C. If it had reported its preferences truthfully it would have received a grant according to the $PCC\beta_t$ curve and would have located at B. The local authority

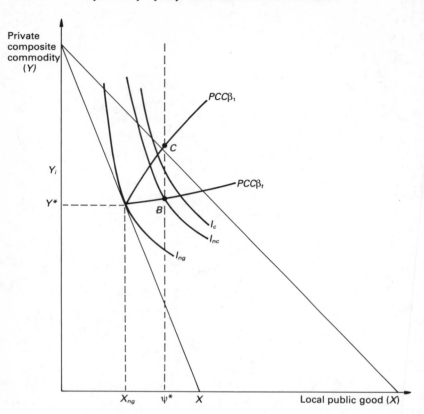

FIGURE 10.5   Cheating case: periods one to three

is clearly better off by cheating since any point north-east of B conveys a greater utility than B. In order to be consistent with its cheating the local authority has, however, to choose a point on the straight line BC. The actual location will depend on the true preferences for local goods of that particular authority.[23] The cheating and spending below point C allows the local authority to save up resources for the last period, as Figure 10.6 shows.

In period four our local authority's budget constraint can be written as:

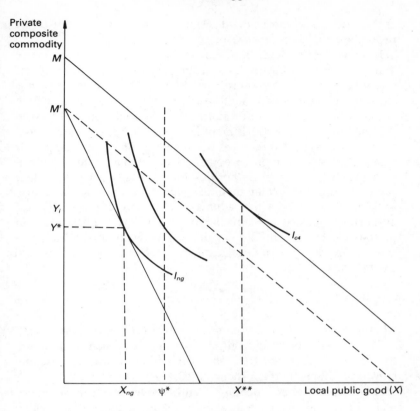

FIGURE 10.6 Cheating case: period four

$$g_4 X_4 + y_4 = M + \sum_{i=1}^{3} (y^* - y_i)$$

where $\Sigma(.)$ represents the savings from previous periods. As a result of its cheating the budget constraint for our local authority in the last period shifts upwards and the price it faces is less than it should have been had it revealed its true preference in the previous periods.

The model presented here considers behaviour of a local government within one four-year political cycle and this is the reason why at the end of period four the decision-making body is better off by revealing its true preferences.

In period four, then, our local authority chooses an optimum point and it uses the savings from previous years to shift its expenditure for public goods from Ψ^* to X^{**}. As a result of this cheating, central government is worse off because the matching grant has to be provided for more units of public goods. To avoid the cheating, central government has to devise a system of incentives such that local authorities will be better off by revealing their true preferences. One of the possible ways in which central government can reward local authorities for truthfully revealling their preferences is by allowing them to spend more than Ψ^*. The form of incentive received will be a function of the preferences that local authorities declare to central government before the start of period one and I will assume that, as a result of the incentive scheme, expenditure on local services is boosted up in each period by the amount:

$$\Psi_t^* \, \theta_t^*, \qquad t = 1, 4$$

where θ_t^* represents the optimal incentive that avoids cheating.

The problem faced by central government is then to minimise the grant to be given to each local authority with the double constraint of having them spend at least Ψ^* in local public services and of stopping them cheating. Central government must choose θ^* in such a way that each local authority is, throughout the whole of its life-cycle, better off by revealing the truth (see Levaggi, 1991, for a formal treatment).

A two-prices system for the grant allocation rule

In the previous system it is possible to show that the loss suffered by central government for its inability to know local government's preferences is equal to:

$$\Psi^*(\theta_t - 1)^{24}$$

I will now slightly modify the system in order to make central government learn the true preference parameter for each local authority by using a lower incentive scheme which reduces the amount central government has to pay to learn β. The new system foresees a set of rules by which local authorities will never be able to spend more than Ψ^{*25} in each period. The implementation I will present requires the introduction of penalties in the form of grant withdrawals for expenditure in excess of the desired level. Each year is characterised by a double price system such that for expenditure up to Ψ^* the matching rate is:

$$(1 - g_t) = \left(1 - \frac{\beta_d{}^* M}{\Psi^*} \right)$$

For expenditure in excess of Ψ^* the matching rate will be:

$$(1 - g_{t, 2})$$

where $g_{t, 2}$ is the price level assuring that any authority, irrespective of its true preferences, will not spend more than Ψ^*. Under the new assumption the budget constraint for the representative local authority has a kink at Ψ^*. This means that in each period the local authority will not be allowed to spend more than this amount on local public goods. Let us, for example, examine what happens in period four. Figure 10.7 is equivalent to Figure 10.6 under the new assumption.

The optimal point C on the IC_{c4} curve is no longer feasible, and the best our local authority can do is to locate at the kink (K) since g_{2t} has been chosen in such a way as to assure that the higher spenders locate at the kinks. Central government has then to offer an incentive to make preferences be truthfully revealed. The new scheme will be labelled $\Psi^* \Omega^*$ and is lower than the previous one. The intuitive reason for this statement is that, since local authorities cannot reach the same high level of indirect utility from their cheating, the incentive to make them reveal their private information can be reduced. It must be noted that the budget has to contain a kink each year, otherwise local authorities might be better off by not accepting the scheme proposed, cheat on their preferences but reveal them before the first period in which the budget presents a kink.

The loss suffered by central government is equal to $\Psi^*(\Omega_t - 1)$,[26] and this represents the 'price' it has to pay for its inability to be fully informed; local authorities are instead better

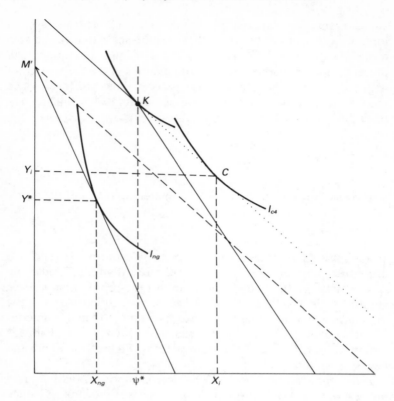

FIGURE 10.7 Two-price system: cheating in period four

off since they are allowed to spend more than Ψ^* and this brings them on to a higher indifference curve.

10.3 CONCLUSIONS

In this chapter I have presented two public finance examples of a class of economic models that is receiving more and more attention from economists. The models I described can be broadly classified in the asymmetry of information framework and reflect situations in which two parties signing a contract have different amounts of information. The party which is better informed always has an incentive to cheat, but under some well-specified circumstances it is possible to have this information truthfully revealed. The asymmetry of information framework seems to be quite useful in the context of public finance and in this chapter I have presented a new way of approaching the grants-in-aid problem. Although local governments are better informed than the central planners about their preferences, it is possible to devise systems by which they report the true parameters. The system is not optimal in a strict Paretian sense since they receive more money than the amount to which they are entitled, and this represents, *per se*, a loss in efficiency, especially in the context of public finance, since central government will have to use some distortionary instrument[27] to finance this 'overspending'.

APPENDIX 10.1

As I showed in the text, the problem faced by the principal in the first case can be written as:

$$\text{MAX}_{(\gamma,\ Y_1,\ Y_2)}\ :\ (1 - \gamma)\Big[pY_1 + (1 - p)\ Y_2\Big] \tag{A10.1}$$

subject to $\gamma Y_i - x^2 \geqslant 0$ (A10.2)

Using the relationship $Y = \alpha x$, x can be written as $x = Y / \alpha$ then (A10.2) can be written as:

$$\text{subject to}\ \left[\gamma Y_2 - \left(\frac{Y_2}{\alpha_2}\right)^2\right] \geqslant 0$$

$$\text{subject to}\ \left[\gamma Y_1 - \left(\frac{Y_1}{\alpha_1}\right)^2\right] \geqslant 0$$

which can be finally written as:

$$\text{subject to}\ \left[\ \gamma\ - \frac{Y_2}{\alpha_1^2}\right] \geqslant 0$$

$$\text{subject to}\ \left[\ \gamma\ - \frac{Y_1}{\alpha_1^2}\right] \geqslant 0$$

This problem can be solved using a standard Lagrange approach to constrained maximisation. The Lagrangian for the problem can be written as:

$$L = (1 - \gamma)\left[pY_1 + (1 - p)Y_2 \right] + \lambda_1\left[\gamma - \frac{Y_1}{\alpha_1^2} \right] + \lambda_2\left[\gamma - \frac{Y_2}{\alpha_2^2} \right]$$

The problem can be solved using the Arrow Entoven method as follows:

$$\frac{\partial L}{\partial Y_1} = (1 - \gamma)p - \lambda(1 / \alpha_1^2) \tag{a}$$

$$\frac{\partial L}{\partial Y_2} = (1 - \gamma)(1 - p) - \lambda_2(1 / \alpha_2^2) \tag{b}$$

$$\frac{\partial L}{\partial \gamma} = -\left[pY_1 + (1 - p)Y_2 \right] + \lambda_1 + \lambda_2 \tag{c}$$

$$\frac{\partial L}{\partial \lambda_1} = \gamma - \frac{Y_1}{\alpha_1^2} \tag{d}$$

$$\frac{\partial L}{\partial \lambda_2} = \gamma - \frac{Y_2}{\alpha_2^2} \tag{e}$$

From (c) we know that either λ_1 or λ_2 cannot be equal to zero, and from (a) and (b) we can derive that both λ should be positive. This means that the constraints are binding as equalities and then it is possible to derive from (d) and (e) that $Y_i = \lambda\alpha_i^2$. Finally, by using equations (a), (b), (c) it is possible to solve for γ and λ. The optimal value of γ will be equal to 1/2. The same result can be obtained by reformulating the problem at this stage as follows:

$$\begin{array}{c} \text{MAX} \\ (\gamma) \end{array} \quad (1 - \gamma)\left[p\alpha_1^2\gamma + (1 - p)\alpha_2^2\gamma \right]$$

If the agent is better informed than the principal the new problem has to be rewritten as follows:

$$\begin{array}{c} \text{MAX} : (1 - \gamma)\left[pY_1 + (1 - p) Y_2 \right] \\ (\gamma, Y_1, Y_2) \end{array} \tag{A10.1a}$$

$$\text{subject to } \left[\gamma - \frac{Y_2}{\alpha_1^2} \right] \geq 0 \tag{A10.1b}$$

$$\text{subject to } \left[\gamma - \frac{Y_1}{\alpha_2^2} \right] \geq 0 \tag{A10.1c}$$

which corresponds to the problem I presented before. The presence of asymmetry of information adds two new constraints to the problem, the so-called incentive compatible constraints:

subject to $\left[\gamma Y_2 - \left(\dfrac{Y_2}{\alpha_2} \right)^2 \right] \geqslant \left[\gamma Y_1 - \left(\dfrac{Y_1}{\alpha_2} \right)^2 \right]$ (A10.3)

subject to $\left[\gamma Y_1 - \left(\dfrac{Y_1}{\alpha_1} \right)^2 \right] \geqslant \left[\gamma Y_2 - \left(\dfrac{Y_2}{\alpha_1} \right)^2 \right]$ (A10.4)

that can be rewritten as:

subject to $\left[\gamma - \dfrac{Y_2 + Y_1}{\alpha_2^2} \right] \geqslant 0$ (A10.3a)

subject to $\left[\gamma - \dfrac{Y_1 + Y_2}{\alpha_1^2} \right] \leqslant 0$ (A10.4a)

If we observe the constraint we realise that, since Y cannot be negative (A10.1c) is always satisfied because (A10.4a) requires a greater γ. Using the same kind of process it is possible to show that (A10.4a) is made redundant by (A102). The problem can be solved using a standard Lagrange approach to constrained maximisation. The Lagrangian for the problem can be written as:

$$L = (1 - \gamma) \left[pY_1 + (1 - p)Y_2 \right] + \lambda_1 \left[\gamma - \frac{Y_1}{\alpha_1^2} \right] + \lambda_2 \left[\gamma - \frac{Y_2 + Y_1}{\alpha_2^2} \right]$$

The problem can be solved using the Arrow Entoven method as follows:

$\dfrac{\partial L}{\partial Y_1} = (1 - \gamma)p - \lambda_1(1 / \alpha_1^2) - \lambda_2(1 / \alpha_2^2)$ (a)

$\dfrac{\partial L}{\partial Y_2} = (1 - \gamma)(1 - p) - \lambda_2(1 / \alpha_2^2)$ (b)

$\dfrac{\partial L}{\partial \gamma} = -\left[pY_1 + (1 - p)Y_2 \right] + \lambda_1 + \lambda_2$ (c)

$\dfrac{\partial L}{\partial \lambda_1} = \gamma - \dfrac{Y_1}{\alpha_1^2}$ (d)

$\dfrac{\partial L}{\partial \lambda_2} = \gamma - \dfrac{Y_2 + Y_1}{\alpha_2^2}$ (e)

The optimal solution is found when both constraints bind, implying the result reported in the text.

APPENDIX 10.2

If no grant is made available for local authorities the demand for local public expenditure of a generic local government would be:

$$X_{NG} = \beta * M.$$

When the grant distribution formula is introduced the budget constraint will be written as:

$$gX + y = M + G_L$$

and the demand equation will be equal to:

$$X_{GR} = \beta \frac{(M + G_L)}{g}.$$

If all the grant is distributed in a lump-sum form, then $(1 - g) = 0$ and the problem faced by central government can be described as follows:

$$\text{MAX} \ (-G_L)$$
$$\text{subject to} \ -(\beta * M + \beta * G_L) \leqslant -\Psi^*$$

and the optimal solution is given by:

$$G_L = \frac{\Psi^* - X}{\beta} = \frac{\Psi^*}{\beta} - M.$$

If central government wants to offer a matching grant, G_L will be set equal to zero and the problem faced by central government will be:

$$\text{MAX} - (1 - g) * \Psi^*$$
$$\text{subject to} \ -\left(-\beta \frac{M}{g} \right) \geqslant \Psi^*.$$

In order to allow local authorities to spend Ψ^* the price they have to face has to be equal to:

$$g = \frac{\beta * M}{\Psi^*}$$

from which it follows that the optimal matching rate is:

$$1 - \frac{\beta * M}{\Psi^*}.$$

The grant in a lump-sum form will be equal to:

$$G_L = \frac{\Psi^*}{\beta} - M$$

and under matching grant will be equal to:

$$G_M = (1 - g) * \Psi^* = \Psi^* - X = \Psi^* - \beta M$$
$$G_M = \beta G_L.$$

Since $\beta < 1$ the matching grant is less than the lump-sum grant.

End Notes

CHAPTER 3

1. See Killingsworth (1983) and Pencavel (1986), for surveys of the extensive literature on labour supply.
2. Throughout, subscripts can generally be interpreted as partial derivatives. Thus, $U_c = \partial U/\partial c$.
3. See Deaton and Muellbauer (1980) for further details of the expenditure function.
4. See Deaton and Muellbauer (1980).
5. There are of course other objections that could be raised about rationality and choice that may have more general applicability and which we do not consider here.
6. See Killingsworth (1983).
7. See Deaton and Muellbauer (1980) ch 5.
8. See Sandmo (1976).
9. See Killingsworth (1983).
10. See Chiaporri (1988) and Brown and Manser (1980).
11. See Apps and Savage (1989).
12. This was at a time when the UK tax system was rather more complex than now, and before pay-as-you-earn was instigated.
13. It is clearly difficult for individuals to know the extent to which they can put into practice hypothetical plans. Nevertheless the Brown *et al.* findings are consistent with the results in Blundell and Walker (1982) and Ham (1986) which allow for the possibility that individuals may be constrained in their decision-making.
14. See, for example, the annual exercise in *Social Trends*.
15. There are age allowances for those over 65, and those over 75. There are also allowances for a housekeeper and for those who depend on assistance from caring relatives.
16. There is provision for married couples to be taxed as single individuals although only a very small percentage of couples would benefit financially from doing so.
17. Lone parents receive an additional personal allowance (APA) whose

254

value is the difference between the MMA and the SA so that lone parents effectively receive the MMA. Similarly widows receive the widow's bereavement allowance which takes their tax allowance up to the MMA for the year of the spouse's death.

18. But only up to a loan size of £30 000. In August 1989 only one such deduction was allowed per property. Prior to this date unmarried couples could claim one such deduction each – i.e. a deduction for a loan up to £60 000.

19. There is a universal child benefit paid at a flat rate per child per week.

20. From April 1990 receipts will be taxable and payments will be tax deductible. Different rules apply to maintenance for wives as opposed to children, and for voluntary payments.

21. See Dilnot and Webb (1989) for further details of the impact of the NI LEL on the distribution of earnings.

22. It is not clear what the incidence of these contributions (or indeed any other taxes and benefits) are, and there has been no systematic research conducted on this important question.

23. The thresholds were changed in April 1986 and both sets are marked in the figure.

24. 31 hours per week (25 for lone parents).

25. For example, earnings up to £9300 for a family with 2 children aged between 11 and 15.

26. FC also provides a passport to a number of other benefits: such as free dental treatment and free medication.

27. 25 per cent plus 9 per cent for NI plus 70 per cent of $(100 - 9 - 25)$ per cent.

28. The proportion of those thought to be entitled, on the basis of their current incomes, who are actually receiving.

29. No official estimates are yet available but Family Income Supplement, the precursor to FC, had a take-up rate of only 62 per cent in 1983/4.

30. 80 per cent as explained above plus 85 per cent of $(100 - 80)$ per cent.

31. 70 per cent plus 85 per cent of $(100 - 70)$ per cent.

32. In April 1990 domestic rates (a tax related to property values) is being replaced by a poll tax known as the Community Charge. There are transitory arrangements made for those on HB (and Income Support).

33. See Dilnot and Kell (1987) for empirical evidence on the wives of unemployed men.

34. The IS system also allows for discretionary payments for unanticipated contingencies in the form of loans to be repaid from future earnings. Expected ability to repay is an element of the decision to make such a payment.

35. The disregard for lone parents is £15. However, since the disregard is against earnings it cannot be used against maintenance payments

from former husbands. Thus and extra £1 of maintenance reduces IS receipt by £1. Not surprisingly the maintenance received by IS recipients is a great deal lower than for non-recipients and the proportion of lone mothers on IS who receive any maintenance is less than 20 per cent.

36. See Pechman (1990) for an international compendium of tax reforms.

37. 23 per cent for both HB rebates plus 50 per cent for FIS and the first £5 was disregarded for HB purposes.

38. Indeed, for lone parents the old tapered disregard, that disregarded half the earnings between £4 and £20, was abolished and replaced by the £15 disregard.

39. These last two jumps were in fact introduced into the NI system in 1985 in the hope of improving incentives to work.

40. £140 post April.

41. For a critique based on the adverse incentive effects of the proposals for married women, see Symons and Walker (1988).

42. See also Brown (1986) for a textbook treatment that contains good coverage of UK evidence.

43. This work is based on an annual budget constraint and is not comparable with the other studies.

44. A result that the compensated labour supply elasticity is negative is inconsistent with the theoretical apparatus, outlined in section 3.2, that economists use to interpret empirical analyses of labour supply. See Blundell *et al.* (1988) for further comment on the problem of such concavity failures for policy analysis.

45. See Killingsworth (1983) and Moffitt (1986) for elementary expositions of the difficulties of dealing with nonlinear budget constraints.

46. Simulation Package for the Analysis of Incentives, written by Symons and Walker (1988).

47. We omit the small category of higher-rate taxpaying women.

48. This chapter has not considered the impact of childcare provision on labour supply. Clearly those countries with extensive childcare provision, such as Denmark and France, have high labour force participation rates, while those that have little provision, such as the UK, have much lower participation rates. However, this does not imply that childcare provision is all-important. It could be that in countries where women wish to work (because of the nature of the tax system, say) the demand for childcare creates a supply which does not appear in countries where women have less of a desire for paid work. That is, childcare provision may be endogenous and, unless it can be shown that the childcare industry is subject to some market failure (that occurs in some countries and not others), there is little case for state intervention.

49. Major changes to arrangements for child support have been announced in *Children Come First*, Cmd 1264, HMSO, 1990.

CHAPTER 4

1. The boundaries between evasion and avoidance may at times be blurred. For an interesting attempt to distinguish between them *for analytical purposes*, see Cowell (1985b). Cowell argues that the essential difference is that avoidance implies certainty on the part of the taxpayer, whereas evasion involves risk.

2. The slope of an indifference curve in Z, W space is clearly given by

$$\frac{dZ}{dW}\bigg|_u = \frac{-(1-p)U^1(W)}{p\ U^1(Z)}$$

    At point A, $W = Z$ and so the slope of the indifference curve is given by $-(1-p)/p$. The slope of the budget constraint is $(t - F)/t$. For an individual to be willing to engage in tax evasion the budget constraint must be flatter than the indifference curve passing through A.

    In other words $\dfrac{t - F}{t} > \dfrac{-(1-p)}{p}$. This reduces to $t > pF$.

3. With a progressive income tax, the budget constraint AB would become concave to the origin. In practice with a series of steps in the tax schedule it would be kinked rather than smooth. Srinivasan also assumes that individuals are risk neutral, so that their indifference curves are linear.

4. For example, Andersen (1977) assumes that the utility function can be written as $U = U_1(Y) + U_2(L)$, where Y is income and L is leisure. Isachsen and Strom (1980) go further and express the utility function as $U = ln\ Y + ln\ L$. This seems to be a well-established tactic for obtaining unambiguous comparative static predictions. See Ehrlich (1973).

5. Clotfelter estimates regression equations for ten different tax groups. He distinguishes between non-business, non-farm business and farm accounts and within each groups segregates by income level.

6. In a 'Yitzhaki' world (see section 4.3(ii)), the entry condition would be

$$1 - F > -\frac{(1-p)}{p}$$

    which reduces to $pF < 1$. For further detail see Fishburn (1979).

7. In addition, the objective of the policy has not been to eliminate evasion entirely, but to reduce it to some socially acceptable level, whatever that might be.

8. Various authors (e.g. Sandmo, 1981, and Skinner and Slemrod, 1985) have argued against equating marginal enforcement costs with marginal tax revenues (MTR) although for different reasons! Skinner and Slemrod argue that the extra revenue is merely a transfer

payment and so its social value is less than the revenue gained i.e. at the optimum $MC < MTR$. Sandmo argues that risk aversion on the part of evaders should lead to $MC > MTR$. See Pyle (1989, pp. 157–9.)

9. Baldry (1984) investigates the option of marginally reducing p and at the same time reducing t. He argues that a policy of full compliance cannot be optimal.

CHAPTER 5

* This work was undertaken whilst the author was a visiting member of the Faculty at Queen's University, Canada. Thanks are due to members of the public finance workshop at Queen's for discussion.

1. For a derivation of the Pareto efficiency conditions for the supply of a public good, see, for example, Brown and Jackson (1990) or Boadway and Wildasin (1984). In addition to the Samuelson condition, which relates to consumption efficiency, Pareto efficiency also requires the achievement of production efficiency.

2. For an introduction to the economics of information, see Varian (1990). Rasmusen (1989) provides a more detailed and highly readable treatment of this literature.

3. Such goods are often analysed within the context of the economic theory of clubs. The seminal work is Buchanan (1965). For a modern treatment of this literature, see Sandler and Tschirhart (1980) and Cornes and Sandler (1986.)

4. It might be noted that nature is more generous than the private sector in that it does provide non-excludable goods. However, without some kind of regulation of the use of these goods (which may simply entail allocating somebody or group the property right), it is unlikely that nature will be able to provide these goods at a Pareto-efficient level.

5. By publicly provided private goods I mean goods which are provided free at the point of use to the consumer but are rival and on technological grounds alone could be excludable. An example is state education. Public provision does not, of course, necessitate public production.

6. In this chapter we are not concerned with the normative aspects of Tiebout's analysis. That is, we do not consider the issue of whether there is an equilibrium in a Tiebout world, and if so, whether it is Pareto efficient. For discussion of these issues, see Stiglitz (1983).

7. From time to time I use the terms 'his' and 'him' when referring to an individual. This is simply due to the fact that there is no gender-free term in the English language for an individual and it is clumsy to write his/her etc.

8. Even if each individual does not free-ride at all (i.e. each individual states his true preference) it is generally argued that public goods will

be under-supplied in the small numbers case. For a discussion of these issues, see Cornes and Sandler (1983).

9. This is a stricter definition of lump-sum taxation than is generally used in the economics literature. More generally a lump-sum tax is defined as a tax which is levied on something which is invariant in quantity – for example, a poll (head) tax is such a lump-sum tax. However, using this more general definition allows the level of the tax to vary with the quantity of the publicly provided good, and hence with state preferences. Such a tax resembles a 'tax price' system which is discussed.

10. For an extensive discussion of these issues, see Mueller (1989).

11. It might be noted that this type of auction would not work if, say, the third highest price was paid by the highest bidder. In this case, bidding their true variation is not the dominant strategy for the two individuals with the highest true valuations.

12. The notion of an externality tax used in this section should not be confused with Pigovian taxes which can be used to correct for externalities.

13. Without this assumption it is possible that the Clarke–Groves mechanism would not be stable. Each individual's preference for the public good would be revised when he discovered how much Clarke–Groves tax he has to pay; this may then lead to a change in the amount of tax to be paid by other individuals, which would lead them to revise this stated preference, etc., etc.

14. Readers interested in a formal proof should consult Laffont (1987 or 1988).

15. Clearly each needs to register a preference of only 101. But being unsure of individual c's valuation they have an incentive to register a large valuation.

16. See, for example, Green and Laffont (1979). If this is so, then like the problem associated with coalition formation, the inefficiency created by the surplus, diminishes as the size of the relevant population increases.

17. For further discussion of these issues, see Inman (1987b) and Laffont (1987).

18. Tiebout bias was first noted by Goldstein and Pauly (1981); an intuitive discussion of it is given in Wildasin (1989). See also Rubinfeld, Shapiro and Roberts (1987).

19. For an analysis of median voter models, see Mueller (1989). The predictive content of median voter models is less clear-cut in multi-dimensional settings.

20. Readers interested in the rationale for the payment of grants are referred to Oates (1972), Topham (1983) or King (1984). Alternatively there are good introductory treatments in texts such as Brown and Jackson (1990) and Boadway and Wildasin (1984).

21. It should be noted that when a local government provides several goods, each of the above types of grant can be either specific or general in form. Specific grants are paid with the objective of aiding

the finance of a particular good; general grants are paid with the aim of aiding the finance of all goods. Since we are assuming that the local government provides just one good there is no distinction to be made between specific and general grants.

22. For an analysis of these issues, see Barnett, Levaggi and Smith (1990, 1991b, 1992).

23. For a discussion of these econometric issues, see Hausman (1985) and Moffitt (1986). For a discussion in the context of the piecewise linear budget constraints faced by British local governments in the 1980s, see Barnett, Levaggi and Smith (1992).

24. This analysis follows Barnett (forthcoming).

25. Wildasin's analysis is similar in nature to that of Stiglitz and Dasgupta (1971) and Atkinson and Stern (1974) referred to in the introduction.

26. See, for example, the discussion in Topham (1983).

27. As we also saw, care must be taken in calculating the equivalent personal income supplements especially where there are matching grants in addition to lump-sum grants.

28. In analyses of a misrepresented budget constraint the argument is usually that local public officials misrepresent the constraint in order to encourage the median voter to demand more locally provided goods. This line of reasoning introduces a supply-side argument into the analysis, which for the time being I want to avoid. The analysis of the flypaper effect presented here follows Barnett (1985). Other key references are Courant, Gramlich and Rubinfeld (1979) and Oates (1979).

29. It should be noted, however, that Barnett, Levaggi and Smith do not use a median voter model, but instead assume that local government expenditure decisions are explained by a local social welfare function.

30. In the literature on the demand for locally provided goods, the survey approach is sometimes referred to as micro-studies, the idea being that the estimation procedure uses a (survey generated) micro data set. Median voter type models, as reviewed in section 5.4, are referred to as macro-studies.

31. In addition to Bergstrom, Rubinfeld and Shapiro (1982), see Rubinfeld and Shapiro (1989).

32. See, for example, Brookshire and Crocker (1981), Brookshire, Thayer, Schulze and d'Arge (1982) and especially Brookshire and Coursey (1987).

33. We might expect some difference due to income effects: the difference between compensating and equivalent variations. But the actual difference in responses seems to be too large to be explained by income effects alone. Also of relevance here is the work of Kahneman and Tversky (1984).

CHAPTER 6

1. Utility maximisation for households and profit maximisation for firms.
2. In 1988, 46 per cent of GDP in the United Kingdom was the result of government activity.
3. See Sen (1977) for a discussion of the limitations of 'rational' behaviour.
4. See Borooah and van der Ploeg (1983) for a relaxation of these assumptions.
5. The false revelation of preferences is a major topic of interest in the literature on voting. See Miller (1987) for a discussion of the issues.

CHAPTER 8

1. In this connection, it should be emphasised, however, that the line between what is called 'consumption' and what is called 'investment' in the national income accounts need not correspond to the developmentally relevant content of these concepts. Shoup (1969), for example, has properly stressed the growth-facilitating virtues of what he calls 'gainful consumption', or increased consumption by poor people which increases their productivity. Equally, every observer of developing countries has his or her favorite story of clearly 'unproductive' investment in presidential palaces, military installations, and so on.
2. Note that there is no evidence, however, that the *marginal* propensity to save of the rich is particularly high.
3. A case in point is Pakistan, once praised for policies like those sketched in the text (e.g. Papanek, 1967), where subsequent political turmoil has underlined the dangers of overtly inegalitarian policies.

CHAPTER 9

1. And in Lambert (1989a), with all the trimmings.
2. For example, Lecaillon *et al.* (1984, pp. 26–7) show top decile shares for 39 countries, all pre-tax, ranging from 56.3 per cent (Kenya 1969, income unit = economically active person) to 28 per cent (Republic of Korea 1970, income unit = household). Of course, the top decile's share of income in any distribution must exceed 10 per cent so long as there is inequality. For the bottom two deciles (20 per cent), the income shares in this study range from a mere 1.9 per cent (South Africa, 1965) to 8.0 per cent (Dahomey 1959, Chad 1958 and Togo 1957) (income unit = individual in all cases).
3. The Lorenz curve does not convey information about absolute income differentials. For example, suppose that two distributions C and D are identical in every respect except that all the incomes in C

are double (or ten, or fifty times . . .) the corresponding ones in D. Then C and D have identical Lorenz curves, but we might not want to judge them as 'equally unequal' if we care about absolute differentials between poor and rich incomes. If concern is over absolute rather than relative income differentials, then the 'absolute Lorenz curve' is the appropriate vehicle. See Moyes (1987).

4. This question was first posed by Garvy (1952). It has most recently been subjected to analysis by Jenkins and O'Higgins (1989).

5. See Lambert (1989a, ch. 4) for more detail on this. In fact, inequality aversion can be ensured of the social evaluation function without the assumption of additive separability and concavity of a common utility-of-own-income function $U(x)$, and Atkinson's theorem can be generalised accordingly. See Dasgupta *et al.* (1973).

6. The von Neumann–Morgenstern Axioms must be satisfied. See Harsanyi (1987) for discussion of the relevance of these axioms in the context of social choice.

7. See Kakwani (1980, p. 204).

8. An independent proof of the Shorrocks (1983) result may be found in Kakwani (1984).

9. See Lambert (1989a, chs 3 and 4) for a proof of this assertion, and for further discussion of Kolm's principle.

10. Full details can be found in Lambert (1989a, chs 3 and 4).

11. Pollak and Wales (1979) and Fisher (1987) discuss the problems involved in deeming two income units 'equally well-off'. Deaton and Muellbauer (1980, ch. 8) describe derivations of equivalence scales.

12. The restriction that post-tax income be an increasing function of pre-tax income ensures that the tax does not induce a re-ranking of income units. Without such an assumption the theorem would be false. Just consider the following very simple example, of an economy with three people:

Income x:	50	100	150
Tax $t(x)$:	35	90	145
Post-tax income $x - t(x)$:	15	10	5

The poorest person before tax becomes the richest after tax, and (as the reader may verify) the tax is progressive. Yet it is not inequality-reducing. Indeed, this tax has no effect whatever on inequality: $L_X \equiv L_X - T$.

13. See Lambert (1989a, ch. 10).

14. A proportional tax is called 'distributionally neutral' here because it preserves *relative* pre-tax income differentials. A progressive tax is *relative*-inequality-reducing. However, somebody for whom absolute inequality is the primitive concept would find a poll tax to be inequality-preserving, and any tax with a positive marginal rate to be inequality-reducing. A recent development, allowing for this and other possible viewpoints when defining income tax progression, was

originated by Pfingsten (1986) and has been fruitfully extended by Besley and Preston (1988).

15. For a first attempt, see Lambert (1989b). The question is not a trivial one, as the following example shows:

Type	Single			Married		
Income	3	4	5	6	7	8
Tax	1	2	3	0	1	2

The tax is progressive, indeed perfectly equalising, on each income unit type. However, as you may check for yourself, overall the Lorenz curve for money income is shifted outwards by this tax; hence it is welfare-inferior to an equal-yield proportional income tax on all income units for the class W_1. *A fortiori*, it could not be welfare-superior when differences in needs are taken into account (i.e. for the class W_3).

16. The degree of variance-reduction that validates such reform is:

$$\text{post-reform variance} < \text{pre-reform variance} - 2\mu^2[t^2 - t^1].$$

$$[\tau - 1 + \tfrac{1}{2}(t^1 - t^2)]$$

where t^1 and $t^2 > t^1$ are the average rates of tax before and after reform, and τ is defined as the ratio of the highest post-tax income before the reform to mean pre-tax income. See Lambert (1989a, ch. 9) for more on this.

17. Since variance reduction is sufficient for a welfare gain, variance increase for the reverse type of reform is sufficient for a welfare loss.

18. A recent example is Atkinson *et al.* (1988), in which the sequential generalised Lorenz dominance criterion is brought to bear on the question: What would be the consequences of replacing the French income tax by a British-style one?

19. Limited social welfare support for such recommendations can sometimes be given (see Lambert, 1989a, ch 5 and 7); but much of the literature on summary inequality measurement takes an axiomatic approach, and this can be seen as incorporating ethical judgements *ab initio*.

20. Preston (1989) has recently made a significant theoretical advance.

CHAPTER 10

* would like to thank Prof. R. R. Barnett, Prof. P. Simmons, and P. C. Smith for their invaluable help.

1. In this first part I shall refer to the model as master–servant relationship to stress the difference between this broader class of models and the principal and agent literature.

2. This classification is clearly very simple; real-world problems sometimes have both aspects together: for example, a bank lending money to a firm may not exactly know the total debt of that firm (private information) and how the money will be used (principal and agent.

3. U' denotes the first derivative of utility and U'' denotes the second derivatives. This notation will be used throughout the chapter.

4. The model presented here has been developed from one of the question set up for the graduate advance microeconomic exam paper, University of York, 1986.

5. In the example the reservation utility level has been set to zero in order to stress the fact that the agent has to receive a non-negative reward for his effort. In more realistic cases this parameter could be greater than a fixed amount representing the utility that could be obtained by using the same effort in other activities.

6. The proofs of those results can be found in appendix 1 of this chapter.

7. The real-world parallel here could be a public enterprise producing under conditions of monopoly.

8. The two new constraints have been obtained by using the relationship $Y = x\alpha$ from which it follows that $x = Y/\alpha$.

9. See appendix 1 to this chapter for a formal proof.

10. The diagram has been drawn for a fixed level of γ to keep it in two dimensions.

11. The term 'adverse selection' is here borrowed from insurance market studies and it is intended to apply to situations in which one party possesses information relevant to the optimisation process of other economic subjects but it is his selfish interest not to disclose it.

12. Borooah and van der Ploeg (1985) explains and tests this theory at length.

13. This method of dealing with incentive problems has been suggested by Rees (1985a).

14. See King (1984) for a more detailed analysis.

15. The problem of defining the length and the problem correlated with dealing with life-cycle models when applied to local governments has been widely described in Levaggi (1991).

16. This assumption rules out the possibility of describing by using this model the behaviour of local authorities that elects one-third of their representatives each year.

17. That is, when both parties are perfectly informed.

18. In other words, β is either a simple political or regional parameter.

19. The separation is based on the assumption that no ceiling exists on the total amount of grant available to be redistributed among local authorities.

20. That is, $p(\beta_i) = k$ for all i.

21. It is clear that this does not mean that all authorities will receive the same incentive: what it means is that the general formula will be the same for all authorities but the actual value will depend on the parameters characterising each authority.

22. In this case, in fact, central government, from observing expenditure will infer $\beta_x = \beta_d$.
23. Figure 10.5 shows the budget constraint for the first period of the life-cycle. The diagram for period 2 and 3 is analogous, but the line shifts upwards according to the savings of the local authority.
24. This is the loss for each period and for a representative authority. The total loss suffered by central government will then be:

$$\sum_{t=1}^{4} \sum_{j=1}^{n} \Psi_{tj}^{*} (\theta_{tj} - 1).$$

25. The actual level of expenditure at the kink is, for the reasons I will show later, $\Psi^{*}\Omega_i$.
26. This is the loss for each period and for a representative authority. The total loss suffered by central government will then be:

$$\sum_{t=1}^{4} \sum_{j=1}^{n} \Psi_{tj}^{*} (\theta_{tj} - 1).$$

27. Either taxation or debt or both.

Bibliography

Aaron, H. J. (1975) *Who Pays the Property Tax? A New View* (Washington, DC, Brookings Institution).

Aaron, H. J. (1982) *Economics Effects of Social Security* (Washington, DC, Brookings Institution).

Akerlof, G. (1970) 'The Market for "Lemons": Quality Uncertainty and the Market Mechanism', *Quarterly Journal of Economics*, 84, 488–500.

Allingham, M. G. and Sandmo, A. (1972) 'Income Tax Evasion: A Theoretical Analysis', *Journal of Public Economics*, 1, 323–38.

Alm, J. (1985) 'The Welfare Cost of the Underground Economy', *Economic Inquiry*, 23, 243–63.

Alm, J. (1988) 'Compliance Costs and the Tax Avoidance – Tax Evasion Decision', *Public Finance Quarterly*, 16, 31–66.

Andersen, P. (1977) 'Tax Evasion and Labor Supply', *Scandinavian Journal of Economics*, 79, 375–83.

Ando, A. and Kennickell, A. (1987) 'How Much (or Little) Life Cycle Is There in Micro Data? The Cases of the United States and Japan', in R. Dounbush, S. Fischer and J. Bossons (eds), *Macroeconomics and Finance: Essays in Honour of Franco Modigliani* (Cambridge, Mass., MIT Press) 159–223.

Andreoni, J. (1988) 'Why Free Ride?', *Journal of Public Economics*, 37, 291–304.

Ang, J. S. and Peterson, D. R. (1986) 'Optimal Debt vs. Debt Capacity: A Disequilibrium Model of Corporate Debt Behaviour', in A. W. Chen (ed.), *Research in Finance*, vol. 6 (Greenwich, Conn. JAI Press).

Apps, P. and Savage E. (1989) 'Modelling Household Labour Supply and the Welfare Effects of Tax Reforms', *Journal of Public Economics* 136, 97–112.

Arrow, K. J. (1963) *Social Choice and Individual Values*, 2nd edn. (New York, John Wiley).

Arrow, K. (1970) *Essays in the Theory of Risk-Bearing* (Amsterdam, North-Holland).

Arrow, K. J. (1987) 'Arrow's Theorem', in J. Eatwell, M. Milgate and P. Newman (eds), *The New Palgrave* (London, Macmillan) 124–6.

Ashworth, J. A. and Ulph, D. T. (1981) 'Endogeneity I: Estimating

Labour Supply with Piecewise Linear Budget Constraints', in C. V. Brown (ed.) *Taxation and Labour Supply* (London, Allen & Unwin).

Ashworth, J. and Ulph, D. (1981) 'Endogeniety I: Estimating Labour Supply with Nonlinear Budget Constraints', in C. Brown (ed.), *Taxation and Labour Supply* (London, Allen & Unwin).

Atkinson, A. B. (1970) 'On the Measurement of Inequality', *Journal of Economic Theory*, 2, 244–63.

Atkinson, A. B. and Bourguignon, F. (1987) 'Income Distribution and Differences in Needs', ch. 12 in G. R. Feiwel (ed.) *Arrow and the Foundations of the Theory of Economic Policy* (London, Macmillan).

Atkinson, A. B., Bourguignon, F. and Chiappori, P. A. (1987) 'What Do We Learn About Tax Reform From International Comparisons?', *European Economic Review*, 32, 343–52.

Atkinson, A. B., Bourguignon, F. and Chiappori, P. A. (1988) 'What Do We Learn about Tax Reform from International Comparisons? France and Britain', mimeo, ERSC Taxation Incentives and Distribution of Income Programme (London, London School of Economics).

Atkinson, A. B. and Stern, N. H. (1974) 'Pigou, Taxation and Public Goods', *Review of Economic Studies*, 41, 119–28.

Atkinson, A. B. and Stiglitz, J. E. (1980) *Lectures on Public Economics* (New York, McGraw-Hill).

Auerbach, A. J. (1979) 'Wealth Maximization and the Cost of Capital', *Quarterly Journal of Economics*, 94, 433–6.

Auerbach, A. J. (1983) 'Taxation, Corporate Financial Policy and the Cost of Capital', *Journal of Economic Literature*, 21, 905–40.

Auerbach, A. J. (1985) 'The Theory of Excess Burden and Optimal Taxation', in A. J. Auerbach and M. Feldstein (eds), *Handbook of Public Economics*, vol. 1 (Amsterdam, North-Holland) 61–127.

Auerbach, A. J., Kotlikoff, L. J. and Skinner, J. (1983) 'The Efficiency Gains from Dynamic Tax Reform', *International Economic Review*, 24, 81–100.

Auerbach, A. J. and Feldstein, M. S. (1985) *Handbook of Public Economics*, vols 1 and 2 (Amsterdam, North-Holland).

Auerbach, A. J., and Poterba, J. M., (1986) 'Tax Loss Carry Forwards and Corporate Tax Incentives', Working Paper, Department of Economics, MIT.

Baldry, J. C. (1984) 'The Enforcement of Income Tax Laws: Efficiency Implications', *Economic Record*, 60, 156–9.

Ballard, C. L., Fullerton, D., Shoven, J. B. and Whalley, J. (1985) *A General Equilibrium Model for Tax Policy Evaluation* (Chicago, Chicago University Press).

Barnett, R. R. (1985) 'On the Flypaper Theory of Local Government Response to Grants-in-Aid', *Government and Policy: Environment and Planning C*, 3, 341–8.

Barnett, R. R. (forthcoming) 'The (Non) Equivalence Theorem When There Are Matching Grants As Well As Lump Sum Grants, *Public Choice*.

Barnett, R. R., Levaggi, R. and Smith, P. C. (1990) 'An Assessment of the Regional Impact of the Introduction of a Community Charge (or Poll Tax) in England, *Regional Studies*, 69, 289–97.

Barnett, R. R., Levaggi, R. and Smith, P. C. (1991a) 'Does the Flypaper Model Stick? A Test of the Relative Performance of the Flypaper and Conventional Models of Local Government Budgetary Behaviour', *Public Choice*, 69, 1–18.

Barnett, R. R., Levaggi, R. and Smith, P. C. (1991b) 'An Incremental Budgeting Model of Local Public Expenditure Setting in the Presence of Piecewise Linear Budget Constraints', *Applied Economics*, 23, 949–56.

Barnett, R. R., Levaggi, R. and Smith, P. C. (1992) 'Local Authority Expenditure Decisions: A Maximum Likelihood Analysis of Budget Setting in the Face of Piecewise Linear Budget Constraints', *Oxford Economic Papers*.

Barr J. L. and Davies O. A. (1966) An Elementary Political and Economic Theory of the Expenditures of Local Governments, *Southern Economic Journal*, 22, 149–65.

Barro, R. J. (1974) 'Are Government Bonds Net Wealth?', *Journal of Political Economy*, 82, 1095–117.

Barro, R. J. and McDonald, G. M. (1979) 'Social Security and Consumer Spending in an International Cross Section', *Journal of Public Economics*, 11, 275–89.

Barry, B. (1970) *Sociologists, Economists, and Democracy* (London, Macmillan).

Bauer, Peter T. and Yamey, B. S. (1957) *The Economics of Under-Developed Countries* (Cambridge, Cambridge University Press).

Baum, D. N. (1988) 'Consumption, Wealth and the Real Rate of Interest: A Re-examination', *Journal of Macroeconomics*, 10, 83–102.

Beach, C. M., Boadway, R. W. and Bruce, N. (1988) *Taxation and Savings in Canada* (Ottawa, Economic Council of Canada).

Becker, G. S. (1968) 'Crime and Punishment: An Economic Approach', *Journal of Political Economy*, 76, 169–217.

Bell, C. R. (1988) 'The Assignment of Fiscal Responsibility in a Federal State: An Empirical Assessment', *National Tax Journal*, 41, 191–208.

Benjamini, Y. and Maital, S. (1985) 'Optimal Tax Evasion and Optimal Tax Evasion Policy: Behavioural Aspects', in Gaertner and Wenig (1985).

Bennett, R. J. (1990) 'Decentralization and Economic Development', in R. J. Bennet (ed.), *Decentralization, Local Governments and Markets: Towards a Post-Welfare Agenda* (Oxford, Clarendon) 221–44.

Bergstrom, T. C. and Goodman, R. P. (1973) 'Private Demands for Public Goods', *American Economic Review*, 63, 280–96.

Bergstrom, T. C., Rubinfeld, D. L. and Shapiro, P. (1982) 'Micro-Based Estimates of Demand Functions for Local School Expenditures', *Econometrica*, 50, 1183–206.

Berlin, I. (1958) *Two Concepts of Liberty*, Inaugural lecture (Oxford, Clarendon Press). Reprinted in *Four Essays on Liberty* (Oxford, Oxford University Press, 1969).

Besley, T. J. and Preston I. P. (1988) 'Invariance and the Axiomatics of Income Tax Progression: A Comment', *Bulletin of Economic Research*, 40, 159–63.

Bhagwati, J. (1982) 'Directly Unproductive Profit Seeking Activities', *Journal of Political Economy*, 90, 988–1002.

Bird, Richard M. (1970) *Taxation and Development: Lessons from Colombian Experience* (Cambridge, Mass., Harvard University Press).

Bird, Richard M. (1974) *Taxing Agricultural Land in Developing Countries* (Cambridge, Mass., Harvard University Press).

Bird, R. M. (1976) *Charging for Public Services: A New Look at an Old Idea* (Toronto, Canadian Tax Foundation).

Bird, Richard M. (1983) 'Income Tax Reform in Developing Countries: The Administrative Dimension', *Bulletin for International Fiscal Documentation*, 37, 3–14.

Bird, Richard M. (1984) *Intergovernmental Finance in Colombia* (Cambridge, Mass., Harvard Law School International Tax Program).

Bird, Richard M. (1989a) 'The Administrative Dimension of Tax Reform in Developing Countries', in Malcolm Gillis (ed.), *Fiscal Reform in Developing Countries* (Durham, NC, Duke University Press).

Bird, Richard M. (1989b) 'Taxation in Papua New Guinea: Backwards to the Future?', *World Development*, 17, 1145–57.

Bird, Richard M. and Horton, Susan (eds) (1989) *Government Policy and the Poor in Developing Countries* (Toronto, University of Toronto Press).

Black, D. (1948) 'On the Rationale of Group Decision-Making', *Journal of Political Economy*, 56, 23–34.

Black, D. (1958) *Theory of Committees and Elections* (Cambridge, Cambridge University Press).

Blinder, A. S. (1975) 'Distribution Effects and the Aggregate Consumption Function', *Journal of Political Economy*, 83, 447–75.

Blinder, A. S. (1987) '"Comment and Discussion" on "Why is U.S. National Saving So Low?" by L. H. Summers and C. Carroll', in *Brookings Papers on Economic Activity*, 636–8.

Blundell, R. W. (1988) 'Econometric Issues in Public Sector Economics', in P. G. Hare (ed.), *Surveys in Public Sector Economics* (Oxford, Blackwell) 219–47.

Blundell, R. and Walker, I., (1982) 'Modelling Household Commodity Demands and Labour Supplies', *Economic Journal*, 92, 351–64.

Blundell, R. and Walker, I., (1986) 'A Lifecycle Model of Family Labour Supply', *Review of Economic Studies*, 54, 163–82.

Blundell, R. and Meghir, C. (1988) 'Female Labour Supply and Unemployment', *Economic Journal*, 98, 76–91.

Blundell, R. Meghir, C., Symons E. and Walker, I. (1988) 'Labour Supply Specification and the Evaluation of Tax Reforms', *Journal of Public Economics*, 14, 144–68.

Boadway, R. W. and Wildasin, D. E. (1984) *Public Sector Economics*, 2nd edn (Boston, Little Brown).

Bohm, P. (1984) 'Revealing Demand for an Actual Public Good', *Journal of Public Economics*, 24, 133–52.

Borcherding, T. E. (1985) 'The Causes of Government Expenditure Growth: A Survey of the US Evidence', *Journal of Public Economics*, 28, 359–82.

Borcherding, T. E. and Deacon, R. T. (1972) 'The Demand for Services of Non-Federal Governments', *American Economic Review*, 62, 891–901.

Borges, A. (1986) 'Applied General Equilibrium Models: An Assessment of the Usefulness for Policy Analysis', *OECD Economic Studies*, Autumn.

Borooah, V. K. and van der Ploeg, F. (1984) *Political Aspects of the Economy* (Cambridge, Cambridge University Press).

Boskin, M. and G. Gale (1986) 'The Effects of Taxation on Capital Formation', (Washington, DC) National Bureau of Economic Research mimeo.

Boskin, M. J. (1978) 'Taxation, Saving, and the Rate of Interest', *Journal of Political Economy*, 86, S3–S27.

Boskin, M. J. and Lau, L. J. (1978) 'A Closer Look at Saving Rates in the US and Japan', Working Paper No. 9, American Enterprise Institute, June.

Boyle, P. and Murray, J. (1979) 'Social Security Wealth and Private Savings in Canada', *Canadian Journal of Economics*, 12, 456–68.

Bradford, D. F. (1980) 'The Economics of Tax Policy Toward Savings', in G. M. von Furstenberg (ed.), *The Government and Capital Formation* (Cambridge, Mass., Ballinger).

Bradford, D. F. (1981) 'The Incidence and Allocation Effects of a Tax on Corporate Distributions', *Journal of Public Economics*, 15, 1–22.

Bradford D. F. and Oates, W. E. (1971) 'The Analysis of Revenue Sharing in a New Approach to Fiscal Federalism', *Quarterly Journal of Economics*, 35, 416–39.

Bradley, M., Jarrell, G. A. and Kim, E. H. (1984) 'On the Existence of an Optimal Capital Structure: Theory and Evidence', *Journal of Finance*, 39, 857–78.

Bramley, G. (1990) *Equalization Grants and Local Expenditure Needs* (Aldershot, Avebury).

Bramley, G. J., Le Grand, J. and Low, W. (1989) 'How Far is the Poll Tax a "Community Charge"? The Implications of Service Usage Evidence', *Policy and Politics*, 17, 187–206.

Brennan, G. and Buchanan, J. M. (1980) *The Power to Tax: Analytical Foundations of a Fiscal Constitution* (Cambridge, Cambridge University Press).

Breton, A. (1966) 'A Theory of the Demand for Public Goods', *Canadian Journal of Economics*, 32, 455–67.

Breton, A. and Scott, A. D. (1978) *The Economic Constitution of Federal States* (Canberra, Australian National University Press).

Brittan, S. (1975) 'The Economic Consequences of Democracy', *British Journal of Political Science* 5, 129–159.

Brookshire, D. S. and Crocker, T. D. (1981) 'The Advantages of Contingent Valuation Methods for Benefit–Cost Analysis', *Public Choice*, 36, 235–52.

Brookshire, D. S., Thayer, M., Schulze, W. and d'Arge, R. (1982) 'Valuing Public Goods: A Comparison of Survey and Hedonic Methods', *American Economic Review*, 72, 165–77.

Brookshire, D. S. and Coursey, D. L. (1987) 'Measuring the Value of a Public Good: An Empirical Comparison of Elicitation Procedures', *American Economic Review*, 77, 554–66.

Brown, C. C. and Oates, W. E. (1987) 'Assistance to the Poor in a Federal System', *Journal of Public Economics*, 32 307–30.

Brown, C. V. (1968) 'Misconceptions about Income Tax and Incentives', *Scottish Journal of Political Economy*. 12, 82–98.

Brown, C. V. (1981) *Taxation and Labour Supply* (London, Allen & Unwin).

Brown, C. V. (1986) *Labour Supply and Taxation* (Oxford, Oxford University Press).

Brown, C. V. and Dawson, D. (1969) *Personal Taxation, Incentives and Tax Reform* (London, Political and Economic Planning).

Brown, C. V. and Jackson, P. M. (1990) *Public Sector Economics*, 4th edn (Oxford, Blackwell).

Brown, C. V., Levin, E. J. and Ulph, D. T. (1976) 'Estimates of labour hours supplied by married male workers in Great Britain', *Scottish Journal of Political Economy*, November, 20, 127–36.

Brown, C. V., Levin E. J., Rosa, P. J., Ruffell, R. J. and Ulph, D. T. (1986) *Taxation and Family Labour Supply in Great Britain: The Final Report of a Project on Direct Taxation and Labour Supply* (funded by H.M. Treasury).

Brown, M. and Manser, M. (1980) 'Marriage and Household Decision-Making: A Bargaining Analysis, *International Economic Review*, 46, 221–37.

Browning, E. K. and Johnson, W. R. (1984) 'The Trade-off Between Equity and Efficiency', *Journal of Political Economy*, 92, 175–203.

Browning, M. J. (1982) 'Savings and Pensions, Some UK Evidence', *Economic Journal*, 92, 954–63.

Bruton, Henry J. (1965) *Principles of Development Economics* (New York, Prentice-Hall).

Buchanan, J. M. (1960) *Fiscal Theory and Political Economy* (Chapel Hill, University of North Carolina Press).

Buchanan, J. M. (1965) 'An Economic Theory of Clubs', *Economica*, 32, 1–14.

Buchanan, J. M. (1975) *The Limits of Liberty: Between Anarchy and Leviathan* (Chicago, Chicago University Press).

Buchanan, J. M. (1980) 'Rent Seeking and Profit Seeking', in Buchanan, Tollison and Tullock (1980).

Buchanan, J. M. (1984) 'The Ethical Limits of Taxation', *Scandinavian Journal of Economics*, April, 102–14.

Buchanan, J. M. and Brennan, G. (1985) *The Reason of Rules* (Cambridge, Cambridge University Press).

Buchanan, J. M. and Tullock, G. (1962) *The Calculus of Consent: Logical Foundations of Constitutional Democracy* (Ann Arbor, University of Michigan Press).

Buchanan, J. M., Tollison, R. D. and Tullock, G. (1980) *Towards a Theory of the Rent Seeking Society* (College Station, Texas A & M Press).

Butler, D. and Stokes, D. (1974) *Political Change in Britain* (London, Macmillan).

Byrne, W. J. (1976) 'Fiscal Incentives for Household Saving', *IMF Staff Papers*, vol. 23, no. 2, 455–89.

Carroll, C. and Summers, L. H. (1987) 'Why Have Private Saving Rates in the United States and Canada Diverged?', *Journal of Monetary Economics*, 20, 247–79.

Chiappori, P. (1988) 'Rational Labour Supply', *Econometrica* 52, 71–90.

Clarke E. H. (1971) 'Multipart Pricing of Public Goods', *Public Choice*, 11, 17–33.

Clarke, E. H. (1972) 'Multipart Pricing of Public Goods: An Example', in S. Mushkin (ed), *Public Prices for Public Products* (Washington, DC, Urban Institute) 125–130.

Clotfelter, C. T. (1983) 'Tax Evasion and Tax Rates: An Analysis of Individual Returns', *Review of Economics and Statistics*, 65, 363–73.

Cnossen, Sijbren (1977) *Excise Systems* (Baltimore, Md., Johns Hopkins University Press).

Colander, D. (1984) *Neoclassical Political Economy: The Analysis of Rent Seeking and DUP Activities* (Cambridge, Mass., Ballinger).

Collard, D. (1978) *Altruism and Economy* (Oxford, Martin Robertson).

Converse, P. E. (1958) 'The Shifting Role of Class in Political Attitudes and Behaviour', in E. E. Maccoby, T. M. Newcomb and E. L. Hartley (eds), *Readings in Social Psychology* (London, Methuen).

Cornes, R. C. and Sandler, T. (1983) 'On Commons and Tragedies', *American Economic Review*, 73, 787–92.

Cornes, R. and Sandler, T. (1986) *The Theory of Externalities, Public Goods, and Club Goods* (Cambridge, Cambridge University Press).

Courant, P. N., Gramlich, E. M. and Rubinfeld, D. L. (1979) 'The Stimulative Effects of Intergovernmental Grants: Or Why Money Sticks Where It Hits', in P. M. Mieszkowski and W. H. Oakland (eds), *Fiscal Federalism and Grants-in-Aid* (Washington, DC, Urban Institute) 23–30.

Cowell, F. (1985a) 'Tax Evasion with Labour Income', *Journal of Public Economics*, 26, 19–34.

Cowell, F. (1985b) 'The Economic Analysis of Tax Evasion', *Bulletin of Economic Research*, 37, 163–93.

Cowell, F. A. (1986) *Microeconomic Principles* (Deddington, Philip Allan).

Cowell, F. (1987) 'Honesty is Sometimes the Best Policy', ESRC Programme on Taxation, Incentives and The Distribution of Income, Discussion Paper No. 107.

Cowell, F. A. (1990) *Cheating the Government* (Cambridge, Mass., MIT Press).

Crane, S. E. and Nourzad, F. (1986) 'Inflation and Tax Evasion: An Empirical Analysis', *Review of Economics and Statistics*, 68, 217–23.

Cross, R. and Shaw, G. K. (1982) 'The Economics of Tax Aversion', *Public Finance*, 37, 36–47.

Daly, M., Jun, J., Mercier, P. and Schweitzer, T. (1985) 'The Taxation of Capital Income in Canada: A Comparison with Sweden, the UK, the USA and West Germany', *Economic Council of Canada Discussion Paper No. 289*, September.

Dardanoni, V. and Lambert, P. J. (1987) 'Welfare Rankings of Income Distributions: A Rôle for the Variance and Some Insights for Tax Reform', *Social Choice and Welfare*, 5, 1–17.

Dasgupta, P. (1985) 'Positive Freedom, Markets and the Welfare State', *Oxford Review of Economic Policy*, 2.

Dasgupta, P., Sen, A. and Starrett, D. (1973) 'Notes on the Measurement of Inequality', *Journal of Economic Theory*, 6, 180–7.

Davies, J. and Hoy, M. (1987) 'Making Inequality Comparisons When Lorenz Curves Intersect', mimeo INBER Discussion Paper, Washington.

Dean, P., Keenan, T. and Kenney, F. (1980) 'Taxpayers' Attitudes to Income Tax Evasion: An Empirical Survey', *British Tax Review*, pp. 28–44.

Deaton, A. and Muellbauer, J. (1980) *Economics and Consumer Behaviour* (Cambridge, Cambridge University Press).

Denny, M. and Rea, S. A. (1979) 'Pensions and Savings in Canada', in George von Furstenberg (ed.), *Social Security versus Private Saving* (Cambridge, Mass., Ballinger) 135–65.

Devereux, M. and Pearson, M. (1989) 'Corporate Tax Harmonisation and Economic Efficiency', Institute for Fiscal Studies, Working Paper No. 35, October.

DeWulf, Luc (1975) 'Fiscal Incidence Studies in Developing Countries', *International Monetary Fund Staff Papers*, 22, 61–131.

Diamond, P. A. and Hausman, J. A. (1984) 'Individual Retirement and Savings Behaviour', *Journal of Public Economics*, 23, 81–114.

Dilnot, A. and Kell, M. (1987) 'Male Unemployment and Women's Work', *Fiscal Sudies*, 8, 6–14.

Dilnot, A. and Webb, S. (1989) 'Reforming National Insurance Contributions', *Fiscal Studies*, 10, 21–8.

Downs, A. (1958) *An Economic Theory of Democracy* (Boston, Harper & Row).

Dubin, J. A., Graetz, M. J. and Wilde, L. L. (1987) 'Are We A Nation of Tax Cheaters? New Econometric Evidence on Tax Compliance', *American Economic Review*, 77, 240–5.

Dubin, J. A., Graetz, M. J. and Wilde, L. L. (1989) *The Report of The United States to The International Fiscal Association on The Costs of Tax Administration and Compliance*, California Institute of Technology, Social Science Working Paper 689.

Due, John F. (1988) *Indirect Taxation in Developing Economies*, rev. edn (Baltimore, Md., Johns Hopkins University Press).

Edwards, J. S. S. and Keen, M. J. (1984) 'Wealth Maximization and the Cost of Capital: A Comment', *Quarterly Journal of Economics*, 99, 211–14.

Ehrlich, I. (1973) 'Participation in Illegitimate Activities: A Theoretical and Empirical Investigation', *Journal of Political Economy*, 81, 521–64.

Evans, O. (1983) 'Tax Policy, and the Interest Elasticity of Saving, and Capital Accumulation', *American Economic Review*, 73, 398–410.

Evans, P. (1988) 'Are Consumers Ricardian? Evidence for the United States', *Journal of Political Economy*, 96, 983–1004.

Fallon, P. and Verry, D. (1989) *The Economics of Labour Markets* (Deddington, Philip Allan).

Feldstein, M. S. (1974a) 'Social Security, Induced Retirement, and Aggregate Capital Accumulation', *Journal of Political Economy*, 82, 905–26.

Feldstein, M. S. (1974b) 'Does the United States Save Too Little?', *American Economic Review*, 67, 116–21.

Feldstein, M. S. (1977) 'Social Security and Private Savings: International Evidence in an Extended Life Cycle Model', in M. S. Feldstein and R. P. Inman (eds), *The Economics of Public Services* (London, Macmillan) 174–205.

Feldstein, M. S. (1978) 'Reply', in R. J. Barro, *The Impact of Social Security on Private Saving: Evidence from the US Time Series* (Washington, DC, American Enterprise Institute).

Feldstein, M. S. (1980) 'International Difference in Social Security and Savings', *Journal of Public Economics*, 14, 225–44.

Feldstein, M. S. (1982) 'Social Security and Private Saving: A Reply', *Journal of Political Economy*, 90, 630–42.

Feldstein, M. S. (1983a) 'Social Security Benefits and the Accumulation of Pre-retirement Wealth', in F. Modigliani and R. Hemming (eds), *The Determinants of National Savings and Wealth* (New York, St Martin's Press) 3–23.

Feldstein, M. S. (1983b) 'Domestic Saving and International Capital Movements in the Long-Run and Short-Run', *European Economic Review*, 21, 129–51.

Feldstein, M. and Hartman, D. (1979) 'The Optimal Taxation of Foreign Source Income', *Quarterly Journal of Economics*, 82, 138–59.

Feldstein, M. S. and Pellechio, A. (1979) 'Social Security and Household Wealth Accumulation', *Review of Economics and Statistics*, 61, 361–8.

Fellman, J. (1976) 'The Effect of Transformation on Lorenz Curves', *Econometrica*, 44, 823–4.

Fischer, E., Heinkel, R. and Zechner, J. (1989) 'Dynamic Capital Structure Choice: Theory and Tests', *Journal of Finance*, 44, 19–40.

Fishburn, G. (1979) 'On How to Keep Taxpayers Honest (Or Almost So)', *Economic Record*, 55, 267–70.

Fisher, F. M. (1987) 'Household Equivalence Scales and Interpersonal Comparisons', *Review of Economic Studies*, 54, 519–24.

Foster, C. D., Jackman, R. A. and Perlman, M. (1980) *Local Government Finance in a Unitary State* (London, Allen & Unwin).

Frank, R. H. (1987) 'If Homo Economicus Could Choose His Own Utility

Function, Would He Want One With a Conscience?', *American Economic Review*, 77, 593–604.

Frank, R. H. (1988) *Passions Within Reasons* (New York, Norton).

Frey, B. (1978) *Modern Political Economy* (London, Macmillan).

Frey, B. S. and Schneider, F. (1978) 'A Politico-Economic Model of the United Kingdom', *Economic Journal*, 88, 243–53.

Friedland, N., Maital, S. and Rutenberg, A. (1978) 'A Simulation Study of Income Tax Evasion', *Journal of Public Economics*, 10, 107–16.

Friedman, M. (1962) 'The Methodology of Positive Economics', in his *Essays in Positive Economics* (Chicago, University of Chicago Press).

Friend, I. and Hasbrouck, J. (1983) 'Saving and After Tax Rates of Return', *Review of Economics and Statistics*, 65, 537–43.

Frisch, D. and Hartman, D. (1983) 'Taxation and the Location of US Investment Abroad', Working Paper No. 1241 (Washington DC, National Bureau of Economic Research).

Fullerton, D., Henderson, Y. K. and Shoven, J. (1984) 'A Comparison of Methodologies in Empirical General Equilibrium Models of Taxation', in Scarf and Shoven (1984).

Fullerton, D. and Henderson, Y. K. (1986) 'The Impact of Fundamental Tax Reform on the Allocation of Resources', *AEI Occasional Papers: Working Paper No. 8*, April.

Fullerton, D. and King, M. (1984) *The Taxation of Income from Capital: A Comparative Study of the United States, the United Kingdom, Sweden and West Germany* (Chicago, University of Chicago Press).

Fullerton, D., Shoven, J. B. and Whalley, J. (1983) 'Replacing the U. S. Income Tax with a Progressive Consumption Tax: A Sequenced General Equilibrium Approach', *Journal of Public Economics*, 20, 1–21.

Gaertner, W. and Wenig, A. (eds) (1985) *The Economics of the Shadow Economy* (Berlin; Springer-Verlag).

Gandhi, Ved P. *et al.* (1987) *Supply-Side Taxation and Its Relevance to Developing Countries* (Washington, International Monetary Fund).

Garvy, G. (1952) 'Inequality of Income: Causes and Measurement', in *Studies in Income and Wealth, Volume 15: Eight Papers on the Size Distribution of Income* (New York, NBER) 27–47.

Gillis, Malcolm, and McLure, Charles E. (1971) 'The Coordination of Tariffs and Internal Indirect Taxes', in Richard A. Musgrave and Malcolm Gillis (eds), *Fiscal Reform in Colombia* (Cambridge, Mass., Harvard Law School International Tax Program).

Gillis, Malcolm *et al.* (1987) *Economics of Development*, 2nd edn (New York, Norton).

Glennerster, H. (1979) 'The Determinants of Public Expenditures', in T. Booth (ed.), *Planning for Welfare: Social Policy and the Expenditure Process* (Oxford, Blackwell).

Goldstein, G. S. and Pauly, M. V. (1981) 'Tiebout Bias on the Demand for Local Public Goods', *Journal of Public Economics*, 16, 131–44.

Goodhart, C. A. E. and Bhansali, R. J. (1970) 'Political Economy', *Political Studies*, 18, 43–106.

Goodspeed, T. (1989) 'A Re-examination of the Use of Ability to Pay Taxes by Local Governments', *Journal of Public Economics*, 38, 319–42.

Gordon, R. (1983) 'An Optimal Taxation Approach to Fiscal Federalism', *Quarterly Journal of Economics*, 98, 567–86.

Graetz, M. J. and Wilde, L. L. (1985) 'The Economics of Tax Compliance: Fact and Fantasy', *National Tax Journal*, 38, 355–63.

Gramlich, E. M. (1977) 'Intergovernmental Grants: A Review of the Empirical Literature', in W. E. Oates (ed.), *The Political Economy of Fiscal Federalism* (Lexington, Mass., D.C. Heath) 219–39.

Gramlich, E. M. (1987) 'Federalism and Federal Deficit Reduction', *National Tax Journal*, 40, 299–313.

Green, J. R. and Laffont, J. J. (1979) *Incentives in Public Decision Making* (New York, North-Holland).

Greenberg, J. (1984) 'Avoiding Tax Avoidance: A (Repeated) Game-Theoretic Approach', *Journal of Economic Theory*, 32, 1–13.

Greenwald, B. and Stiglitz, J. (1988) 'Pareto Inefficiency of Market Economics: Search and Efficiency Wage Models', *American Economic Review Papers and Proceedings*, May, 351–5.

Groenwegen, P. (1990) 'Taxation and Decentralization: A Reconsideration of the Costs and Benefits of a Decentralized Tax System', in R. J. Bennett (ed.), *Decentralization, Local Governments and Markets: Towards a Post-Welfare Agenda* (Oxford, Clarendon) 87–115.

Grossman, P. J. (1989) 'Intergovernmental Grants and Grantor Government Own-Purpose Expenditures', *National Tax Journal*, 42, 487–94.

Grossman, S. J. and Hart, O. D. (1983) 'An Analysis of the Principal–Agent Problem', *Econometrica*, 51, 7–45.

Groves, T. (1973) 'Incentives in Teams', *Econometrica*, 41, 617–31.

Gultekin, N. B. and Logue, D. E. (1979) 'Social Security and Personal Saving: Survey and New Evidence', in George Von Furstenberg (ed.), *Social Security versus Private Saving* (Cambridge, Mass., Ballinger) 65–132.

Ham, J. (1986) 'On the Interpretation of Unemployment in Empirical Labour Supply Analysis', in R. Blundell and I. Walker (eds), *Unemployment, Search and Labour Supply* (Cambridge, Cambridge University Press).

Hamada, K. (1966) 'Strategic Aspects of Taxation on Foreign Investment Income', *Quarterly Journal of Economics*, 80, 361–75.

Hamilton, B. W. (1983) 'The Flypaper Effect and Other Anomalies', *Journal of Public Economics*, 22, 347–61.

Hamilton, J. (1980) 'The Flypaper Effect and the Deadweight Loss from Taxation', *Journal of Urban Economics*, 19, pp. 148–55.

Hamilton, J. (1986) 'The Fly Paper Effect and the Deadweight Loss from Taxation', *Journal of Urban Economics*, 19, pp. 148–55.

Hanley, N. D. (1989) 'Valuing Non-Market Goods Using Contingent Valuation', *Journal of Economic Surveys*, 3, 235–50.

Harberger, A. C. (1959) 'The Corporation Income Tax: An Empirical Appraisal', in *Tax Revision Compendium*, vol. 1, House Committee on Ways and Means (Washington, DC, Government Printing Office).

Harberger, A. C. (1962) 'The Incidence of the Corporation Income Tax', *Journal of Political Economy*, 70, 215–40.

Harberger, A. C. (1964) 'Taxation, Resource Allocation and Welfare', in *The Role of Direct and Indirect Taxes in the Federal Reserve System* (Princeton, NJ Princeton University Press).

Harberger, A. C. (1966) 'Efficiency Effects of Taxes on Income from Capital', in M. Krzyzamiak (ed.), *Effects of Corporation Income Tax* (Detroit, Mich., Wayne State University Press).

Hare, P. G. (ed.) (1988) *Surveys in Public Sector Economics* (Oxford, Blackwell).

Harris, M. and Townsend, R. M. (1981) 'Resources Allocation Under Asymmetric Information', *Econometrica*, 49, 33–64.

Harsanyi, J. C. (1953) 'Cardinal Utility in Welfare Economics and Theory of Risk Taking', *Journal of Political Economy*, 61, 434–5.

Harsanyi, J. C. (1955) 'Cardinal Welfare, Individual Ethics and Interpersonal Comparisons of Utility', *Journal of Political Economy*, 63, 309–21.

Harsanyi, J. C. (1987) 'Von Neumann–Morgenstern Utilities, Risk Taking and Welfare', in G. R. Feiwel (ed.), *Arrow and the Ascent of Modern Economic Theory* (London, Macmillan) ch. 17.

Hartwick, J. and Olewiler, N. (1986) *The Economics of Natural Resource Use* (New York, Harper & Row).

Hausman, J. (1985) 'The Econometrics of Non-Linear Budget Sets', *Econometrica*, 53, 1255–82.

Hayek, F. (1944) *The Road to Serfdom* (London, Routledge & Kegan Paul).

Henderschott, P. H. and Peck, J. (1985) 'Household Saving: An Econometric Investigation', in P. H. Henderschott (ed.), *The Level and Composition of Household Saving*, (Cambridge, Mass., Ballinger) 63–100.

Hettich, Walter, and Winer, Stanley L. (1988) 'Economic and Political Foundations of Tax Structure', *American Economic Review*, 78, 701–12.

HMSO (1980) *The Taxation of Husband and Wife*, Cmnd 8093.

HMSO (1986) *The Reform of Personal Taxation*, Cmnd 9756.

Horioka, C. Y. (1986) 'Why is Japan's Private Savings Rate So High?, IMF Working Paper DM/86/44.

Hotelling, H. (1929) 'Stability in Competition', *Economic Journal*, 39, 41–57.

Howrey, E. P. and Hymans, S. H. (1978) 'The Measurement and Determination of Loanable Funds', *Brookings Papers on Economic Activity*, 655–85.

Hubbard, R. G. (1986) 'Pension Wealth and Individual Savings: Some New Evidence', *Journal of Money, Credit and Banking*, 17, 167–78.

Inman, R. P. (1978) 'Testing Political Economy's "As If" Proposition: Is

The Median Voter Really Decisive?', *Public Choice*, 33, 45–65.

Inman, R. P. (1979) 'The Fiscal Performance of Local Governments: An Interpretative Review', in P. Mieszkowski and M. Straszheim (eds), *Current Issues in Urban Economics* (Baltimore, Md., Johns Hopkins University Press) 270–321.

Inman, R. P. (1987a) 'Markets, Governments, and the "New" Political Economy', in A. J. Auerbach and M. S. Feldstein (eds), *Handbook of Public Economics* (Amsterdam, North-Holland) 647–777.

Inman, R. P. (1987b) 'The "New" Political Economy', in A. J. Auerbach and M. S. Feldstein (eds), *Handbook of Public Economics*, Vol. 2 (New York, North-Holland) 647–777.

Isaac, R. M., McCue, K. and Plott, C. (1985) 'Public Goods Provision in an Experimental Environment', *Journal of Public Economics*, 26, 51–74.

Isachsen, A. J. and Strom, S. (1980) 'The Hidden Economy: The Labour Market and Tax Evasion', *Scandinavian Journal of Economics*, 82, 304–11.

Ize, Alain. (1989) 'Savings, Investment, and Growth in Mexico: Five Years After the Crisis', International Monetary Fund Working Paper 89/18.

Jackson, P. M. (1982) *The Political Economy of Bureaucracy* (Oxford, Philip Allan).

Jackson, P. M. (1989) 'The Boundaries of the Public Domain', in W. J. Sammuels (ed.), *Fundamentals of The Economic Role of Government* (London, Greenwood Press) 105–16.

Jackson, P. M. (1990) 'Public Choice and Public Sector Management', *Public Money and Management*, 10, 13–20.

Jakobsson, U. (1976) 'On the Measurement of the Degree of Progression', *Journal of Public Economics*, 5, 161–8.

Jenkins, S. (1985) '"The Star Chamber", PESC and the Cabinet', *Political Quarterly*, 56, 113–21.

Jenkins, S. and O'Higgins, M. (1989) 'Inequality Measurement Using "Norm Incomes": Were Garvy and Paglin Onto Something After All?', *Review of Income and Wealth*, 35, 265–82.

Johansen, L. (1977) 'The Theory of Public Goods: Misplaced Emphasis', *Journal of Public Economics*, 7, 147–52.

Johansson, P. O. (1987) *The Economic Theory and Measurement of Environmental Benefits* (Cambridge, Cambridge University Press).

Jones-Lee, M. W., Hammerton, M. and Philips, P. R. (1985) 'The Value of Safety: Results of a National Sample Survey'. *Economic Journal*, 95, 49–72.

Jun, J. (1989) 'Tax Policy and International Investment', *NBER* Working Paper 3034, July.

Kahnemann, D. and Tversky, A. (1984) 'Choices, Values and Frames', *American Psychologist*, 39, 341–50.

Kakwani, N. C. (1977) 'Applications of Lorenz Curves in Economic Analysis', *Econometrica*, 45, 719–27.

Kakwani, N. C. (1980) *Income, Inequality and Poverty: Methods of*

Estimation and Policy Applications (Oxford, Oxford University Press).

Kakwani, N. C. (1984) Welfare Ranking of Income Distributions', *Advances in Econometrics*, 3, 191–213.

Kaldor, Nicholas (1965) 'The Role of Taxation in Economic Development', in Organization of American States, Joint Tax Program, *Fiscal Policy for Economic Growth in Latin America* (Baltimore, Md., Johns Hopkins University Press).

Kay, J. A. (1990) 'Tax Policy: A Survey', *Economic Journal*, 100, 18–75.

Keith Report, The (1983) Committee on Enforcement Powers of the Revenue Departments, Cmnd 8822, 9120 and 9440 (London, HMSO).

Keller, W. J. (1980) Tax Incidence: A General Equilibrium Approach (Amsterdam, North-Holland).

Kikutani, T. and Tachibanaki, T. (1986) *Tax incidence: A General Equilibrium Approach* (Amsterdam, North-Holland).

Killingsworth, M. (1983) *Labour Supply* (Cambridge, Cambridge University Press).

Killingsworth, M. and Heckman, J. (1986) 'Female Labour Supply', in O. Ashenfelter and R. Layard (eds), *Handbook of Labour Supply* (Amsterdam, North-Holland).

King, D. N. (1984) *Fiscal Tiers: The Economics of Multi-Level Government* (London, Allen & Unwin).

King, D. N. (1990) 'Accountability and Equity in British Local Finance: The Poll Tax', in R. J. Bennett (ed.), *Decentralization, Local Governments and Markets: Towards a Post-Welfare Agenda* (Oxford, Clarendon) 143–56.

King, D. N. (1991) 'Developments in the Theory of Fiscal Federalism', in D. N. King and G. Pola (eds), *Local Government Finance in Theory and Practice* (London, Routledge).

King, M. A. (1974a) 'Taxation and the Cost of Capital', *Review of Economic Studies*, 42, 21–35.

King, M. A. (1974b) 'Dividend Behaviour and the Theory of The Firm', *Economica*, 41, 25–34.

King, M. A. (1977) *Public Policy and The Corporation* (London, Chapman & Hall).

Klein, R. (1976) 'The Politics of Public Expenditure: American Theory and British Practice', *British Journal of Political Science*, 6, 401–32.

Kolm, S. -C. (1976) 'Unequal Inequalities, II', *Journal of Economic Theory*, 13, 82–111.

Kopits, G. and Gotur, P. (1980) 'The Influence of Social Security on Household Savings: A Cross Country Investigation', IMF *Staff Papers*, 27, 161–90.

Koskela, E. and Viren, M. (1983) 'Social Security and Household Saving: An International Cross Section', *American Economic Review*, 73, 212–17.

Krueger, A. O. (1974) 'The Political Economy of the Rent Seeking Society', *American Economic Review*, 64, 291–303.

Laffer, A. B. (1982) 'Government Exactions and Revenue Deficiencies', in R. H. Fink (ed.), *Supply Side Economics: A Critical Appraisal* (Frederic, Md., University Publications of America).

Laffont, J. J. (1987) 'Allocation of Public Goods', in A. J. Auerbach and M. S. Feldstein (eds), *Handbook of Public Economics*, vol. 2 (New York, North-Holland) 537–69.

Laffont, J. J. (1988) *Fundamentals of Public Economics* (Cambridge, Mass., MIT Press).

Lambert, P. J. (1989a) *The Distribution and Redistribution of Income: A Mathematical Analysis* (Cambridge, Mass., Blackwell).

Lambert, P. J. (1989b) 'Progression and Differences in Need: Can We Justify Our Income Taxes?', *Institute for Fiscal Studies Working Paper No. 89/7*.

Landsberger, M. and Meilijson, I. (1982) 'Incentive Generating State Dependent Penalty System', *Journal of Public Economics*, 19, 333–52.

Layard, R., Barton, A. and Zabalza, A. (1980) 'The Labour Supply of Married Women in the UK', *Economica*, 46, 186–99.

Lecaillon, J., Paukert, F., Morrison, C. and Germidis, D. (1984) *Income Distribution and Economic Development: An Analytical Survey* (Geneva, ILO).

Levaggi, R. (1991) 'Fiscal Federalism, Asymmetry of Information and Grants-in-Aid: The problem of asymmetrical information (Aldershor, Gower).

Lewis, A. (1979) 'An Empirical Assessment of Tax Mentality', *Public Finance*, 34, 245–57.

Lewis, W. Arthur (1966) *Development Planning* (London, Allen & Unwin).

Lijphart, A. (1977) *Democracy in Plural Societies* (New Haven, Yale University Press).

Lijphart, A. (1984) *Democracies: Patterns of Majoritarian and Consensus Government in Twenty-One Countries* (New Haven, Yale University Press).

Lin, C. (1986) 'A General Equilibrium Analysis of Property Tax Incidence', *Journal of Public Economics*, 29, 113–30.

Lindbeck, A. (1977) *The Political Economy of the New Left: An Outsider's View* (New York, Harper & Row).

Logan, R. R. (1986) 'Fiscal Illusion and the Grantor Government', *Journal of Political Economy*, 94, 1304–18.

Long, M. S. and Malitz, I. B. (1985) 'Investment Patterns and Financial Leverage', in B. M. Friedman (ed.), *Corporate Capital Structures in the United States* (Chicago, University of Chicago Press).

Macrae, C. D. (1977) 'A Political Model of the Business Cycle', *Journal of Political Economy* Vol 85, April, pp. 239–263.

Makin, J. H. (1986) 'Savings Rates in Japan and the United States: The Roles of Tax Policy and Other Factors', in F. Gerard Adams and S. M. Wachter (eds), *Savings and Capital Formation* (Lexington, D. C. Heath) 91–126.

Margolis, H. (1982) *Selfishness, Altruism and Rationality* (Cambridge, Cambridge University Press).

Markowski, A. and Palmer, E. E. (1979) 'Social Insurance and Saving in

Sweden', in George von Furstenberg (ed.), *Social Security versus Private Saving* (Cambridge, Mass., Ballinger) 167–228.

Marsh, P. R. (1982) 'The Choice Between Equity and Debt: An Empirical Study', *Journal of Finance*, 37, 121–44.

Marshall, T. H. (1964) *Clan Citizenship and Social Development* (New York, Doubleday).

Marwell, G. and Ames, R. (1981) 'Economists Free Ride, Does Anyone Else?', *Journal of Public Economics*, 15, 295–310.

Mason, R. and Calvin, L. D. (1984) 'Public Confidence and Admitted Tax Evasion', *National Tax Journal*, 37, 489–98.

May, K. O. (1952) 'A Set of Independent, Necessary and Sufficient Conditions for Simple Majority Rule', *Econometrica*, 20, 680–4.

McKee, M. J., Visser, J. J. C. and Saunders, P. G. (1986) 'Marginal Tax Rates on the use of Labour and Capital in OECD Countries', *OECD Economic Studies*, Autumn.

McKinnon, Ronald I. (1964) 'Foreign Exchange Constraints in Economic Development and Efficient Aid Allocation', *Economic Journal*, June.

McLure, C. E. (1967) 'The Interstate Exporting of State and Local Taxes', *National Tax Journal*, 20, 145–58.

McLure, C. E. (1979) *Must Corporate Income Be Taxed Twice?* (Washington DC, Brookings Institution).

McLure, C. (1986) 'Tax Competition: Is What's Good for the Private Goose Also Good for the Public Gander?', *National Tax Journal*, 39, 341–8.

Micklewright, J. (1985) 'Fiction versus Facts: Unemployment Benefits in Britain', *National Westminster Bank Quarterly Review*, May, 52–62.

Mieszkowski, P. (1972) 'The Property Tax: An Excise Tax or a Profits Tax?', *Journal of Public Economics*, 1, 73–96.

Mieszkowski, P. and Zodrow, G. R. (1989) 'Taxation and the Tiebout Model: The Differential Effects of Head Taxes, Taxes on Land Rents, and Property Taxes', *Journal of Economic Literature*, 27, 1098–146.

Miller, N. R. (1987) 'Voting', in J. Eatwell, M. Milgate and P. Newman (eds), *The New Palgrave* (London, Macmillan) 826–9.

Miller, W. L. and Mackie, M. (1973) 'The Electoral Cycle and the Asymmetry of Government and Opposition Popularity: An Alternative Model of the Relationship Between Economic Conditions and Political Popularity', *Political Studies*, 21, 263–79.

Minarik, J. J. (1982) 'The Future of the Individual Income Tax', *National Tax Journal*, 35, 231–41.

Minford, P. and Ashton, P. (1989) 'The Poverty Trap and Labour Supply: What does the GHS Tell Us?', mimeo, University of Liverpool.

Mintz, J. and Tulkens, H. (1986) 'Commodity Tax Competition Between Member States of a Federation: Equilibrium and Efficiency', *Journal of Public Economics*, 29, 133–72.

Mitchell, R. and Carson, R. T. (1989) *Using Surveys to Value Public Goods: The Contingent Valuation Method* (Washington, DC, Resources for the Future).

Modigliani, F. and Sterling, A. (1983) 'Determinants of Private Saving with Special Reference to the Role of Social Security', in F. Modigliani and R. Hemming (eds), *The Determinants of National Savings and Wealth* (New York, St Martin's Press) 24–55.

Moffitt, R. (1986) 'The Econometrics of Piecewise Linear Budget Constraints', *Journal of Business and Economic Statistics*, 4, 317–28.

Montgomery, E. (1986) 'Where Did All the Saving Go?', *Economic Inquiry*, 24, 681–97.

Moyes, P. (1987) 'A New Concept of Lorenz Domination', *Economics Letters*, 23, 203–7.

Mueller, Dennis C. (1989) *Public Choice II* (Cambridge, Cambridge University Press).

Munnell, A. H. (1974) 'The Impact of Social Security on Personal Savings', *National Tax Journal*, 27, 553–67.

Munnell, A. H. (1976) 'Private Pensions and Savings: New Evidence', *Journal of Political Economy*, 84, 1013–32.

Munnell, A. H. (1982) *The Economics of Private Pensions* (Washington, DC, Brookings Institution).

Musgrave, R. A. (1959) *The Theory of Public Finance* (New York, McGraw-Hill).

Musgrave, Richard A. (1969) *Fiscal Systems* (New Haven, Yale University Press).

Musgrave, R. A. (1983) 'Who Should Tax, Where, and What?', in C. McLure (ed.), *Tax Assignment in Federal Countries* (Canberra, Australian National University Press).

Musgrave, R. A. (1985) 'Excess Bias and The Nature of Budget Growth', *Journal of Public Economics*, 28, 287–305.

Musgrave, R. A. and Musgrave, P. B. (1976) *Public Finance in Theory and Practice* (Tokyo, McGraw-Hill).

Myers, S. C. (1984) 'The Capital Structure Puzzle', *Journal of Finance*, 39, 572–92.

Newbery, D. and Stern, N. (1987) *The Theory of Taxation of Developing Countries* (Oxford, Oxford University Press for the World Bank).

Ng, Yew-Kwang (1979) *Welfare Economics* (London, Macmillan).

Niskanen, W. A. (1971) *Bureaucracy and Representative Government* (Chicago, Aldine Atherton).

Nordhaus, W. D (1975) 'The Political Business Cycle', *Review of Economic Studies*, 42, 169–90.

Nozick, R. (1974) *Anarchy, State and Utopia* (New York, Basic Books).

Oakland, W. H. (1987) 'Theory of Public Goods', in A. J. Auerbach and M. S. Feldstein (eds), *Handbook of Public Economics* (Amsterdam, North-Holland) 485–535.

Oates, W. E. (1969) 'The Effects of Property Taxes and Local Public Spending on Property Values: An Empirical Study of Tax Capitalisation and the Tiebout Hypothesis', *Journal of Political Economy*, 77, pp. 957–71.

Oates, W. E. (1972) *Fiscal Federalism* (New York, Harcourt Brace Jovanovich).

Oates, W. E. (1979) 'Lump Sum Intergovernmental Grants Have Price Effects', in P. M. Mieskowski and W. H. Oakland (eds), *Fiscal Federalism and Grants-in-Aid* (Washington, DC, Urban Institute).

OECD (1983) *Taxes and Immovable Property* (Paris).

Olson, M. (1965) *The Logic of Collective Actions* (Cambridge, Mass., Harvard University Press).

Olson, M. (1982) *The Rise and Decline of Nations: Economic Growth, Stagflation and Social Rigidities* (New Haven, Yale University Press).

Ouder, B. A. (1979) 'Data and Studies on Savings in France: A Survey', in George von Furstenberg (ed.), *Social Security versus Private Saving* (Cambridge, Mass., Ballinger) 257–76.

Papanek, Gustav F. (1967) *Pakistan's Development* (Cambridge, Mass., Harvard University Press).

Pauly, M. V. (1973) 'Income Redistribution as a Local Public Good', *Journal of Public Economics*, 2, 35–58.

Peacock, A. and Wiseman, J. (1961) *The Growth of Public Expenditure in the United Kingdom* (London, Allen & Unwin).

Peacock, Alan T. and Jack Wiseman (1967) *The Growth of Public Expenditure in the United Kingdom*, rev. edn (London, Allen & Unwin).

Pechman, J. (1990) 'Tax Reforms', National Bureau of Economic Research, Working Paper 3254, Washington.

Pechman, J. A. and Okner, B. A. (1974) *Who Bears The Tax Burden?* (Washington, DC, Brookings Institution).

Pencavel, J. H. (1979) 'A Note on Income Tax Evasion, Labour Supply and Non-Linear Tax Schedules', *Journal of Public Economics*, 12, 115–24.

Pencavel, J. (1986) 'Labour Supply of Men: A Survey', in O. Ashenfelter and R. Layard (eds), *Handbook of Labour Economics* (Amsterdam, North-Holland).

Pfaff, M., Hurler P. and Dennerlein, R. (1979) 'Old-Age Security and Saving in the Federal Republic of Germany', in George von Furstenberg (ed.), *Social Security versus Private Saving* (Cambridge, Mass., Ballinger) 277–312.

Pfingsten, A. (1986) *The Measurement of Tax Progression*, Studies in Contemporary Economics, 20 (Berlin, Springer-Verlag).

Phillips, A. W. (1954) 'Stabilisation Policy in a Closed Economy', *Economic Journal*, 64, 290–322.

Piggott, J. (1980) 'A General Equilibrium Evaluation of Australian Tax Policy', Ph.D. dissertation, University of London.

Piggott, J. and Whalley, J. (1984) 'Economic Effects of UK Tax-Subsidy Policies: A General Equilibrium Appraisal', in Scarf and Shoven (1984).

Pissarides, C. A. (1980) 'British Government Popularity and Economic Performance', *Economic Journal*, 90, 569–81.

Please, Stanley (1967) 'Saving Through Taxation–Reality or Mirage?', *Finance and Development*, 4, 24–32.

Plott, C. (1967) 'A Notion of Equilibrium and its Possibility Under Majority Rule', *American Economic Review*, 57, 787–806.

Pollak, R. and Wales, T. (1979) 'Welfare Comparisons and Equivalence

Scales', *American Economic Review*, 69, 216–22.

Pommerehne, W. W. and Schneider, F. (1983) 'Does Government in a Representative Democracy Follow a Majority of Voters' Preferences? – An Empirical Examination', in H. Hanusch (ed.), *Anatomy of Government Deficiences* (Berlin, Springer Verlag) 61–84.

Poterba, J. M. (1986) 'Taxation and Corporate Capital Structure', Comments presented for the IV John Deutsch Roundtable of Economic Policy, The Impact of Taxation on Business Activity, Ottawa, November 11–13, 1985.

Premchand, A. (1983) *Government Budgetting and Expenditure Controls* (Washington, International Monetary Fund).

Preston, I. P. (1989) 'The Redistributive Effect of Progressive Taxation', Oxford University D.Phil. thesis.

Pyle, D. J. (1983) *The Economics of Crime and Law Enforcement* (London, Macmillan).

Pyle, D. J. (1989) *Tax Evasion and The Black Economy* (London, Macmillan).

Rasmusen, E. (1989) *Games and Information: An Introduction to Game Theory* (Oxford, Blackwell).

Rawls, J. (1971) *A Theory of Justice* (Cambridge, Mass., Harvard University Press).

Rees, R. (1985a) 'The Theory of Principal and Agent, Part I', *Bulletin of Economic Research*, 37, 3–25.

Rees, R. (1985b) 'The Theory of Principal and Agent, Part II', *Bulletin of Economic Research*, 37, 75–95.

Reinganum, J. F. and Wilde, L. L. (1983) 'An Equilibrium Model of Tax Compliance with a Bayesian Auditor and Some "Honest Taxpayers"', California Institute of Technology, Social Science Working Paper 506.

Riker, W. H. (1982) *Liberalism Against Populism* (New York, Freeman).

Romer, T. and Rosenthal, H. (1978) 'Political Resource Allocation, Controlled Agendas and the Status Quo', *Public Choice*, 33, 27–43.

Romer, T. and Rosenthal, H. (1979a) 'The Elusive Median Voter', *Journal of Public Economics*, 12, 143–70.

Romer, T. and Rosenthal, H. (1979b) 'Bureaucrats versus Voters: On the Political Economy of Resource Allocation by Director Democracy', *Quarterly Journal of Economics*, 93, 563–87.

Romer, T. and Rosenthal, H. (1980) 'An Institutional Theory of the Effect of Intergovernmental Grants, *National Tax Journal*, 33, 451–8.

Romer, T. and Rosenthal, H. (1982) 'Median Voters on Budget Maximizers: Evidence from School Expenditure Referenda', *Economic Inquiry*, 20, 556–78.

Rosen, H. (1976) 'Taxes in a Labour Supply Model with Joint Wage–Hours Determination', *Econometrica*, 44, 91–106.

Rosen, S. (1974) 'Hedonic Prices and Implicit Markets', *Journal of Political Economy*, 82, 34–55.

Ross, S. A. (1973) 'The Economic Theory of Agency: The Principal Problem', *American Economic Review*, 63, 208–312.

Rubinfeld, D. L. (1987) 'The Economics of the Local Public Sector', in A. J. Auerbach and M. S. Feldstein (eds), *Handbook of Public Economics* (Amsterdam, North-Holland) 571–645.

Rubinfeld, D. L., Shapiro, P. and Roberts, J. (1987) 'Tiebout Bias and the Demand for Local Public Schooling', *Review of Economics and Statistics*, 69, 426–37.

Rubinfeld, D. L. and Shapiro, P. (1989) 'Micro-Estimation of the Demand for Schooling', *Regional Science and Urban Economics*, 19, 381–98.

Samuelson, P. A. (1954) 'Pure Theory of Public Expenditures', *Review of Economics and Statistics*, 36, 387–9.

Samuelson, P. A. (1955) 'Diagrammatic Exposition of a Theory of Public Expenditures', *Review of Economics and Statistics*, 37, 350–6.

Sandford, C. T. (1973) *Hidden Costs of Taxation* (London, Institute of Fiscal Studies).

Sandford, C. T. (1989) *Administrative and Compliance Costs of Taxation*, (Bath, Fiscal Publications).

Sandler, T. and Tschirhart, J. (1980) 'The Economic Theory of Clubs', *Journal of Economic Literature*, 18, 1481–521.

Sandmo, A. (1976) 'Optimal Tax Theory: A Survey', *Journal of Public Economics*, 13, 149–62.

Sandmo, A. (1981) 'Income Tax Evasion, Labour Supply and the Equity-Efficiency Trade-off', *Journal of Public Economics*, 16, 265–88.

Saunders, P. and Klau, F. (1985) *The Role of the Public Sector* (Paris, OECD).

Scarf, H. E. (1984) 'The Computation of Equilibrium Prices', in Scarf and Shoven (1984).

Scarf, H. E. and Shoven, J. (eds) (1984) *Applied General Equilibrium Analysis* (Cambridge, Cambridge University Press).

Schokkaert, E. (1987) 'Preferences and Demand for Local Spending', *Journal of Public Economics*, 34, 175–88.

Scholes, M., Wilson, R. and Wolfson, M. (1989) 'Tax Planning, Regulatory Capital Planning and Financial Reporting Strategy for Commercial Banks', Stanford Graduate School of Business Working Paper.

Schumpeter, J. A. (1918) 'Die Krise des Steverstaates' (translated as 'The Crisis of the Tax State'), in W. F. Stolper and R. A. Musgrave (eds), *International Economic Papers* (London, Macmillan).

Seldon, A. (1977) *Charge* (London, Temple Smith).

Self, P. (1980) 'Public Expenditure and Welfare', in M. Wright (ed.), *Public Spending Decisions* (London, Allen & Unwin).

Sen, A. K. (1977) 'The Rational Fools: A Critique of the Behavioural Foundations of Economic Theory', *Philosophy and Public Affairs*, 6, 317–44.

Sen, A. K. (1982) *Choice Welfare and Measurement* (Oxford, Basil Blackwell).

Serra-Puche, J. (1984) 'A General Equilibrium Model of the Mexican Economy', in Scarf and Shoven (1984).

Shibuya, H. (1987) 'Japan's Household Savings Rate: An Application of the Life-Cycle Hypothesis', IMF Working Paper, WP/87/15, March.

Shibuya, H. (1988) 'Japan's Household Savings: A Life-Cycle Model with Implicit Annuity Contracts and Rational Expectations', mimeo.

Schlicht, E. (1985) 'The Shadow Economy and Morals: A Note', in Gaertner and Wenig (1985).

Shorrocks, A. F. (1983) 'Ranking Income Distributions', *Economica*, 50, 1–17.

Shorrocks, A. F. and Foster, J. (1987) 'Transfer Sensitive Inequality Measures', *Review of Economic Studies*, 54, 485–97.

Shoup, Carl S. (1969) *Public Finance* (Chicago, Aldine).

Shoven, J. (1983) 'Applied General Equilibrium Tax Modelling', *IMF Staff Papers*, September, 394–420.

Shoven, J. B. and Whalley, J. (1972) 'A General Equilibrium Calculation of Differential Taxation of Income from Capital in the US', *Journal of Public Economics*, 2, 211–24.

Sinn, H. W. (1985) *Kapitaleinkommensbesteuerung* (Tubingen, Mohr). English edition: *Capital Income Taxation and Resource Allocation* (Amsterdam, New York, etc., North-Holland, 1987).

Sinn, H. W. (1990) 'The Vanishing Harberger Triangle', National Bureau of Economic Research Working Paper, No. 3225, January.

Skinner, J. and Slemrod, J. (1985) 'An Economic Perspective on Tax Evasion', *National Tax Journal*, 38, 345–53.

Slemrod, J. B. (1983) 'A General Equilibrium Model of Taxation with Endogenous Financial Behaviour', in M. S. Feldstein (ed.), *Behavioural Simulation Methods in Tax Policy Analysis* (Chicago, Chicago University Press).

Slemrod, J. (1990) 'Optimal Taxation and Optimal Tax Systems', *Journal of Economic Perspectives*, 4, 157–78.

Slemrod, J. and Sorum, N. (1984) 'The Compliance Costs of The U.S. Individual Income Tax System', *National Tax Journal*, 37, 461–74.

Slemrod, J. B. and Razin, A. (1990) *Taxation in The Global Economy* (Chicago, Chicago University Press).

Smith, L. B., Rosen, K. T. and Fallis, G. (1988) 'Recent Developments in Economic Models of Housing Markets', *Journal of Economic Literature*, 26, 29–64.

Song, Y. D. and Yarbrough, T. E. (1978) 'Tax Ethics and Taxpayer Attitudes: A Survey', *Public Administration Review*, 38, 442–52.

Spicer, M. W. and Becker, L. A. (1980) 'Fiscal Inequity and Tax Evasion: An Experimental Approach', *National Tax Journal*, 33, 171–5.

Spicer, M. W. and Hero, R. E. (1985) 'Tax Evasion and Heuristics', *Journal of Public Economics*, 26, 263–7.

Spicer, M. W. and Lundstedt, S. B. (1976) 'Understanding Tax Evasion', *Public Finance*, 31, 295–305.

Srinivasan, T. N. (1973) 'Tax Evasion: A Model', *Journal of Public Economics*, 2, 339–46.

Starret, D. A. (1988a) *Foundations of Public Economics*, Cambridge Economic Handbooks (Cambridge, Cambridge University Press).

Starrett, D. A. (1988b) 'Effects of Taxes on Saving', in H. J. Aaron, H. Galper and J. A. Pechman (eds), *Uneasy Compromise: Problem of a Hybrid Income–Consumption Tax* (Washington, DC, The Brookings Institution) 237–59.

Stern, N. H. (1987) 'The Theory of Optimal Commodity and Income Taxation', in David Newbery and N. H. Stern (eds), *The Theory of Taxation for Developing Countries* (Oxford, Oxford University Press) 22–59.

Stigler, G. J. (1970) 'The Optimum Enforcement of Laws', *Journal of Political Economy*, 78, 526–36.

Stiglitz, J. E. (1983) 'The Theory of Local Public Goods Twenty Five Years After Tiebout', in G. Zodrow (ed.), *Local Provision of Public Services: The Tiebout Model After Twenty Five Years* (New York, Academic Press) 17–54.

Stiglitz, J. E. (1987) 'On the Causes and Consequences of the Dependence of Quality on Price', *Journal of Economic Literature*, March, 1–48.

Stiglitz, J. E. and Dasgupta, P. (1971) 'Differential Taxation, Public Goods and Economic Efficiency, *Review of Economic Studies*, 38, 151–74.

Sugden, R. (1984) 'Reciprocity: The Supply of Public Goods Through Voluntary Contributions', *Economic Journal*, 94, 772–87.

Summers, L. H. (1981) 'Capital Taxation and Accumulation in a Life Cycle Growth Model', *American Economic Review*, 71, 533–44.

Summers, L. H. (1983) 'The After Tax Rate of Return Affects Private Savings', *American Economic Review*, 74, 249–53.

Symons, E. and Walker, I. (1988) 'The Reform of Personal Taxation: A Brief Analysis', *Fiscal Studies*, 9, 15–26.

Szentes, T. (1983) *The Political Economy of Underdevelopment* (Budapest, Akademiai Kiado).

Tanzi, Vito (1977) 'Inflation, Lags in Collection, and the Real Value of Tax Revenue', *International Monetary Fund Staff Papers*, 24, 154–67.

Tanzi, Vito (1987a) 'Quantitative Characteristics of the Tax Systems of Developing Countries', in Newbery and Stern (1987).

Tanzi, V. (1987b) 'The Response of other Industrial Countries to the US Tax Reform Act', *National Tax Journal*, 40, 339–55.

Tanzi, V. (1991) *Public Finance in Developing Countries* (Aldershot: Edward Elgar Publishing).

Tideman, T. N. and Tullock, G. (1976) 'A New and Superior Process for Making Social Choices', *Journal of Political Economy*, 84, 1145–59.

Tiebout, C. M. (1956) 'A Pure Theory of Local Expenditures', *Journal of Political Economy*, 64, 416–24.

Titman, S. and Wessels, R. (1988) 'The Determinants of Capital Structure Choice', *Journal of Finance*, 43, 1–19.

Topham, N. (1983) 'Local Government Economics', in R. Millward *et al.* (eds), *Public Sector Economics* (Harlow, Longman).

Tullio, G. and Contesso, F. (1986) 'Do After Tax Interest Rates Affect Private Consumption and Savings? Empirical Evidence for 8 Industrial Countries: 1970–83', *Economic Papers*, Commission of the European

Communities, No. 51, December.

Tullock, G. (1967) 'The Welfare Costs of Tariffs, Monopolies and Theft', *Western Economic Journal*, 5, 224–32.

Tullock, G. (1988) *Wealth, Poverty and Politics* (Oxford, Basil Blackwell).

Tustin, A. (1954) *The Mechanism of Economic Systems* (London, Heinemann).

Varian, H. R. (1990) *Intermediate Microeconomics*, 2nd edn (New York, W. W. Norton).

Venti, S. F. and Wise, D. A. (1987) 'IRAs and Saving', in M. Feldstein (ed.) *The Effects of Taxation on Capital Accumulation* (Chicago, Chicago University Press) 7–48.

Vickrey, W. (1961) 'Counterspeculation, Auctions and Competitive Sealed Tenders', *Journal of Finance*, 16, 8–37.

Wallerstein, I. (1979) *The Capitalist World Economy* (Cambridge, Cambridge University Press).

Waud, R. (1988) 'Tax Aversion, Optimal Tax Rates and Indexation', *Public Finance*, 43, 310–25.

Whalley, J. (1975) 'A General Equilibrium Assessment of the 1973 United Kingdom Tax Reform', *Economica*, May.

Wicksell, K. (1896) 'A New Principle of Just Taxation', reprinted (1958) in R. A. Musgrave and A. T. Peacock (eds), *Classics in the Theory of Public Finance* (London, Macmillan) 72–118.

Wildasin, D. E. (1987a) 'Theoretical Analyses of Local Public Economics', in E. S. Mills (ed.), *Handbook of Urban Economics*, vol. II (Amsterdam, North-Holland) 1131–78.

Wildasin, D. (1987b) 'The Demand for Public Goods in the Presence of Tax Exporting', *National Tax Journal*, 40, 591–601.

Wildasin, D. E. (1986) *Urban Public Finance* (New York, Harwood Academic Publishers).

Wildasin, D. (1989) 'Demand Estimation for Public Goods: Distortionary Taxation and Other Sources of Bias', *Regional Science and Urban Economics* 19, 353–79.

Willis, R. and Rosen, S. (1981) 'Education and Self Selection', *Journal of Political Economy*, 89, 341–66.

Wilson, J. (1986) 'A Theory of Interregional Tax Competition', *Journal of Urban Economics*, 19, 155–78.

Wilson, J. D. (1987) 'Trade, Capital Mobility and Tax Competition', *Journal of Political Economy*, 95, 835–56.

Witte, A. D. and Woodbury, D. F. (1985) 'The Effect of Tax Laws and Tax Administration on Tax Compliance: The Case of the US Individual Income Tax', *National Tax Journal*, 38, 1–13.

Wolfson, Dirk (1979) *Public Finance and Development Strategy* (Baltimore, Md., Johns Hopkins University Press).

World Bank (1988) *World Development Report 1988* (New York, Oxford University Press for the World Bank).

Wright, C. (1969) 'Saving and The Rate of Interest', in *The Taxation of*

Income from Capital, ed. M. J. Bailey (Washington, DC, Brookings Institution) 275–300.

Yamada, T. and Yamada, T. (1988) 'The Effects of Japanese Social Security Retirement Benefits on Personal Saving and Elderly Labour Force Behaviour', NBER Working Paper, No. 2661, July.

Yitzhaki, S. (1974) 'Income Tax Evasion: A Theoretical Analysis', *Journal of Public Economics*, 3, 201–2.

Zabalza, A. (1983) 'The CES Utility Function, Nonlinear Budget Constraints and Labour Supply', *Economic Journal*, 93, 213–27.

Zabalza, A. and Arrufat, J. (1988) 'Female Labour Supply with Taxation, Random Preferences and Optimization Errors', *Econometrica*, 44, 63–78.

Zabalza, A., Pissarides, C. and Barton, M. (1980) 'Social Security and the Choice between Full-Time, Part-Time and Retirement', *Journal of Public Economics*, 9, 245–58.

Zodrow, G. R. and Mieszkowski, P. (1986) 'Pigou, Tiebout, Property Taxation and the Underprovision of Public Goods', *Journal of Urban Economics*, 19, 356–70.

Author Index

Subject Index

296